4839629

SAINTLY BILLY

SAINTLY BILLY

A Catholic Boyhood

BILL NAUGHTON

Oxford   New York
OXFORD UNIVERSITY PRESS
1988

Oxford University Press, Walton Street, Oxford OX2 6DP
Oxford New York Toronto
Delhi Bombay Calcutta Madras Karachi
Petaling Jaya Singapore Hong Kong Tokyo
Nairobi Dar es Salaam Cape Town
Melbourne Auckland
and associated companies in
Beirut Berlin Ibadan Nicosia

Oxford is a trade mark of Oxford University Press

British Library Cataloguing in Publication Data
Naughton, Bill
Saintly Billy: a Catholic boyhood.
1. Naughton, Bill — Biography
2. Authors, English — 20th century
— Biography
I. Title
823'.914   PR6027.A9Z/
ISBN 0-19-212270-3

Library of Congress Cataloging in Publication Data
Naughton, Bill.
Saintly Billy: a Catholic boyhood / Bill Naughton.
p.   cm.
1. Naughton, Bill—Biography—Youth.   2. Authors, English—20th
century—Biography.   3. Lancashire—Social life and customs.
4. Catholics—England—Lancashire—Biography.   I. Title.
PR6027.A9Z468   1988
828'.91409—dc19
[B]   87-16120
ISBN 0-19-212270-3

Set by Wyvern Typesetting Ltd.
Printed in Great Britain by
Biddles Ltd.
Guildford and King's Lynn

CONTENTS

I

The Backstreet Gamblers

ONE could hardly have wished for a more animated scene than that of our backstreet in Bolton on a Saturday afternoon during the early spring of 1920, when the marble season had got going. At least I, in my tenth year, could not; and although all my mates have gone off to the 'penny rush' at the nearby Derby Picture Palace, to see the latest episode of the Eddie Polo following-up film, *The Broken Coin*—Eddie hanging on to a rope over a cliff, with a vivid close-up of the various strands tearing apart, was how we last saw our hero—I prefer the real live drama of the backstreet. The players are youths from the age of seventeen upwards to men of thirty, around half of whom are colliers—a couple of them, in their pit dirt, haven't even had the time or energy for a proper wash after working the early shift down pit, so eager are they to get playing—and most of the others are mill workers, but there is one chap who works at the foundry, another at Walker's tannery, also a glass-blower, a firewood hawker, a soldier said to be on leave, and others.

They are every one single men—not a one of them with a girlfriend of any kind: 'What—start bloody courtin'—an' a tuppenny meat pie costs a chap fourpence! Not bloody likely!' And even the miners among them never visit pubs— they seem to be wedded to their mates and the street-corner. Living, as they all do, in small crowded homes, with Mam in charge, feeding and caring for them, scrubbing their backs at the kitchen sink after their shift down pit, buying them all their clothes, taking their wages and giving them spending money, they don't appear to need a wife. Once home from work, with their meal eaten, it seems they can't get to their mates quick enough at the Big Corner—the spacious corner of Birkdale Street and Can Row. Corner mates don't want someone who turns up for an hour or so and then goes off to meet a girl, and such a one is soon made to feel out of it. Nor do they accept someone who goes off to a pub for an hour and comes back after closing time.

Once a member of the Corner gets married—and it seems the odd one does get nabbed—he is no longer welcome among his old pals. Often he will try to ease himself in again, usually after a couple of boring evenings at home, but he is likely to turn up at the Corner rather late, and will receive a cool reception, and find that his once regular place has been filled. It is not merely a question of split loyalties—those of wife and home and those of his old mates—but married life restricts his interests and outlook, seems to emasculate a man in some way, or at least softens him up, so that he will bring much less vitality or interest in either personality or talk to the Corner—and domestic chat is unacceptable. Even more, should there be trouble of any kind a married man cannot be relied upon to support a mate.

As I watch the marble players, seeing how between shots they yell out to each other, argue fiercely, cackle, yodel, offer a cigarette to a close mate, even do a few steps of a clog dance, and generally display an independence, vigour, and spontaneity seldom seen in the married man, I decide they could be nearly right when they say a man is a fool who lets himself get roped into marriage: 'It's nourishment I want,' they say, 'not bloody punishment.' (Except, of course, he be in love, as I am, with a wonderful girl like my Alice.) These youths and men are not playing marbles for love of the game but for ready cash. Having gone to work in the mill at the age of twelve for ten shillings a week seems to have made them set a value on every activity, so that even a game of football is usually played for a 'tanner a man'.

The marble players are spread out along the length of the backstreet, with three or four separate games going on, about four players in each group, divided according to skill and the size of stakes, and at a penny and twopence a hit there is much handing out of money. Nor are they using the common stone or glass marbles, which they would consider childish, but each player has his own iron bobber. Aside from the marble players there is a game of pitch-and-toss going on, with money won and lost at every toss of the two pennies in the air; then up against our midden door is a banker school— 'Peter pays Paul,' calls Tommy Burton as he turns up the cards and switches the stakes from a losing to a winning card, 'an' the banker gets sod all.' There is even a little crown-and-anchor game, 'The more you put down the more you pick up,' comes the invitation, '—you come in rags an' go away in motor-cars.'

If our backstreet isn't actually the hub of the world, I feel it cannot be far from it, with all that money changing hands. It makes you feel hoarse in the throat from excitement. And very few places that could boast such powerful figures as Jud Burns and Louis Arpino—they are all a bit on the short side of course, welterweights as they call them—young men never been known to duck a challenge. Why, there's one fellow with a stiff leg, Knocky Bolton, who for a tanner bet, or sometimes for fun, will take a rat and actually worry it to death between his teeth, shaking it violently until it expires. You won't get many doing that.

It seems that the faintly sweet stink from the privy closets lined along each side of the backstreet—the pails emptied on Thursday nights—adds to the atmosphere and excitement. What's all this about spring, the cuckoo, and the birds that sing tra-la-la—never heard in our part of the world—and spring flowers and all the rest of it! Around here we're happy with the occasional singing canary in a cage, the aspidistra in the window, and the privet hedge here and there—and these we have all the year round. To heck with poets and all the rest of them—you can't beat the cosy feeling of your own backstreet, and all the young miners and others playing marps for money. After all, they do say, 'Where's there's muck there's money.'

We're not what could be called posh in Unsworth Street, but there aren't many backstreets in Bolton to compare with ours for liveliness. Walk a couple of hundred yards away to

Maybank Street where all the spinners and overlookers live, people who think that they and their families are somebodies, where each home has a tippler closet, and their backstreets will be deserted. A few streets away, around Isabel Street and Walter Street, where there are lots of pigeon flyers, there might even be more going on, lots of gambling, with big crowds of youths and men gathered on the spare ground beside the gable-end, many of them miners, with a few whippets to be seen beside their masters, but then that area is said to be common, and certainly it isn't as respectable as our street. Every house except three in our street of some thirty-two families has its front doorstep and windowsill mopped and stoned for the weekend—'I've just got to finish my front an' then I'm done,' is a frequent exchange beween housewives—but they don't seem to go in for that in Isabel Street, they just aren't houseproud; besides, the worst thing of all, they say some homes there have bugs; so far as I am aware, bugs are more or less unknown in our street.

Ours is not a mining district, being a good tram ride or two from the pits, which lie clear of the town; studded about as it is with cotton mills, weaving sheds, a foundry or two, and a big brewery in among the rows of terraced houses and cobbled streets, three out of four workers are employed in the mill, and only about one in seven families have a man working down the mine. The less posh the locality the more miners there are, and what they might take away in tone they make up for in character. The reason the miners are more prominent in the backstreet is that they are still earning the higher wages they procured during the Great War years, and can afford a gamble, which they enjoy. Spinning-mill workers the same age as the younger miners are badly paid, because from the age of seventeen, when they usually become side-piecers, they have to wait a dozen years or more for a rise until a minder or spinner dies and they can get his wheels. As it happens, owing to spinner's cancer and other diseases related to the work, that aristocrat of the cotton mill, the spinner, is not long-lived.

Apart from a few toddlers making mud pies—they scrape

dirt from between cobblestones and pee on it to make the sludge which they pack into the lids of shoe-polish tins to shape the pies—I am the only young lad there, and I would have been shooed off early on were it not that I live at number 8, and it seems you can't be sent away from your own backstreet. And, as I say, my own feeling toward all that is going on around me is that I wouldn't wish to be anywhere else in the world but there in our backstreet, it is all so exciting, to see those cocky young miners darting around and showing off with their swinging shoulders, and also to feel myself part of some lawbreaking activity, for the detectives are always on the watch-out for gambling, and a nixer, Bally Selby, has been posted at the far end of the backstreet on the look-out for them. The marble players in no way reflect the tone of the neighbourhood, as a number of families are Methodists and abhor gambling of any kind, and somehow make that an accepted attitude, and of course many young men are either too poor or too mean to play. Mixed with the prosperity is a lot of poverty. In fact, old Mr Whittle, a gingery man, palefaced and fragile, wearing an old waistcoat and frayed trousers, old shoes serving as slippers, opens the back gate behind me and surveys the scene with a bemused look. 'By gum, Billy,' he remarks, 'it seems like there's plenty of money around.'

I nod my head in agreement as I recall an incident in Bibby's chip shop that very dinnertime. Mrs Tiplady, a woman who had the well-paid job of working the hoist at a cotton mill, had been getting served with a few parcels of fish and chips; 'Just wrap 'em up,' she had said to Mrs Bibby, the shop being full and this did save time and allow others to get served, '—we've plenty of vinegar at home.' Then as she took her fat bulging purse out of her basket and began to finger for the money a seam must have given way, and the next thing a shower of silver and copper coins went cascading on to the floor. Everybody around bent down to help pick them up and hand them over, after which Mrs Tiplady said: 'Ta very much—I think that's the lot.' Then I spotted a small silver coin down between the well-scrubbed floorboards, stooped to get it, and as I handed it to her she held back and said, 'Ee it's only a threepenny bit, luv—I don't know as it matters all that—' as much as to say I could keep it, but out of shame's sake I pressed it on her. Then a small girl called out, 'There's a penny here—' but Mrs Tiplady was on the move and called back, 'You can keep it, luv—an' owt else you find,' and off she went, laughing away, with all her parcels of fish and chips. 'Ee fancy that!' remarked old Mrs Entwistle, an old-age pensioner, 'I've seen the time when a woman 'ud be down on her hands an' knees scrawpin' around for a lost ha'penny.' 'Aye,' said Mr Bibby, delving with his big wire ladle into the huge pan of boiling fat, scooping out a pile of chips and fingering one or two to see if they were ready, 'an' the way things are lookin' happen you'll see it again before long.'

Still standing at his back gate old Mr Whittle pipes out in a squeaky voice: 'It aren't any of it comin' my way,' and spotting a few nuts of coal that had dropped off some coal-cart he hurries out to get them, placing them carefully along his left arm which is pressed against his greasy waistcoat. He comes back slowly, breathless from the exertion of stooping: 'I'll tell you one thing,' he says to me, since it seems I'm the only one who will listen, 'it won't last. It can't—the country won't stand for it. These bloody miners, they keep askin' for rises, they haven't the sense to see that the war's over—they're not needed the same—we can get coal from Germany. You just mark my words—' and, shaking his head and giving a last look at the eager young men, he goes inside, bolting the back gate behind him. I get the feeling he's having a dig at our family with that talk of miners, but he's mistaken if he imagines I'll tell my father what he's said. The life I see out-of-doors I never mention in our home.

I turn once more to the marble players and wonder at their skill. They are drawn from various streets in the area, and will all gather at the Big Corner in the evening, when the miners may be fewer in number than mill workers, yet it is miners, always perched down on their haunches, who seem to give the Big Corner its vitality. It seems that the hard sweating labour of the coal-mine brings out character in the

face, and also toughens the figure, but the humidity of the
spinning mill seems to drain the colour and life out of the
workers, producing a 'mill face' over the years and a feeble
figure. (The odd spinner will resist deterioration by a routine
of physical training, and some even become weight-lifters.) It
also happens that many of those who move from mill to mine
somehow fail to survive the change from the delicate work of
the spinning room to the strenuous labour of delving for coal,
and have to give the job up; whilst those who do endure feel a
reasonable pride in the achievement and the hard knotty
muscles that accompany it.

'Bloody 'ell!' calls Billy Burton, as Gilbert Clegg is seen to
hit the iron bobber which he has just tawed down in a niche
at the edge of the kerb and sent it flying. As Billy hands over
the coppers, Louis Arpino calls out, 'Sarves thee reet, tha
pillock—tha left too much showin'.' A young player keeps
getting in the way of Jud Burns, a big handsome miner: 'Get
from under t'bloody feet,' warns Jud, '—or I'll ding thy soddin' lug for thee!' Threats of this kind are frequent, but the
words, short and hard, suffice, and never have I seen a blow
struck or a fight take place—a necessary understanding is
always reached.

Every single one in the backstreet, from the youngest to the
oldest, with the sole exception of myself, wears a cap. They
cannot understand why I go around bareheaded, especially in
the rain, and seem to put it down to my being Irish and not
knowing any better. The cloth cap—the adjective never heard
among those who wear such—is an indispensable item of
dress. It is worn by every male from the age of five until
death; almost literally so in certain cases, for when I go
errands for Mrs Hardman I often see Mr Hardman sat up in
bed in the front kitchen—he suffers from bronchitis and the
upstairs bedroom is too cold—with his cap on. A cap worn
for such long periods—as in the case of spectacles—becomes
closely identified with the face, and often there is an astonishing change when the headgear is removed. Just as wire spectacles produce a furrow across the bridge of the nose, the
constant wearing of a heavy cap brings about a decided

groove around the lower part of the head of the wearer, and also flattens the hair. These caps are bulky, bulging out an inch or two at the side, with huge nebs at the front which protrude over the forehead. The cap on your head tells a lot about you: your job, of course—the greasy cap of the mill worker distinct from that of the miner—but also your personality and character, what you are and what you would like others to think you are. The timid child will want to pull down his cap at the front, whilst the bolder child will cock it back a bit—and with variations these traits will persist throughout life. The average male would as soon go out of the front door without trousers as without his cap; 'I feel undressed without mi cap,' or 'I'm lost without a cap,' is often heard. Even in the tidy homes caps rate a place on the dresser, mostly over an ornament, the heads of bronze horses being a regular hanging place; Dad has the favourite place, the horse's head nearest the door, and each member of the family his own place in order of seniority downwards.

Suddenly Bally Selby, the bow-legged youth with a lined face, big pale nose peppered with blackheads, and grinning eyes, springs to life from his nixing post at the corner of the backstreet, and with a hand beside the corner of his mouth yells out to the players: 'Look out! Look out, everybody! 'Tecs!—two of 'um!' All the games stop at once. Tommy Burton looks at the stakes on the cards and calls back: 'Bally—art' coddin'? 'Am I bloody hell as like!' yells Bally '—they're comin' down Thomas Rostron Street!' The banker players snatch their stakes amid shouts and argument, the crown-and-anchor and pontoon schools break up with the youths climbing over gates and backyard walls, the marble players grab their iron bobbers. I make a dash to the safety of our backyard, and as I open the gate a half-dozen young men almost bowl me over as they follow me inside. It seems that in the backstreet there is only one figure left, Jud Burns, calling out to his departed mates: 'What the bloody 'ell's up with you all! A chap can play marps after his day's work! I'm buggered if I'm gooin'.'

The young men who have followed me get down against

our privy closet wall out of sight; young miners balanced comfortably in their usual pose, knees wide apart, the spinners unable to squat with ease have their knees together. Jack Dalton, a young soldier of twenty, home on leave and wearing old civvy clothes, is left standing, and he opens our coalshed, looks inside, turns to us all, and puts a finger to his lips for us to say nothing. He is about to go in when the back door opens and my mother stands there, just fastening a nice clean pinafore and smiling: 'Well, gents,' she says quietly, 'what is it?' Jack Dalton turns to her at once: 'It's the 'tecs, Missis Naughton,' he says, '—after us for gamblin'. I'm on leave from the army—I don't want to get in trouble—could you let me hide inside?' 'Oh surely,' says my mother at once, '—come in, come in now.' She looks at me, but I like the company of the young men and don't wish to go inside.

Jack Dalton quickly follows my mother inside, making a swift turn to us, finger once more to his lips. 'Old Jack's got the wind up proper,' says one youth. 'Aye,' says Billy Burton, 'he's frickened of bein' picked up. He's not on leave, y'know—he's on the run.' 'Aye,' says another, 'absent without leave—a deserter. An' they're after him.' 'They were shippin' him off to India with all his mob when he did a bunk,' says Billy Burton. 'He detests the bloody army—an' reckons they'll never get him to India.' 'They will,' remarks one, '—they got their hands on mi dad after five bloody year. T'army never lets go.'

Bally Selby is now heard yelling: 'False alarm, chaps! You can all bloody come out. It weren't 'tecs, it were two other buggers.' They jump to their feet and make for the backstreet, myself in among them. Jud Burns surveys them: 'Windy sods, the soddin' lot of you—' he calls out. They all get playing once more. I now go inside to tell Jack Dalton that the coast is clear. He is standing in the back kitchen, drinking a cup of tea and talking to my mother. 'I got as I couldn't stand it, Missis Naughton,' he is telling her. 'All that discipline an' drillin', an' polishin' your brass an' one thing and another. They're allus on at you. It near drove me mad. I love bein' back home with my mam—an' at the Corner with my mates.

I'm not cut out for army life. They'll not get me back if I can help it.'

(Alas, poor Jack, they picked him up at six o'clock the following Monday morning, when he was fast asleep in the back bedroom of his mother's home in Back Cannon Street. He managed to get out of the bedroom window and on to the outdoor privy closet, but a detective was waiting there and nabbed him. He had to do a spell of detention in the Glass House—so I heard—everything to be done at the double wearing full kit; then they shipped him off to India. He was a much changed man when he next came back to the Big Corner years later, hard and stiff and soldier-like, the coolest man there, and certainly not one with whom to start an argument.)

2

Meeting Uncle William

I HAD returned to the backstreet with Jack Dalton, and after a time I saw my mother standing at the back gate, smiling away and chatting to the marble players in her usual bright manner. She gave me a look and nod which meant she wanted me in; that was the way we Irish liked to communicate, expecting the other person to understand what was in mind without explanations, and giving a wink or a beckon to anyone who was slow of understanding. I went into the back kitchen beside her, knowing I was expected to wash and change and take my young brother Jim to the tram-stop to meet Uncle William coming in for his weekend visit from Chequerbent, a mining village a few miles away. It was a duty I undertook with a certain ill humour, for when we had first arrived in England around Christmas 1914 I had been Uncle's favourite, then a year later my young brother James had been born. 'The only one belonging to us ever born on English soil!' Uncle William had once declared with pride, for he had great respect and affection for the English. As though that were some distinction, I used to think to myself, in a place where anyone would have been hard put to scrape a bucket of soil from an entire neighbourhood of massed cobbled streets and spinning mills. Almost at once young James had taken my place in Uncle William's affections, and he would dandle him on his knee, and lilt away jigs and reels, and on occasion offer him pound notes to burn, should he wish to fling them on the fire. My brother Edward had never found favour with Uncle William, and as Uncle didn't seem to care for girls neither had my sister May, I had been the fair-haired boy until the arrival of young James, but he had clearly ousted me. My resentment had been aggravated by

two incidents which stuck in mind: the first was at the age of
five when Uncle William had attempted to carry me to school
against my will—but failed; the second a year later, when he
was giving me a bath as I stood naked on the kitchen slopstone—preparatory to taking us to the photographer in
town—and then had swilled me down with a gallon pitcher
of cold water. It had made me so breathless that I had
thought I would die of shock.

I stripped down to the waist to have a good wash at the
slopstone in the back kitchen, with old newspaper spread
around my feet to keep the bare kitchen flags from getting too
wet. I made a big affair of a wash, which I always enjoyed,
even though all I had was the rickety cold-water tap; procur-
ing hot water demanded much trouble with saucepans and
kettles, and I chose to have lashings of cold water. My mind
was throbbing with self-examination of one kind and another
as I stooped over the stone slopstone and worked up a lather
of carbolic soap suds—taking care to keep it out of my eyes—
in an effort to rid myself of all traces of the backstreet stench,
which became unpleasant when one left the scene.

On my mind were a number of problems about how best to
work out the evening before me without missing out on anything, and yet at the same time avoiding getting any unwhole-
some blob of sin on my soul, since I would be going to Holy
Communion at the nine o'clock Mass next morning. There
was a duty monthly Communion Sunday for all the schoolboys, when every boy was expected to receive the Eucharist,
but the odd boy made Communion a weekly practice. It
would not have been surprising had this been an outlet for
boys putting on a pious attitude, but so far as I could judge it
was not so; we were a mixed bunch, and, although the
majority were from the more respectable families, where one
or other parent may have been a weekly communicant, some
of them were from poor homes, and may well, like myself,
have been mildly discouraged. Also, the obligatory Confession on Friday evening, mostly with queues of kneelers at
every confessional box, was irksome to some, as was the
morning fast before Communion. Although I found such

waiting before Confession rather wearisome, the feeling of leaving the confessional with spotless soul more than compensated. It was like a boxer or runner who had to keep in prime physical condition for some Sunday morning event—I had to keep a constant eye on my spiritual state. And I much preferred such discipline to the aimless and disordered way of life of most boys, who being without any objective seemed errant and unguided; the best substitute the non-Catholic boy could muster in that area was the boy scouts or boys' brigade. As for the idea of pride or vanity in my aspiration, I must admit there was a little, but only a little; when I was kneeling at the altar rails about to receive the Host on my outstretched tongue it seemed that usually I was so puffed up by humility that I could never quite escape a spasm of sympathy for those nearby who were clearly less piously transported than myself.

When I had finished washing, and had liberally splashed my chest with cold water, I took down the old family toothbrush from the ledge of the window, rubbed away the dry stiffness of the bristles with my thumb, lightly dipped the brush into the carbolic soap, and gave my teeth and mouth a good cleansing with it; it seemed the backstreet reek made its presence felt all over one. I resolved that when I next got the opportunity I would trim down the bristles of the toothbrush—a tip I had picked up from *My Weekly*, one of Mother's women's magazines. I now felt the physical and spiritual selves to be more in tune as I gave myself a good drying down. I longed for purity of body and soul, to be immaculate inside and out, and at times in bed at night I would imagine myself standing at the mast of a sailing ship crossing the ocean and breathing in ozone, or traversing a desert on a camel, or away in the Yukon where many of my heroes drove their teams across the spotless snow. I whispered an Act of Contrition to get rid of the venial sin or two—listening to bad language of the backstreet, and somehow enjoying it—that might have stained the soul within. I saw this soul as a large white wing poised there over the back of my heart and poking out a bit unseen from my body, which soul I would now and again adjust into position.

Deficient in much of the energy and most of the skills of the
native Lancastrian boys—who enjoyed kicking a tin can
around, heading a pig's bladder, or doing acrobatics on the
pavement, such as standing or walking on their hands—and
above all shrinking from the yelling and din that so often
accompanied such—the average Irish boy of the day was of
an oddly quiet disposition—I found my own energy coursing
through my head rather than my limbs. My mind seemed incessantly concerned with whether I should do this or that, alive
with ideas, with wisps of thought and fancy, bits of poetry,
scurrying daydreams and images, creating within the imagination a private world more agreeable and adaptable than the
one outside. It was all I could do not to talk to myself.

Around the time of my First Communion I had felt myself
to be taken over by the magical sensation which was the gift
of the Holy Spirit. And, failing to find happiness in my school
life, or the sort of quiet comfort I longed for in my home life
and that of the street-corner, I turned from what the catechism described as the temporal world to that which promised eternal life. I told myself to forget happiness and accept
misery—of that, at least, one could always be sure. But in
moments of uplift, which often visited me during my penance
prayer after Confession, I was inclined to make vows and
pledges to the Virgin Mary which later proved difficult to
fulfil. I would promise that for a month I would say a decade
of the Rosary on top of my night prayers—only an extra Our
Father, ten Hail Marys and a Glory be, which seemed simple
enough. It would have been possible except for a stipulation I
made, which was that, on any occasion I caught my con-
centration slipping, straying into daydreams, I would release
my fingers on the rosary bead and start all over again.

I used to kneel on the wooden floor, elbows resting on the
bed, in my shirt—we had neither pyjamas nor nightshirt of
course, and, although my mother tried to persuade me to
wear some old tattered shirt at night, I found that changing in
a cold bedroom was not only uncomfortable but kept me
awake—and some nights, no matter how hard I tried, I could
never finish off the decade without wandering of mind or

dropping off to sleep. Then I would be forced to get into bed from the chilled and weary feeling, and in this way I became in arrears with my prayers, and ashamed to look the Virgin Mary in the face when I closed my eyes at night in the dark. I always liked to feel free of prayer debts by Sunday morning, and to this end had been including the Rosary always said before Benediction on Tuesdays and Thursdays, which was perhaps stretching it a little, but I had somehow persuaded God it was not a cheat.

Mother came into the kitchen as I was finally rubbing my back down and expanding my chest. 'You're a great man altogether,' she said. She had my Sunday trousers which fastened just below the knee, a clean shirt, and jersey, also fresh socks, all of which she placed on a chair. 'Ta, Mam,' I said, for I appreciated being waited upon, and there were few pleasures I enjoyed more than putting on a clean shirt, freshly washed socks, and polished boots.

'Do you think you have your ears well washed?' asked Mother.

'I've 'um almost scrubbed off,' I said, still sensing the tingling of my ears after all the rubbing. I looked at her. Mother never gave a disapproving look of any kind—it seemed such was beyond her—and the usual expression on her face, always warm and motherly but never weak, stood out from that of most other women—for, although Lancashire women were mostly good and kindhearted, it seemed that those early years of working, tending machines from the age of twelve among all the din of a cotton mill, which she of course had been spared, did tend to bring to the face a set look, from which it seemed a smile or gentle glow had to force its way through. 'Have a look if you want,' I said to her.

Her face had a look of quiet concern as she took a small white linen handkerchief from her pinafore pocket, put it over her short forefinger, dabbed it on the damp board beside the sink, and firmly held the left side of my head as she moved her finger along the outer furrow above the earhole, and into an inner one with a tight corner at which point she gave a twirl of her finger: 'Ow!—go easy, Mam!' I called out. 'That hurt.' Without speaking she removed the handkerchief and displayed the spot under which her finger had put the pressure. There was a coating of fine dark dirt there. 'That—' I declared, 'never came out of my ear!' After all, hadn't I washed that ear with enough soap to clean my entire body!

She took hold of a spotless corner of the white handkerchief, 'Would you try it yourself over the other ear,' she said, placing it over my right index finger. 'Just wet it on your tongue,' she said, 'an' then give it a scratch or two up there in the corner.' I moistened the handkerchief on my tongue and put it up to my ear. I'll show her, I thought. Oddly enough that one spot did seem untouched as I gave a twist or two. I then took my finger out and looked down at the handkerchief—there before my eyes was a large smudge of what looked like old dirt facing me on the white linen. And that after all my washing and scrubbing! I was filled with an apprehension of what might have happened should Mother not have spoken to me—the thought of meeting Alice with such a shocking thing as dirty ears, which I detested, was too much for me. 'Tell me, Mother,' I said, '—did all that dirt come out of my ears? I'll have to wash all over again.'

'You will not,' she said. 'Wasn't it only a smudge—that you got out there in the backstreet. Sure I wouldn't have told you if I'd known it was going to trouble you at all.' And surely I was upset to discover I wasn't exactly the immaculate lad I thought myself to be. 'I never in this world knew a one as clean as yourself,' she went on, 'and aren't you as fine a young man as one would meet in a day's walk.' She had the Irish way of never praising her own except in a joking way— all such pride was better hidden—and even in fun she would often invoke God's blessing. She then put down further old newspapers for under my feet, and went out of the kitchen whilst I washed them and my lower body, taking scrupulous care this time.

I heard the heavy tones of Paddy, the St Vincent de Paul collector, who came every Saturday for the weekly sixpence Mother gave for the poor. Paddy was something of a trial, an intense young man with a spotted face, inclined to come out in sweat on the forehead, who never knew when or how to make his departure, and who hadn't a word to say, so that Mother would be exhausted making talk to cover up the emptiness of his company. Only once in all the years he came round had we known him to help at all in that direction. Mother had finally given up on this occasion and started doing odd jobs around the place, and I myself, not a bad hand at keeping talk on the flow, had run out of subjects, when suddenly Paddy blurted out to Mother, 'Did you ever try to wring a wet towel dry, ma'am?' Mother stopped what she was doing and gave him a look of great interest: 'You'd be amazed,' he went on, 'if you began to wring out a wet towel with your hands, how much you can get out of it—I mean if you keep opening out the towel an' startin' all over again. You can wring an' wring an' keepin' gettin' a few extra drops out, long after you'd think you had them all out.' 'Now isn't that an extraordinary thing you're after tellin' me,' said Mother, putting on a rather refined accent which she kept in reserve for special occasions. 'Musha I'll put the kettle on again an' go an' make a second pot of tea,' she said, 'after hearing that.' And she did.

On this present visit she managed by some adroit twist to indicate to Paddy that she was awfully busy, and got the message across before he had time to sit down and become settled in, and the next thing he was going off with the sixpence in his hand, with Mother uttering Godspeeds and telling him to book it down next week. The next thing she was in the back kitchen scraping candle grease off the seats of two chairs she had brought down from upstairs. 'I've a feeling', she said, 'there could be a big gatherin' this evenin', an' that we'd be chairs short.'

I heard the front door opening, and the friendly voice of Mr Leach giving his warm shy greeting: 'Oh hello!—good afternoon!' It was the accepted custom for all such callers for money to give a knock on the door, each one in his own style—the rent-collector with a peremptory rat-rat, the insurance man with the humble tapping of one getting something for as yet nothing—then enter, pick up the book—old and somewhat tattered, but precious in that it recorded all the payments—and the coins, usually the correct amount, swiftly enter the sum, and off again with scarcely a word. Mr Leach was a different class of man from the usual collector: he was tall and spare, wore wire-rimmed spectacles, and had the earnest look of a young and sincere English clergyman. He wore a shiny blue serge suit, large brown boots which fastened above the ankle, just below his bicycle clips, and a faded trilby hat which he always raised high above his head as he gave his usual bow to my mother. Mr Leach was a bespoke tailor of sorts, with his own room in St George's Road, and my father and Cousin Willie, a miner who lived with us, got their suits from him, paid for on the weekly instalment plan, which he collected every Saturday afternoon. It would never have entered their minds to go to anyone else but Mr Leach, for they had the Irish way of keeping to the one tradesman, not only from a sense of loyalty, but to avoid dealing with new people.

There was the odd occasion—a rare one up to 1920—when Mother would approach Mr Leach with an apologetic smile: 'I wonder, Mr Leach,' she would say, 'would you mind leaving it till next week?' She preferred to be alone with him on such occasions, but, liking to hear Mr Leach and being the nosey fellow I was, I might be present, to see Mr Leach flush with embarrassment, as though ashamed of any distress his visit may have caused. 'But of course, of course,' he would say, 'I understand perfectly.' But, unlike other collectors, he would not dart out of the door instantly, which betrayed to the watching neighbours—some people had little to occupy their interest, and tooting, as it was called, from behind curtains on all that went on in the street passed as a sort of entertainment—that the caller in question had been given a miss. Mr Leach would stand there and at once light upon some topic which occupied a minute or two, which would not only deceive the neighbours, but would dismiss all aspects of the missing payment from mind; then he would later leave with the usual hat-raising and a smile on his face. (I tell of such ordinary happenings with more detail than they may merit, simply to give some idea of the countless subleties of working-class domestic and street life.) 'Sure I'm ashamed to miss that decent man,' I had heard Mother remark, 'to see him so troubled that I should be short of money.'

I hurried getting dressed in the kitchen so that I could go in and hear what Mr Leach had to say. He was a man who had a need to express himself on the political state of the world, and on Saturday afternoon in Bolton there may have been a scarcity of listeners, especially so since his opinions were of a radical nature. One strap of my braces had stretched and was in danger of splitting away, there was a button off the back of my trousers, one of my stockings looked as though it might soon spring a hole in the heel, and, as I was finicky about such matters, I had my usual little fantasy of wishing to be in the navy where the trousers held up at the waist, or on a desert island where one didn't have to worry about such things as missing buttons; then I hurried in to hear what new comments on the state of the world Mr Leach had to say this week.

Mr Leach interrupted himself to greet me, a courtesy no other club collector would consider towards a boy, and then went on talking about the disgraceful happenings in Ireland, where in March of that year, 1920, the Royal Irish Constabulary and the Black and Tans had made their way after midnight into the home of the young Lord Mayor of Cork, Tomas MacCurtain, and murdered him. I was a keen patriot at the time, and, although I knew of the murder, for my father often spoke of it, I was moved by this Englishman's account, told in a quiet English manner, as though apologizing for his own countrymen—which I felt few Irishmen would do. It was Mr Leach who inspired in me an affection and respect for this kind of English gentleman, the quiet and often ineffective idealist, who leaves a special memory among those who have actually known him. Curiously enough, Mother failed to respond with the condemnation I should have expected: 'May the Lord have mercy on him,' she said, blessing herself, and added, '—but where there are men with guns, an' maybe have drink taken, isn't there bound to be injury and death.'

Suddenly my father entered from the back kitchen, having come down quietly from his afternoon sleep—he worked nights at the pit—wearing his flannel shirt and old trousers, but respectable enough. He must have heard Mr Leach and he joined in with him, denouncing the thousands of armed raids on homes, the sackings and burnings of towns and shootings of unarmed civilians. Mother beckoned me to follow her into the back kitchen. She put water in the small kettle and put it on the small iron gas stove and lit the single ring, for the one thing my father had to have on getting up was tea.

'You'd need to be ready to take young James up to meet Uncle,' she said.

'I'm hungry,' I said, '—famished.'

Mother had a way of knowing better than myself what I fancied or needed, and producing it without delay, so that in a minute or two I was standing at the big chest of drawers in the kitchen eating a meat sandwich and drinking a freshly brewed cup of hot strong sweet tea, all on my own, the way I liked to eat. Mr Leach had moved the talk with my father from Ireland to Lloyd George and on to Russia. Then he went off. I went in the front kitchen after Mother. My father took the mug of tea from her, had his usual rather dainty sip, and then said, 'That man has the greatest head on him for facts an' figures of any man ever I knew—although he tells me he never takes a drink.' No appraisal of a man had any significance for my father unless it included his drinking habits. He was suspicious of the man who apparently didn't drink, and scornful of the one who avoided drink because of the expense: 'He doesn't drink but he'll sup all you pay for—'; the genuine teetotaller quite mystified him: 'If a man doesn't drink,' he would often ask aloud, 'what does he do?' It was beyond him to conceive of someone abstaining from choice, as though such a one preferred to be less than half alive.

He lowered his voice and gave me one of his intense questioning looks: 'But he's a Communist—an' though they're right in many ways, the first thing they'd do if ever they came to power would be to go round to all the Catholic churches, take out the priests, line them up against the wall, an'—' he went silent and raised his hands in the gesture of a man firing a gun. I found it a most impressive moment, until my mother spoke up: 'That man', she said, 'would not hurt a fly.' And as I took young James's hand to shepherd him off to meet Uncle William it seemed that my father's words faded away and some truth in my mother's words stuck in my mind.

Mother ushered me and my young brother James to the front door to make sure we shouldn't be late for greeting Uncle William as he stepped off the tramcar outside Heap's furniture shop at the corner of Derby Street and Peace Street. Any show of ill humour over a duty or task that had to be done would be considered most ungracious, so that it was rarely indulged, although, as my mother stood at the door all smiling, I let her see by an odd shrug or two that taking James to meet Uncle William was not exactly to my liking. From an early age the Irish child was expected to behave in a quiet and considerate manner, shouldering his share of the family difficulties and responsibilities, so that he cultivated a control and often a cunning, far beyond that of his English counterpart, who was free to grumble as much as he liked, so long as he did the job on hand, and was in time to start work as the mill buzzer blew. I felt like an old man in my behaviour and thinking compared with that of my schoolmates or even street-corner pals.

James, five years younger than myself, was a good-natured and easygoing boy, but uninteresting to me, the elder brother. I pretended to listen to his prattle as we approached the corner, but the thought that was on my mind was how in two hours' time I would be secretly returning to that same place to meet my girlfriend, Alice Varley. It was the only chance she would have of slipping away from the street and her street mates without being noticed. No matter what move you made in our street, if it was at all out of the ordinary it seemed someone spotted you, and wanted to know what you were up to and where you were going. But on Saturday

evenings things were freer, some working girls would go to
the pictures, and somehow it wasn't considered nice to play
street games, being that the next day was Sunday. And the
reason we had arranged to meet at a busy corner was that it
provided any number of excuses for being there, in case
someone came along—you could be waiting for a tram, or
going to Hodgson's toffee shop, or the chemist, or thinking of
getting some tripe bits from Vose's across the road, or just
looking in shop windows.

Two trams came along without Uncle William appearing,
and James said that, since he had threepence, shouldn't we go
lower down Derby Street to Skinny Nancy's shop to see what
he could buy whilst we were waiting. He was a boy who had
no sense about holding on to money—he always wanted to
spend it at once. I was glad to escape the tedium of waiting,
and agreed. Derby Street seemed to have emerged from a
wartime dullness, when the shops had had few goods to put
on display, for now they all seemed dazzling with new goods.
Pearson's bicycle shop had a windowful of lovely bicycles,
Raleighs and Rudge-Whitworths, and Skinny Nancy's shop
had a window crammed with all manner of sports goods:
footballs and cricket bats, fishing rods and lines, roller skates,
tennis rackets, Sandow's developers, dumb-bells and bar-
bells. There was the usual film of dust over everything, for
Nancy Davenport and her brother Mark, who kept the shop,
were reputed to be misers who never washed or dusted. It
didn't seem that threepence would buy very much, but
Nancy, a small witchlike creature in old dark clothes, with
gold-rimmed spectacles so grimy that it was a wonder how
she could see through them, fobbed James off with 'The
Kaiser's Last Stand' for his coppers. It was a little model in
hardened clay of old Kaiser Bill, at stool. With it went three
small pills, one of which was to be placed in his open mouth,
then a lighted cigarette or a match had to be placed under
him, after which he would defecate. I had tried to explain to
Jim that this begrimed model of the Kaiser was old wartime
stuff and had been out of fashion for a year or two, but the
idea of seeing the emperor doing his business so fascinated his

childish mind, together with the hypnotic gaze of Skinny Nancy when out to sell, that he would not heed me—especially when to clinch the deal she gave him three matches as a sort of bonus.

We had to run to the tram-stop, and there was Uncle William, standing on the pavement and not feeling too happy, I thought, at our having failed to be on the spot to greet him, although he did produce his usual smile. The first thing James showed him—which I'd asked him not to—was the squatting figure of Kaiser Bill. It was I who got the cool look from Uncle for letting young James buy such a vulgar toy. That boy will never have a steam of sense, I felt, being born and brought up in England. When we got back home Mother had the hot potato cake ready for Uncle William, and with him ensconced in my father's rocking-chair, drinking tea, his usual good humour soon revived in him. He now allowed James to feel down in the big pocket of his jacket to retrieve a bag of sweets and some coins, and he beckoned me across and slipped sixpence into my hand. The Irish were great at giving money, for soon our cousins Patrick and John arrived from the mining village of Westhoughton, and I got a threepenny-piece and twopence. I always refused, of course, knowing I could be sure they would thrust it on me.

My sister May, eighteen months older than myself, avoided the Saturday evening gatherings, and usually slipped in next door to play with Alice and Lizzie Woods; brother Edward, four years old than I, had got a job at the Maypole Dairy shop and worked until eight o'clock in the evening, and James was too young to enter into things, so that I was the one who hurried to open the door when I spotted a visitor of ours crossing the road; I also did little jobs around the house, such as bringing in coal for the fire, but so far as possible I kept out of my father's way, for I found the man, with his loud voice and manner, a threat to my peace of mind. Around half-past-six I was watching for the time when I should slip off unnoticed to meet Alice, when Cousin Willie beckoned me to go along with him to the outdoor licence shop, Nancy's, to help carry back some jugs and bottles of beer.

Uncle William had handed him a pound note, and, as I had time to spare, I went off up the backstreet with Willie, carrying one of the jugs.

Willie, a good-looking young man in his twenties, a collier in the mine, was my favourite among our cousins. Uncle William was fifty-five, my father forty-five, and to me there was something vaguely old and unlively about them; nor had they the good looks, fresh skin, and fresh smile about them that Willie had, and above all they lacked a youthful spontaneity, a way of making one laugh and feel at ease, and so now it was a pleasure to step it out alongside Willie as we went up our backstreet together, turned right at the end, and there was the outdoor licence at the corner of Birkdale Street. And what was always an ordeal for me when accompanying my father was now a bit of fun, as Nancy blushed and wiped her cherry nose with a small hanky as Willie made jokes, and out of the back place came old Ma Nightingale to join in the chat, and even the old Airedale dog came round for Willie and myself to stroke him.

Then back home we went, carrying three large jugs of beer between us, and Willie with bottles of Crown Ale in his pockets, and myself carrying a large bottle of stout. We slipped in the back gate and into the back kitchen and unloaded ourselves there, and Willie gave me sixpence out of the change—it was really Uncle William's of course—poured out a cupful of best beer for me, the glasses being needed for the young men calling in. I gulped down the beer, but would have enjoyed it more had I been able to take it at my leisure, and with plenty of money in my pocket and the beer in my stomach I sneaked quickly out the back way.

3

The Tryst with Alice

I WENT off in a state of suppressed excitement, keeping my gaze to the ground, as though deep in thought, in case I passed any of my mates. I didn't want to exchange more than a nod, so that I could meet Alice—the girl I loved. When I got to Derby Street the scene was livening up. There were married couples going towards town, perhaps making for the enclosed market, or planning to go the second-house pictures, or maybe for a drink, and groups of mill girls in their Saturday-night clothes, and I found it simple enough to remain unnoticed, as I pretended to wait for a tram, looked in the paper-shop window, and memorized the advertisement for pens on a tin panel in the doorway, 'They come as a boon and a blessing to men, The Pickwick, the Owl, and the Waverley pen.' I wished there were more like that one, I thought, for I enjoyed a rhyme. I crossed the road to Vose's tripe shop, which was managed by a family called Wilkinson, who had a handsome son called Neville, and from there I looked across to Peace Street, and my heart gave a funny turn as I suddenly saw Alice walking along. She was wearing a weekday blue dress—apparently not wishing to give the show away to her parents or other girls—and I could see her thick hair must be in a broad single plait and not in Sunday ringlets, and yet so startlingly different did she look in her quiet beauty and erect bearing from all others, that for a moment it seemed she and I were the only two persons in the world—or at least the only two in the scene—for all the others looked like clockwork figures moving around, their mouths opening and shutting, their limbs moving, but all without significance. How lucky I had been to meet up with Alice—for had our family stayed home in Ireland I should

never have known her! It seemed inconceivable to me, that
she and I would have been languishing away for the rest of
our lives, longing for the ideal sweetheart! Or was it as
Bolton folk said, 'What you never had you never missed'?
No—never!—I had been only half alive until I met Alice.
Stop!—a sin to think like that—setting aside God and the
Holy Spirit. No—I had only *seemed* half alive.

The next thing she saw me, and, although we had arranged
not to recognize each other until we were sure the coast was
clear and there was no one we knew hanging about, I saw her
give a big smile, and her pace quicken, and I smiled back at
her from the distance. I dare not go down High Street, since
two schoolmates were living there, one at number 27 and
another at number 36, and I might easily bump into one or
the other. It was a tricky business, because you did not walk
down other folk's streets—main roads or streets made up of
gable-ends were all right, since they were not considered
private. And so I now turned round by the tripe shop and
casually made my way up Derby Street on the left-hand side,
and she went up on the opposite side; I saw her glancing in
shop windows, making out she was just passing the time. In
Bolton you never saw a boy and girl out together unless they
were brother and sister, which you could always tell by the
way one bossed the other or both were sulking. It felt exciting
to be kidding the world at large about our love affair. I
turned left at a pub called the Pike View, and into Swan Lane,
first making sure that Alice saw me from the other side of the
road, so that she would be sure to follow. Swan Lane wasn't
a proper street like ours, but was a sort of faded posh, and
had no street-corner where lads might gather. Then I dodged
into a short and narrow piece of backstreet behind the pub,
hidden up against a post, and as Alice came along I suddenly
darted out and gave her a little scare, and she gave a cry and
then a laugh, and it felt so jolly to let one's feelings out.

I laughed and lost all control—as it seemed I always did in
the presence of someone I was very fond of, and I started
joking around in a way that would have given the game away
at once. Then, knowing how girls like being complimented

on their clothes, I said, 'I like you in that dress.' 'It's not my best frock,' she said, 'but my Mam says I suit blue.' I hesitated a moment, and then said, 'I think by rights it should be "blue suits you".' She frowned slightly and I quickly said, 'I suppose it's just another way of puttin' it.' I was sorry I had corrected her. 'I say, let's go an' get some toffee, darling,' I added. It was awkward to keep tagging the word 'darling' on to the end of sentences, the same as they spoke in women's magazines, but Alice rather expected it. Her blue eyes now opened wide with admiration. She was an only child, from a respectable family, teetotallers, careful of every penny that was spent, and the open-handed Irish way impressed her. I led her along towards a toffee shop in Derby Street.

'Mind walking under the ladder!' she called out a warning to me. The ladder was outside a house where they were doing some emergency repair to an upstairs window, and after hearing her warning I showed how daring I was by deliberately walking under it. 'Ooh, you are reckless,' she said. 'But you see, you'll have bad luck.' I explained to her that it was only a superstition. 'It might be,' she said, 'but these superstitions have a way of comin' true.'

Then she went on about how her mother once cut her nails on a Sunday and how everything went wrong for her, and as for putting new shoes down on a table, or spilling salt, or breaking a mirror—there was no end of bad luck attached to such careless acts. How is it, I thought, as she detailed what had happened, that a girl can be so beautiful and look so intelligent and talk so daft. The only trouble is, if you're not careful, you find yourself talking just as daft as they do. The liberal buying of the toffee, however—I liked showing off in a modest manner—made her smile and look happy, as it always did. And I enjoyed it, too, for, although Alice could be quietly bossy at times, it was like taking a child out when she was in a sweet shop. When we left the shop Alice had a Fry's cream bar, and a fat bag of Mackintosh's toffees in her hand. I was a shilling short—one-and-a-penny in fact—of what I had had going in but I felt it perhaps worth it.

'You shouldn't spend your money like that,' she said,

'—you should save some.'

'What for?' I said.

'For our future,' she said. I could have kissed her for that.

When we came out I made the way back into Peace Street, and turned sharply up the backstreet which on one side was Derby Street and the other Howcroft Street, which I knew was always deserted; I caught Alice's hand, and pulled her behind a thick telegraph pole and gave her the kiss. It seemed I didn't get the response I was expecting, and I saw a distasteful look cross her face: 'Ugh,' she said, 'you smell of beer!'

I felt awfully hurt. A half-cupful of Magee's best beer, and the way she said it made it sound like something really foul and smelly. My father was right after all, there was something odd about teetotallers.

'*I smell of beer!*' I said. I had to be careful how I spoke since I didn't want to tell an outright lie before Communion next morning.

'I—I thought you did,' she said, faltering. She should have known before, I thought, how easily hurt I am.

'It's all right, Alice,' I said. But I knew it wasn't. How sure of yourself you are, I thought, when you're feeling happy—you don't realize how a word or two can make you just as unhappy.

Somehow nothing went right after that. We wandered along View Street, turned along Brandon Street, went into Willows Lane—but wherever we went I had a schoolmate living there and had to dodge around a bit, going ahead or behind Alice. She seemed to get impatient with my tactics, and almost in tears she burst out: 'I don't care if the whole world knows I love you!' Then added, 'And *passionately*.' With that she actually linked up with me, put her arm through mine, going along the street. I felt I'd have died of shame if a schoolmate had seen us.

'I don't care either,' I said, as I gently disengaged my arm.

'It looks like it!' she exclaimed, in a rather common tone, quite unlike the voice she usually had for me.

'It's just that I don't want any of my mates to know,' I said, 'or they'll never stop pullin' my leg. You see, darling, they don't understand what it is to be in love.'

I found I was sweating a bit, and noticed that she had stopped eating the chocolate, which was a sure sign that she was unhappy. It struck me she might have been right about walking under the ladder—it didn't do to scoff at any super-stition, no matter what. If I'd my time over again, I thought, I'd walk quietly round it and say nothing. Then later she told me that she had to be in by nine o'clock at the latest, so that her mother could wash her hair and put it in curling cloths for Sunday. These were strips of cloth, each of which was wound round a long lock of hair then left for the night to produce ringlets next day.

The moment that thoughts and the like began to break into my feelings, I found myself thinking what a nuisance it could be to go around with a girl. It seemed that you always had to buy them something for a start—then they didn't understand jokes—they never said anything that stuck in your mind—not if you were courting one—and not only had a lad to watch his tongue all the time, but he had to keep talking their way to please them. We had to separate near Gibbon Street, and so miserable were we both that we somehow forgot or didn't feel inclined to make arrangements to meet. It was only as I stood watching her lonely figure as she went off, that once more the love rose up warmly in my heart, and I thought what a beautiful if often painful feeling love was, and how different Alice was from all other girls on earth.

I did not return home when Alice had gone, nor did I go to the Lads' Corner at the gable-end of our street where the lamp-post was, but wandered down Gibbon Street, and then cut across to Cannon Street, and came up that way. By chance I met Ernie Arpino, an older lad with whom, together with his younger brother, Albert, I often went to school. Along the way we used to tell tales, and I would make up poems about fat Mister Bibby who had the fish-and-chip shop. Ernie was allowed to gather with the little-piecers and other young workers on the fringe of the Big Corner, where the youths and men of the neighbourhood met, chatted, and argued. The Arpino family lived at the end house in Back Cannon Street, just opposite the Big Corner, and the big lads played knock-up, a form of hand-ball, against their gable-end; Louis Arpino, the eldest son, a collier and a good wrestler, was one of the main figures at the Big Corner, so that Ernie couldn't be shooed off. I was considered rather big for my age, and being quiet I was able to nudge myself in among Ernie and his mates, Joe Fish, Pierce and Jimmy Naylor, and others. We were off the pavement, but I could hear every word of the big lads' talk. I felt privileged to be there. Then along came Sammy Howarth with his melodeon, and since Sammy, in his twenties, lived next-door-but-one to us, I felt then that I wouldn't be told to clear off. Sammy was a good player, and after a few tunes Jud Burns called out: 'Hy, lads, what about a walk up the Middle Brook?' It was agreed they would all go off on a walk. So they rose up from their hunkers and made off down Cannon Street on their way to the Middle Brook. Ernie Arpino turned to Joe Fish and me and one or two others, 'What about it, lads?' he asked. We all agreed to follow the big lads, but we kept well behind them, six of us in all, and once or twice there were shouts for us to get back home, but Ernie kept going, moving closer to the group, and right close when we came to a tough district known as the Pocket and felt more in need of their protection. It was a warm May evening, and dusk was falling but slowly, and once we got clear of all the houses and factories and mills, going along beside the Middle Brook, near Deane Golf Course, the air suddenly felt beautifully fresh and soft. And now Sammy played songs with scarcely a pause, and they all sang, mostly wartime songs, 'Roses are Blooming in Picardy' and 'Mademoiselle from Armentières'. Sammy always switched from a sad tune to a lively one.

I felt I was somehow coming of age to be close to these older lads, to hear their lively singing voices and occasional wild whoops of laughter. Yet with all the pleasure it seemed there was a tinge of melancholy, one that had clung to me ever since we left Old Ireland, a feeling to which I had grown so used that I felt a bit lost without it. And I kept thinking, this is the best way to enjoy myself, for I'm among young lads like myself, and I can say what I feel like, and I am enjoying all those songs. At the same time I kept dipping deep inside myself and sensing my secret love for my dear Alice—most keenly when Sammy played 'She's the Lassie from Lancashire'—yet without having her clinging to my arm and talking daft. Tomorrow morning, I told myself, with empty stomach, and after a good Act of Contrition with shining white soul, I shall go to Mass and take Holy Communion, and on top of all else I shall have God Himself within me—or at least his Blessed Son, Our Lord Jesus Christ. What a lucky lad am I, I thought, to be me and no one else—and what a pity I spent one-and-a-penny on Alice, and got so little out of it.

4

June Holiday Week, 1920

THE year 1920 turned out to be an odd one all round. At first there was all this money about. There had been money during the War, of course, with everybody working, many of them on overtime, but then there had been precious little to spend it on. But now the toffee shops had any amount of sweets and chocolate of a kind not seen during the War. A neighbour in 1920 could no longer just open her front door, beckon the first lad she saw, send him on a few errands, and then give him a penny; lads held out for a penny an errand.

'That won't pay for the bloomin' clog-irons I've worn out,' I heard Teddy Fairclough tell Mrs Challoner when she gave him a penny for three errands. Of course, she had a cunning way of first asking a lad to go to the corner shop for something, which looked like an easy penny earned, but when he got back she would say, 'I wonder could you run to Warburton's greengrocers for me?' If he refused he got nothing. After Warburton's she might then ask him to take her books back to High Street library and change them. That was what she had done with Teddy. 'You'll not get me for your mug, next time, Missis Jellybelly,' he added as he walked away. 'You impertinent thing,' she called after him in her posh voice, 'you'll be glad of it one day.' Then she remarked to the world at large, 'You don't know where you are with folk these days!'

I agreed with her in my own mind, for now you got lads who had been as humble as could be becoming quite cocky because they had a tanner in the pocket. Money seemed to change the character. Lads who had been glad to spend an evening eating a penny pomegranate with a pin, picking one seed after another, now simply tore a full glossy fruit open and broke it in chunks and finished it off in five minutes. Prices were rising faster than wages, and the knocker-up, who was an old-age pensioner, raised his weekly charge from fourpence to sixpence; my mother had always given him six-pence anyway—she wouldn't take the twopence change—so now there was ninepence waiting for him on the dresser on Saturday afternoon when he called for his money. All the slang terms for money were bandied around with relish: 'I've got some *iron*,' 'Hand over the *shekels*,' 'Don't worry, I'm *carryin'*,' and 'Take a *Bradbury*.' Lads got so cocky once they had a bit of *splosh* in their pockets—they were not as easy to get on with, or so I thought.

When June Holiday Week came round, with all the mills and industry closing down, there were people going off on holiday—even letting lads carry their bags to the station— who had never been away in their lives. You couldn't get into the High Street swimming baths for queues of men trying to get a scrub down before going away. 'I reckon to have one good bath a year,' they used to say, 'whether I need it or not.' Even in our own home we were not to escape the mood. Uncle William arrived on the Friday evening to take Mother and young James back home to Ireland for a week. I had heard talk, although Mother herself had been rather quiet about it; but I could hardly believe it when the moment came for them to go, and my father eagerly picked up Mother's suitcase, and Uncle William his own, ready for off. I had remained silent and unprotesting, but when she came to hug and kiss me the tears began to flow. That she, my own good mother, would go off home to Ireland for a week leaving me at the untender mercy of my father—whom she knew I detested! She slipped a two-shilling piece into my palm, and Uncle William pressed a half-crown on me, which, although amounting to a good sum of money, seemed to be without any power to comfort me. Moreover, I felt it to be bribery. What do they want to take James to Ireland for, I asked myself, who has never seen the place, and leave me, the only one around who loves it, behind! And yet with all the flurry of feelings within I couldn't say a word but silently cry. And from the cut of my father and the way he was going on I could see he was glad to see them off, so that he could enjoy a week's holiday and drinking in peace.

It was the most unhappy week of my life up to then. At the time I had little common interest with my sister May or brother Edward; May had girls in the street who were her close friends, and she would visit their homes; Edward's whole concern appeared to be clothes, and after that girls. It seemed that it was always I who was thrust in the company of my father when he came in after his midday drinking. I had no stomach for the food he prepared for us; he was fond of fat meat, which made me sick. And for Sunday dinner he produced a roast of meat which he was unwise enough to tell us was horsemeat. I wouldn't touch it. But above all I was made uncomfortable by his bouts of drunken cajolery, when he would praise and flatter me in a manner that I could see was utterly false. It seemed that the joy I had been antici-pating in escaping from my teacher, the testy Miss Newsham, was drowned in the misery of daily contact with my father—whom I had always tried to avoid. There was nothing I could say against him, except that he was a man whose feelings were concerned solely with himself. Nobody else, it seemed, ever quite broke through this barrier. And to make matters worse, at a time when Alice and I might have enjoyed a few of our walks together out in the country, her mother and father had taken her to Southport for a week's holiday. The right place for teetotallers, I gathered, so different was it said to be from breezy Blackpool—neither of which Lancashire resorts had I visited, but could not help hearing them being talked about.

I resolved, however, not to fritter my four-shillings-and-sixpence away, but buy myself some chest expanders from Skinny Nancy's. The chest was the one thing the big lads boasted about at the Big Corner, and of anyone who lacked a decent chest he was said to be 'Not as far through as a bloody kipper.' I had decided they wouldn't say that about me. But when I went to try the developers I found I couldn't budge them with the three springs on. Then Mark managed to remove one, but it was still no use. He took another spring off, but even with the one spring I couldn't use them. Skinny Nancy was not going to let me go without spending, and she foisted on me a fishing-line—a sport for which I had no inclination. What the week did for me, however, was to harden me up a bit, for at heart I was a real softie. Had my mother returned by Monday or Tuesday I should have run to her, and perhaps burst sobbing into her arms with relief and love. But by Saturday morning, when the party did return, I had somehow got the worst over, and had realized that misery, if borne long enough, can become an acceptable element of one's life. And so I was able to preserve a cool front when Mother came open-armed to me, and to fend off her concern about me, and not give too much away (until I got a good chance later to tell her about the horsemeat and other tribulations). And I was especially reserved towards Uncle William.

The one happy event of that month of a school holiday was that one fine evening, when the street was a most lively scene with rounders and other games being played by girls in the cobbled roadway—no traffic beyond the occasional ice-cream cart drawn by a pony ventured into the street in the evening—and many homes had the parents on wooden chairs outside their doors, I managed to get a few moments with Alice. We arranged to meet the next day, again near Heap's furniture shop. I still had three shillings left of my money, and was able to slip sixpence into her hand as we were looking into a shop window. Then she got on the next tram going to town, and sat below, and I went up on the top deck. In town we were fairly safe, and we went along together to the tram starting-place opposite Trinity Street Station. And there we caught a tram to Dunscar and went for a walk in a place called the Jumbles. Alice knew it because she had once been in a sanatorium there, when she was said to be 'overgrowing her strength'. That was a wonderful day for us both, walking hand-in-hand by a stream in the country, where I could feel sure I would meet none of my schoolmates. I had learned from my week of misery how to control myself better, to avoid always giving way to impulses and getting too excited.

It all worked well, for I played the silent and masterful man, which role Alice seemed to prefer. She kept gazing at me admiringly with her large blue eyes—an experience I couldn't get too much of. I was rather sorry when a week or so later my reserve began to give way to let in my natural spontaneous self.

The main subject of talk in our home during late summer and early autumn of 1920 was the hunger-strike of Terence MacSwiney in Brixton Prison. Terence MacSwiney, poet and philosopher, was an ardent member of Sinn Fein, and when his friend, Tomas MacCurtain, was murdered, MacSwiney, forty, succeeded him as Lord Mayor of Cork. In August the military arrested him and others in Cork City Hall. They all decided to go on hunger-strike; the others were released but not MacSwiney—who was sentenced to two years' imprisonment by a court-martial. He said he would limit the sentence by a fast, and his stand attracted sympathy from all over the world. Efforts were made to get the British government to release him, but they refused.

It was in October, coinciding with the final days of MacSwiney's seventy-four-day fast, that the miners came out on strike for an increase in wages—the railwaymen and dock workers having got rises. My poor father was distraught over MacSwiney, and would be up early, waiting eagerly for the morning newspapers—he took the *Daily Herald*, the one Labour newspaper, and the *Daily News*, which was Liberal—to learn if MacSwiney was still alive. After attempts to force-feed him, he died in Brixton Prison on 24 October. My father could hardly speak when he read the news, and was greatly upset. Lloyd George settled the strike, largely on the miners' terms, within three weeks. It was not a defeat for him, but a cunning tactic on his part, a temporary solution to the mining problem, since he was preparing to advance the date of decontrol, when the miners and their wages would once again be the concern of the mineowners.

It was around that same time that I suffered one of my frequent bouts of sore throat. But then I began to feel more sick and feverish, and woke up one morning to find myself covered with numerous red spots; and, as it happened, so was my sister May. Word was left at the surgery for Dr Beesley to call when he was on his rounds with his bicycle. Meanwhile there was scared talk between May and myself of our being sent off to the fever hospital in Hulton Lane, which was usual for children with scarlet fever, but which we did not fancy. Dr Beesley arrived and flung back the bedclothes. 'Scarlatina rash,' he said. 'Keep them in bed for a few days.' We did not know that this was another term for scarlet fever, and at once my mother seized upon it as being only a mild disorder in which there was a rash. Since Dr Beesley did not report it, she saw no reason why she should. But after a week or so, when the long pieces of skin began to peel off, there was little doubt about what we had had, although 'scarlet fever' was never mentioned.

Uncle William visited us daily during that short strike, and once again made what later seemed pathetic attempts to create a garden for Mother down one side of our backyard. They were both fond of flowers, something I doubt my father ever gave a thought to. He brought a load of soil on a cart from the farm nearby his lodgings, and, using long boards, partitioned off an area in which there were a few inches of soil. But, alas, there was never a ray of sunshine that reached that yard.

One day when I was recovering from my illness he came with a surprise present for me—a brand new book with stiff backs and nice large print. 'I've heard said,' I heard him say to Mother, 'that this is a good book.' I don't think Uncle had read a book in his life. Secretly I was disappointed with his present, for I should have much preferred comics, or a boy's magazine. But I was always glad of something to read, and so I began *Jane Eyre*.

The picture I got at the opening, of the orphan Jane, seated like a Turk, hidden from the mean and nasty Reed family in the window-seat, reading about birds and wild places, took hold of me almost at once. I read on, and could not bear to be interrupted; I read of the horrible John striking her, of the red room where she was locked away and thought she saw a ghost. I was no longer myself—I was brave little Jane. And what I admired above all was how she spoke up to Mrs Reed before being sent away to Lowood, telling her exactly what she thought about her. If only I had the guts to do the same to Miss Newsham! My eyes became sore and weary, migraine dots danced around in the air—I was impatient at her long talks with Mr Rochester, and began to skip them—until finally I finished that strange story. It was all too much for my ten-year-old imagination. I had nightmares until I almost wished I had never seen the book. It had been such an intense experience that I couldn't wait to get hold of *Film Fun* and read the comic adventures of Ben Turpin and Chester Conklin, and Charlie Chaplin in the *Funny Wonder* comic, to take its place in my mind. I was relieved when someone borrowed the book and never brought it back. (It was sixty years before I came across another copy by chance. Although at first I was reluctant to open it, I did so, and began to read. Again the story took hold of me, as I read with the same engrossment. It revived old memories, and not only did I dream of the old greenwashed back bedroom in Bolton, but had waking images of it, of the sick and sweating hours, the sounds from the backstreet of children playing, the smell of middens, and a keen memory of Uncle William.)

5

Reconciliation with Uncle William

IT WAS at that period that a happy reconciliation took place between Uncle William and myself. It turned out to be one for which I had reason to be deeply grateful, and after which all trace of ill will between us was to vanish. I grew to love and respect the dear man in a new way, and he in turn accorded me a special nod and look of understanding, as though we had some unspoken bond of our own, and our relationship was on another level from that with others. It came about in the first instance because of a piggy. A piggy was a small rounded piece of wood about two-and-a-half inches in length, over an inch in diameter, which might have been cut off a broom handle, with one end tapered down from about one-third the length into a conelike point; for the game of piggy one had to have a useful piece of wood, known as a striker, not too heavy nor too light, something in the form of a boiler stick, which was used for swirling the clothes round in the wash boiler, but the wood had to be hard. The piggy would be placed on a flat stone surface, the striking player would stoop over it, tap the end, causing the piggy to rise in the air, and then he would strike at it, driving the piggy as far as he could. Next he would estimate how many leaping strides he could give for it—and his opponent would then try to cover the distance in that or a lesser number; if he succeeded the striker had lost that number and if he failed the number was added to the striker's total. It was a popular backstreet game; there were said to be variations of it, one known as tipcat or pussy, in which the tipcat was pointed at both ends, and had to be struck twice. Around our neighbourhood in Bolton nothing of that childish sort was allowed, and it had to be a proper piggy.

I had done some sums for a boy named Whittaker in my class—at least I showed him the figures and the answers—and he was so grateful that he insisted on giving me a present of a piggy which he said had belonged to his uncle who was killed in the war. I didn't really want it, and a piggy was not a thing of much value anyway. Indeed you could buy one from Skinny Nancy's for three-halfpence, made by her brother Mark, a wood-turner. But a good piggy was rather like a good cricket bat, in that it would be handed down; a brand new one was not thought very much of, since a piggy had to prove its worth in actual play, and also it had to become seasoned. The piggy I was given did not at first sight impress me much. It was a smaller piggy than usual and, judging from its dark worn appearance, it was obviously old, yet it was not frayed in any way, and was smooth to the touch, pleasant to feel, and heavy for its size. I had gone about with it in my pocket before my illness, and slowly it began to take on some odd significance, in the way a pebble from the beach will from constant handling.

There had been no opportunity to try it out in actual play, although in the backyard when I had practised it for its rising quality—a good riser was an essential quality in a piggy—I had found it responsive. In fact, almost too much so for me, since it had a liveliness that one had to get used to. When struck on the end it was entirely absent in the fault of certain piggies, which was known as back rising—that is, rising in the air in a backward arc, making it difficult to strike any distance. It was perfectly balanced, always rose truly, and even more, if struck correctly, it rose with a slight forward movement, which meant that one could bring the piggy stick forward with a swinging understroke, and so send it much further than most piggies would travel. Once I got used to giving it the right gentle tap, I realized I had a treasure in that piggy.

On the day I felt I had recovered I went out to our street-

corner in the afternoon, and there met a pal called Ernie
Fairclough, who had also been off school. I had the piggy in
my pocket, and after a time I asked Ernie did he fancy a game
of piggy on the Brickfield, an area of rough sloping ground,
some three hundred yards from our street-corner. Ernie was a
good mate, a most reasonable one—which was an unusual
trait at street-corners, where there was a tendency for lads to
behave purely on impulse. Ernie said he would like a game,
and I went in home and found a piece of a worn pick-shaft
near the coalshed and gave it a good wiping; then I joined
Ernie, and, our eyes skinned for the schoolboard officer, we
set off for the Brickfield. It was a clear fresh day, and, going
along the streets in the afternoon quiet, chatting to Ernie, my
piggy in my pocket, a good piggy stick in my hand, I felt a
sense of anticipation about the game. We decided to set our
mort on a spot high up on the Brickfield, well away from
houses, so that we shouldn't break a window. I did a bit of
loosening up with my piggy stick, and then had a light stroke
or two with the piggy, and felt that my eye was in, and my
arm free and fairly strong. We tossed up a piece of slate for
first go and Ernie won. He took his strike, got only a short
one, made it a five, and I didn't bother to jump it, but let him
have his five.

As I put my dark piggy on the stone, and took up my piggy
stick, I surveyed the scene for a moment. In the distance there
was a mass of terraced houses, sloping down away, street
after street, set in amongst countless factories and mill
chimneys, with smoke rising slowly from almost every house-
top chimney and from every mill stack, so that there was a
huge industrial saucer half-buried in grey smoky mist, and
rising away beyond could be seen the hills, Belmont or some
place, and coming from there, and perhaps from the distant
sea itself, was this soft westerly breeze. That was one good
thing about living in a place devoid of beauty: the little that
sneaked in seemed to be touched with some mystical flavour,
beyond ordinary experience. I made a silent prayer of thanks
to God.

'Right, Bill,' said Ernie. Even the most understanding

Boltonian did not care to be left hanging about whilst his opponent meditated. 'Right, Ernie,' I said.

I stooped and first tapped the stone on which the dark piggy was placed, and then I lifted my eyes and looked ahead, again with a sort of contemplative gaze, but reflecting this time on how far I might knock my piggy. Then I turned once more to my prospect of striking, and with a little care, but not too much, I tapped the end of the piggy for the rise. The black piggy rose smoothly, maybe a yard high, and with just enough forward direction for me to swing my pick-handle and strike without changing my balance much, except to bring the weight to my front foot. It was not a swipe, not even a really hard strike, but just a pleasant swing with some nice drive behind it. It connected clean and true, made a crisp sound, pleasant to the ear, and the piggy rose swiftly in the air like a small dark bird. I felt an excited fluttering of the heart as I watched it fly through the air.

'Not a bad shot,' murmured Ernie. He seemed as surprised as I was at the ease and accuracy with which I'd driven it. 'Not bad at all, Bill.' There was even a note of suspicion in his voice—from where had I got this sudden skill?

A huge grey stone was seen amongst the surface of clay and rubble of the Brickfield some distance away, and I could see the piggy flying towards it. Then it landed on top of the stone, and rose up off it with a rebound, and went right into the air towards the far pavement. Next it struck a huge white stone in the distance, and shot clear in the air once more, and went like a tiny dark speck across Gibbon Street. For moments all sign of the piggy disappeared.

'Where the 'ell's it gone?' said Ernie.

'I dunno,' I said.

The next thing there came to my ears the distant but clear report of breaking glass. I felt the usual spasm of uneasiness at that particular sound, distant though it was, for it carried the faint but ominous note of a stone striking a windowpane. I stared hard for a long silent second or two and then it seemed I could just make out a gaping hole in the front window of the end house.

'Bloody 'ell!' breathed Ernie, in a sigh of wonder and dis-
belief, '—it's gun' through t' flappin' house-window! Look,
yon corner 'ouse!'

The rise of the piggy and the effortless swing of the piggy
stick, together with the exactness of the impact and the extraordinary flight of the piggy, had transported me for one fleet-
ing moment—giving me a taste of what those players with a
true eye and natural swing may enjoy for long periods of their
lives. 'Hy, come on, Bill!' whispered Ernie anxiously, 'let's
make a run for it—afore they come out. We'll go back home
t'other way—along View Street. Pretend tha'rt crippled—I
will too.' This was a dodge that boys attempted in our
neighbourhood—if you were spotted or likely to be spotted
running away from such an act, you put on a sort of disguise
of a stiff leg, or humpback, so that you might evoke a spot of
sympathy, and also set off a wrong description of yourself.
Then you swiftly adopted your true height and deportment
once you were round a corner.

'There's nob'dy come out, Ernie,' I said. 'Aye, but they will
come out,' said Ernie, 'an' then tha'll be too late.' And with
that he was already off, moving in some sort of hobble, his
piggy stick left behind.

I stood where I was and watched the house in fear and
dismay. If they don't come out, I thought, I'll be off too. And
I'll not be long about it. Then I saw the door open and out
came a man and woman, an elderly couple, with the mild
stoop some people who live in small dainty homes suffer. I
saw them look at the shattered window, and then up and
down the quiet empty street and across the deserted lower
end of the Brickfield. They never thought to look towards me,
since it seemed I was much too far away to be related to what
had happened. I turned and saw Ernie beckoning to me from
the corner of View Street. Something in me longed to join
him, but I could not give way to it. It was not so much
honesty as the way I had been brought up by Mother and
Uncle William that kept me there. The prospect of admitting
guilt was an awful one, but you couldn't just run away and
leave a decent man and woman wondering, perhaps for the

rest of their days, how this had happened to their front
window. Also, I felt a bit unhappy to think I had lost my
piggy. Ernie had now disappeared, and so I made my way,
nervously, uneasily, across the Brickfield. Along the way I
decided to drop my piggy stick and retrieve it later. I went
down towards the man and woman, who were still inspecting
the broken window, perhaps less with annoyance than mysti-
fication. It seemed a long walk to reach them, and they gave
me a look but no more as I approached and braced myself for
the encounter.

'Excuse me, sir,' I said, going up to them and addressing
the man, 'but I'm afraid 'twas I broke your window—with
my piggy.'

I was young, nervous, yet not without a sense of knowing
how to behave. They both looked at me, then at each other,
unsure how to take what I had told them, for it was surely
the first time they had ever known a boy to come right up to
their front door and admit to having broken a window. The
usual response of the householder in such a situation was to
grab the first boy in sight, and hold him until he confessed or
else split on his mates. They didn't grab me. They were
respectable Lancashire working folk, he was probably
retired, not short of money, and it seems that the best of those
people are amongst the best in the world. They appeared
almost disinclined even to believe me, and waited for me to
explain.

'My name is William Naughton,' I said, as I found myself
talking like one of the decent public school chaps I read about
in the *Gem* and *Magnet*, 'and I live at number 8 Unsworth
Street. I'm sure my parents will pay to have your window put
back in. I'm very sorry. I did it with my piggy. It bounced on
a stone.' By this time I became aware of a touch of heroics in
my performance, and catching on to this I sort of lost confidence in myself, and a lump came in my throat. At this the
dear woman went inside and came out with a piece of cake
(always a sign of a respectable home in those days, where
there was cake actually uneaten, lying around under a cover).
Nor did they insist on coming with me to verify my story, but

instead told me not to worry. How strangely and unexpectedly people behave, I thought.

When I arrived back in our street the schools had loosed, and there were a few lads at the corner of the street, amongst them Ernie, and I sensed that the word had gone round. I waved to them as I passed and went off to our house. I felt uneasy as I opened our front door (I was praying all the time to the Blessed Virgin to get me out of the mess), and I found Uncle William had arrived in my absence, and was having a cup of tea with Mother. I might have broken down if Mother had been there alone—the nervous tension after the illness was proving a bit much—but seeing Uncle I put on a face, but maybe a tear did escape. Then I told them both what had happened. To add to my perplexity Uncle William did not seem the least upset at the terrible mishap, and was inclined to treat it lightly. 'But we must go back and tell them it will be all right,' I said.

So I went back to the house along with Uncle William. The man and woman were more posh than our own family, of course, and so was the house, but Uncle William had this expansive manner, and they all got along very well. The one thing they continually emphasized was that they understood there had been two boys playing piggy, but only one had gone to the house and owned up. 'If only boys would own up—' was something that kept being repeated, much to my embarrassment. I had returned in a stupefied daze which seemed to have little to do with principles. Indeed I was regretting all the fuss, and perhaps even more the fact that nobody mentioned the actual piggy, and I couldn't bring myself to ask for it back. Nor did they think to return it.

Uncle William measured the window, and the next day brought the pane of glass, and I went with him and stood by whilst he put it in himself. That he, an Irishman, could actually put in a window, and do so very neatly, without breaking it, impressed me greatly. And it was that incident which brought about the change in the relationship between Uncle and myself. It seemed that now we each had a more mature understanding of the other, and there was no longer the mock politeness, but more of a special wink and nod carry-on, as though we had some deep secret between us. And somehow I sensed he was not at heart the stalwart man I had taken him to be when I was younger. He was as gracious as ever, always or nearly always with a gentle smile, but at times he was touchy, and it seemed that my mother was much concerned about him at such times, more attentive if that was possible, and also protective, preventing any argument about the Strike arising. And it seemed he turned to her as though he had need to.

6

Lock-out of Miners

THE fact that my father and Cousin Willie had lost three weeks' wages owing to the Strike meant that Mother was short of money to run the home, and was getting more into debt with our corner-shop grocer, Mr Denton. Of course, no mention was made of such, since it wasn't considered the thing to comment on money, one way or another. But to my sharp eye the signs were there, and as we moved into 1921 I became aware of money getting scarce everywhere. It was an uneasy change that few workers were prepared for—excepting perhaps the cautious spinners. (But even they could hardly have envisaged that it would go on for some eighteen years—until there were preparations for the next war—closing down cotton mills almost weekly, putting many thousands of them on the labour market, and the once proud spinner would be queueing up among hundreds of others for a labourer's job.) In the first instance it had been a mystery where all the money had come from, but where it had all gone now seemed an even greater mystery—certainly a more immediate one. In our street and at the Big Corner many men and youths who had had regular jobs were suddenly thrown out of work—'On the Bolsheviks' as the unemployment insurance pay was known locally at the time. Housewives who had been going into the corner shop for half-pounds of roast pork for the family tea could barely afford even two ounces of pig's brawn to spread on butties. In our history lesson at school we were into the eighteenth century, learning about the South Sea Bubble—and it seemed to me that one not unlike it had burst in our midst, for it came out that even a number of spinners, the canniest of men, had lost most of their life's savings in the boom of cotton shares, which had now collapsed.

The ready-money shopkeepers in Derby Street, green-grocers and others, who had become rather snooty when they were selling all they could get hold of, were now putting on smiles of welcome. It was the same all over the place. Even Tutty Booth, the owner of the Derby Picture Palace, would stand outside, watching out for and welcoming every one of his regulars. He would not allow Edgar, the operator, to start up until Mrs Fish and Mrs Hosky and others were safely in their favourite seats. Also, with fewer people being able to afford the fourpence for a good seat, a visit to the pictures took on added importance. A neighbour who had enjoyed the privilege felt it her duty to call in on a less fortunate one the next day, to tell what had happened in the new episode of the following-up film. I occasionally heard one tell the story of the top film, recounting it as though it were a real happening: 'A rotten film—a society film—ee, but this chap the villain, he wur a bad 'un.' 'Geroff!—go on.' 'Aye, his poor wife at home wi' a sick child, an' he's out wi' his fancy woman, spendin' all his money on her.'

One Monday evening I chanced to get hold of twopence to go to the pictures, and my pal Harry dragged me along to his home to see if this could help him soften up his own mother. 'Where's mi purse?' she cried out, '—if I have it I'll give it you an' if I haven't I can't.' She hadn't twopence; but there was none of the ill feeling that might follow the refusal from a better-off parent. Harry didn't give up: 'You 'aven't any empty bottles I could take back, Mam?' 'There's a couple I've put on one side undert'stairs,' she said, 'but tak' 'um an' blast you. An' don't let the others see 'um.' 'Good lad you, Mam,' said Harry, and he gave her a kiss. She was a thin woman, Harry's mother, in her forties, but looking rather old and worn out, her voice hoarse from asthma and use, varicose veins on her legs, her hands bleached and shiny from doing washing, yet she had this bright and vigorous way with her, and could keep his dad and all the family in order. 'She's a wonder is my mam,' said Harry, after he had got his twopence for the bottles, '—she'll allus find money, one way or another.'

Towards the end of 1921 I found I was once again standing in Bibby's chip shop when Mrs Tiplady was getting served, and this time she was asking for two *separate* penn'orths of chips (it was said you got more in separate pennyworths). She was no longer the proud working woman with the cotton-flecked hair, for she had been out of work for months, and her manner was appropriately humble. 'Don't wrap 'um up, please,' she said to Mrs Bibby, as she scratched away in the corner of what appeared to be a fairly empty purse. I looked at her and she looked at me, and it seemed we were both recalling that day a year or so before when her fat purse had burst its seams from the weight of half-crowns and florins, and she had been casually buying fish by the half-dozen. Indeed, there was at that moment a lavish array of beautifully fried plaice and cod, crisp, brown, batter-clad, laid out in the open metal chamber, set back above the boiler; fish that, if they had not looked so dignified, even lying on their backs, one would have sworn were crying out to be bought by some nice hungry customer and eaten up. But few folk, apart from the odd spinner still in work, could afford fish. Mr Bibby seemed suddenly aware that it was almost cruel to display such choice items before hungry eyes, and being the kind man he was he quickly put the lid down and shut them from sight. Mrs Tiplady now produced a handy basin which had been kept under her shawl, asked for a penn'orth of wet beans (beans with some bean gravy, if there was any gravy) and whispered to Mrs Bibby might she have a few scraps to go with them, if there were any left over (these were the burnt scraps which were periodically removed from the huge pans of boiling fat and put at one side). 'Don't wrap 'um up,' she said again to Mrs Bibby about the chips. Mrs Bibby was rather sharp at wrapping up pennyworths, before the customer had got a hand on the vinegar bottle, since the profit hardly paid for the vinegar used.

I watched Mrs Tiplady lift the big vinegar bottle and start squirting the contents on her purchases, which for threepence occupied a fair amount of space on the counter. Suddenly she turned and addressed a loud vehement remark to all the

customers in general who were standing around waiting their
turn, about how she thought it a crying shame that they were
making Princess Mary marry an old chap like Viscount
Lascelles. This turned all eyes from the vinegar squirting to
her face, but she kept on jerking the bottle as she spoke, as
though she was absent-minded. 'You've only to look at that
picture of 'um taken together int'*Daily Sketch*,' she went on,
'—it's as plain as a pikestaff she's not i' love with that fella.
Ee, she did look miserable, poor girl—but makin' the best of
it like. I coulda cried I could for her I could!'

That she had hit upon a subject of warm interest and
concern became clear at once, as other women joined in and
mostly agreed with her. Mr Bibby turned as he lifted the long-
handled chip container with its huge wire basket from the
boiling fat, and remarked that the poor chap was only forty.
Mrs Tiplady retorted that he looked more like eighty to her.
'An' there are rumours goin' round about 'im as well,' she
added darkly—but what these rumours were she would not
say. And to express her distaste she began to shake the vinegar bottle even more forcefully, as though jabbing it into the
Viscount himself. It struck me that Mrs Tiplady's bringing up
of Princess Mary had diverted attention from her lavish use
of the vinegar bottle, allowing her to give a right good sous-
ing to her chips and beans. And I could see from the look Mrs
Bibby gave that she had spotted the dodge. But Mrs Tiplady
had always been a good customer, and times were bad, and
vinegar made a tasty dip for bread after it had soaked the
chips, so all she did was to give one of her quiet knowing
smiles, as though to herself.

'He's got plenty o' money,' remarked Mrs Entwistle,
'—that's one thing.' 'Four million,' said Mr Bibby, 'they say
he's worth four million.'

'Money,' snorted Mrs Tiplady, as she turned from the
counter and made to elbow her way out, with a lovely aroma
steaming up from her parcel; 'money aren't everythin'!'

I watched her go off looking rather pleased with herself,
and could imagine her getting home and the Tiplady kids
enjoying lashings of chip-and-bean butties for their dinner—

nice and savoury too, and, when soaked with vinegar and a few scraps thrown in, delectable. What I most admired was how Mrs Tiplady had carried off the ticklish operation, for she had managed not to humble herself or to lose face in front of neighbours, and at the same time to acquire a tasty feed for the family for threepence—thanks to the engagement of Princess Mary and Lord Lascelles.

The nationalization of the mines in 1916 had come about because of bad labour relations, an urgent need for increased output, and above all the scandal of profiteering; the mineowners in 1916 doubled their 1914 profits even though output and manpower had decreased. The question of decontrol had been shelved at the end of the War; the miners' leaders were resisting the move, since owners were declaring in advance the cuts in miners' pay that would be made, and above all in the poorer coalfields, such as those of Lancashire. The Miners' Federation during the War had got something approaching a national agreement for miners; the owners were now determined to revert to an area system, whereby a miner in a mine where the coal was of inferior quality received lower wages than a miner in an area of rich seams. There were, and always had been, bitter feelings between the mineowners and the miners. The mineowners, most of them wealthy, happened in many cases to be some sort of landed gentry, maybe the odd nobleman amongst them—Lord Ellesmere was the owner of Brackley Pit where my father worked—who had derived much of their wealth from the adventitious discovery of minerals beneath the land they owned.

The working conditions in and around mines, where men wearing nothing but underpants laboured deep underground, with the sweat oozing out of them, and pit brow lasses worked above ground, were harsh and primitive, the accident rate and loss of life shocking. This daily summoning up of a man's total energy, the sweating and exhaustion, followed by a feeling of content and relaxation when, still blackened all over by coal dirt, the miner reached home, ate, curled up on the rug in front of the fire, and went off to sleep with an old topcoat over him—as so many I knew did—produced a human being that had familiarized himself with areas of human experience seldom reached by the average man, and in consequence one that was different. It seems that when it is demanded of a man that he work beyond the normal limits of endurance, he can do so only by setting aside his sensibility, and this tends to harden if not brutalize the person.

There was an incident in the 1920s during which two Lancashire colliers, in one of those sexual pranks in which older workers play some joke on a young novice, grabbed hold of a lad of sixteen during the snap break, inserted the end of the compressed-air pipe into his rectum, and turned on the power. These two callous men unwittingly killed the unfortunate boy. Tragedy of that kind could never have occurred amongst cotton spinners or factory workers—it would have been unthinkable—although a greasing of the private parts of an apprentice with wagon fat was not uncommon. Yet, despite the apparently demoralizing effects of such harsh work, those miners of intelligence and character were enriched and toughened by their work. There had been a spirit of idealism among certain miners, aspirations towards culture and learning, to which the once splendid libraries so many of these miners' groups built up, particularly in South Wales, would testify. These miners were outstanding compared to men of their like from other industries; and when it came to facing politicians and the mineowners' representatives, it would be surprising if their steely—and, it must be said, often stubborn—characters did not detect a flabbiness and hypocrisy about the men they were dealing with; there was also the natural reaction of a man who has known many years of hard work towards the chap who has never handled a pick or spade: one of quiet contempt. The claims made by the miners might well have appeared extravagant to others, but to the miners, who knew what it meant to mine the coal, they seemed modest enough. Arguments taking place in a conference room ignore the real factors, which can be realized only by doing the job.

* * *

The Miners' Strike began on 1 April 1921 (it was in fact a lock-out by the mineowners, but was always spoken of as a strike). The Sankey Commission set up by the government had come to the decision that the industry would be better nationalized, and this had led the miners to believe the findings would be carried out. Lloyd George—who had a score or two to settle with the miners, who had got the better of him during the War—set aside the recommendations of Lord Sankey and the commission, and instead brought forward the decontrol date. Now the boom had collapsed, he was scheming to play certain of the big trade unions one against the other. The mineowners were now insisting on severe wage cuts, which the miners were refusing to accept, and the upshot was the lock-out or strike.

The first thing the Strike did was to whip up a sense of purpose and challenge among the miners–as usually happens with strikers—and a feeling of bold optimism. It should be understood that the miner was something of an outsider in the normal industrial scene. He was not an urban presence in the way the spinner or mechanic was—the miner was never seen crowding the streets at dinnertime, going to and fro between the job and home—nor was he part of the visible working scene, such as a bricklayer or joiner might be; the miner usually went off to work at odd hours, and disappeared down a pit cage to emerge at the end of his shift a black unrecognizable figure wearing old clothes and heavy clogs. This cut him off from the rest of the working community, and he had no secure working rank or dignity, of a kind any mill or factory employee might acquire; you couldn't just go and get a job in a factory or foundry, but almost any man, young and strong, could get a job down pit. It needed guts to keep going, for it was exceptionally hard work, but a young miner could always hold his own among other youths. There was almost always a surplus of miners— except during any emergency such as a war, when extra coal was needed. It was only then that the men had the power to bargain for fair wages. The miners had done this during the Great War, and by 1919 had achieved a new social standing, and a better living for themselves and their families; a young woman did not hesitate as she used to over marrying a miner. The tendency was for a miner's daughter to marry a miner; the miner made a good husband, but he was tougher and less pliable than the mill-worker husband; he drank more beer, took more time off work, and, with his need for a good scrub down after every shift, and the extra washing and mending of his pit clothes, and the larger meals he ate, took more looking after. One had only to be in the company of miners, especially the hardier ones, the men who worked at the coalface, to see that they had a rough dignity and pride all their own.

The 1921 Strike, like most other miners' strikes, was an unfair contest. The situation of the miner coming out on strike was in total contrast to the mineowners, politicians, and others who opposed the Strike. A miner who worked for six shifts a week down a mine, often in danger, appeared to imbibe a sense of grievance with his mother's milk—since it was likely that his father before him had had to endure the same harsh conditions. The miner was wholly involved in the Strike—his livelihood, his job, his family, his social standing and pride, not to mention his stomach, and numerous other subtle aspects of daily life that may affect a man deeply. The public at large, depending solely on the misrepresentation of newspapers for their information, neither understood what it was to be a miner, nor the issues involved, nor had they much political awareness. And, as there was said to be a Triple Alliance of the railwaymen and transport workers with the miners, the newspapers exaggerated the dangers of a General Strike, and played on the fears of the public.

7

The Irish and the English

IN OUR home the Strike set going a holiday mood for the first week or so. There was no immediate lack of money, since the mineowners, like most employers, kept a week's wages in hand; on the Friday of the first week of idleness there was a full week's wages to draw (which meant that on the return to work it would be a fortnight before a man drew any money). My father's normally pale and strained face took on colour and soon filled out, and with this there appeared an almost benign look, and a disconcerting impulse to crack jokes. The dark fringes of coaldust around the eyelids, by which a miner was always recognizable, slowly disappeared. Cousin John now came to live with us, as Willie prepared to leave to get married to a Lancashire woman; Paudric, the eldest son, went home to Ireland to take up the few family acres and to marry a 'Yank'.

Cousins Willie and John had brought a distinct spirit of gaiety to our family life. They were different from my father not only in temperament but in upbringing: from the age of twelve he had been a shopboy in the town of Ballyhaunis, whereas they were from the village of Knock, where much singing and dancing went on; he had a serious manner, but they kept a light laughter going most of the time. Willie had a way of pursing up his mouth before he laughed, as though it was an indulgence he must resist or at least control, and then when he did laugh his lips would part, showing strong white teeth, his face would warm with a clownish humour, and his dark blue eyes would light up—a most infectious state it was; John was more subtle and a good mimic. They had male physiques of a kind seldom seen outside the labouring classes: the figure appeared outlined, no matter what clothes they were wearing, with the upper back, shoulders, and arms so developed from hard work that they had acquired not a thickened appearance so much as a winglike hardness; their waists were lean, below they had a hard-buttocked look, and, despite the muscular power displayed, there was a curious springiness about their movements.

Uncle William had been against the miners coming out on strike, and Willie and John Kirrane tended to agree with him; they had infinite fortitude but no fight; aggression was not in their natures. Uncle abhorred confrontation, and had no feeling about the conflicts that are part of industrial society; he believed that the mineowners were mostly gentlemen and that English gentlemen usually did the right thing. Above all, he couldn't bear to think he was one of those who would put to hardship the decent Lancashire folk, now suffering from a shortage of household coal. He would not argue the matter, for among his kind of Irish to engage in argument was considered coarse behaviour, not the kind of encounter likely to beget good feeling. He was conservative by nature, and what little he knew or cared about politics he regarded in the same way; self-respect and decency, to these qualities he could give his own tacit enthusiasm. He was all for what he took to be quiet reason, for some honourable agreement to be reached, and for all conflict to be peaceably settled. He retained an old-fashioned principle of loyalty to one's employer, and had no notion of the skulduggery that was part of most industrial organizations; indeed he didn't wish to know, and seemed distressed when my father spoke of certain fraudulent practices that had come to light. If the men had to take a cut in wages—as occasionally I would hear him explain to Mother when my father was asleep upstairs—because the price of coal had dropped all over the world, then the best thing was to take the cut, knowing that good times would surely come again and there would be a rise in earnings. Above all, we Irish should remain quiet, since we were strangers in England, and unspeakable happenings were taking place in our own country.

Even as a small boy I was seldom unaware of how vulnerable we Irish were. Although we had a good family sense, which was comforting, we had only a remote feeling of belonging, since we were aliens. That was a feeling I never lost. The attitude towards the Irish in those days, when Ireland was part of Great Britain, and Britain had a vast empire, was different from that of today, although more than a trace of it may remain. The Irish—like many other nations and races—were looked down upon. Nor could one blame the English, since it could hardly be otherwise. At school the huge map of the world would be spread on the blackboard, the vast British Empire marked in red, and Miss Newsham with her long cane would point out the many and various colonies, dependencies, and other possessions, and explain how on the Empire the sun could never set, since it stretched around the globe. I would watch my mates staring agog, as though asking, '*Dominion over palm and pine*—am I an' mi' mum an' dad an' mi Aunt Flo' an' our Sarah Jane included?' Even the Lancashire little-piecer, undersized and underfed, working from the age of thirteen what had customarily been fifty-six hours a week in a cotton-mill—now at last reduced to forty-eight—had somehow been persuaded into considering himself a vital member, or at least a member, of the British Empire. Perhaps he was. At least I, being Irish, would have to admit an inferiority on that score, if on no other; although we were reluctant members of that same empire. Moreover, I found I was drawn to such an English boy; indeed in many ways more than I was drawn to one of my own. I respected and half-feared his cool Englishness. What made him appear superior to me and mine in the first place was that he felt himself so, and I found that a difficult thing to counter, even though it may have been assumed on dubious grounds. The Irish seemed to live in the past and the English always in the present, and that certainly put them ahead. That the Englishman was part of a society more ordered than that of the Irish could not be gainsaid: the English responded to the factory buzzer with a promptness beyond the understanding of the Irish mind, which was quite untrained to punctuality; also they were a people clearly more law-abiding and hard-working, for the Lancashire miner could leave the leisurely Irishman behind.

It was as navvies the Irish came into their own—and this difference seemed to be reflected on their faces. The Irish face—except for those of coal-miners—was ruddy and fresh, set on the broad red neck with the round cleanshaven nape, and it would be simple for anyone to pick out such a one in a crowded English street, especially so since no Irishman ever hurried. The more intelligent Irish face had a lively mobility and friendly expression, quite unlike that of the simian-featured Irishman of English cartoons; even as a small boy I felt offended by this caricature of our people. Yet it was clear that the emotional Irish expression must defer to the stolid English look, and that the swift fluty tones of the Irish lacked the authority of the strong flat English voice. Apart from these and certain racial differences, one further comparison could be made: the Irish face was free of—or possibly had not yet acquired—that certain look which industry stamps upon its subjects. There was no doubt, however, that the countenance which had grown up on familiar terms with machinery, and had acquired that particular concentrated look—a form of sophistication—was the one which would prove superior in a material or wordly sense. The face that told of outdoor labour, of familiarity with the earth, the spade, and the muck fork, must give way to the one acquainted with the spanner. Moreover, a people who have been subject to another nation for centuries need a generation or two to shake off their inadequacies and equal up (if indeed they ever can without the superior nation going down a bit).

Nor was the superiority always of a remote order: the English were a reliable people, the Englishman's word was his bond—allowing the exception of a politician—and, if he promised to see you at the Ram's Head corner at eight o'clock and lend you a pound (or more likely ten shillings), you could bet he would be there, dead on eight, without any of the Irish excuses, and the note safe in his waistcoat pocket. Nor was the Englishman deep, treacherous, or given to feuds or grudges; and, although a peaceful man, never quickly pugnacious, he would seldom duck a fight. Then there would be the calm English ritual of jackets off, and not flung down but folded up carefully, sleeves calmly rolled up, the opponents set facing each other, left fist forward, right hand on guard, and no getting the first blow in, with someone to see fair play, not a move until the call was given; the commands, *Fists only! No feet!* and *Don't hit a man when he's down!* would be followed. (I had soon discovered he might drop his guard, dodge down and grab you by the knees, and flip you on your back in a trice.) Calls of *Play the game!* and *Play the white man!* would be made from the spectators during a fight; calls never heard, I imagine, at an Irish fight. The nature of the Celt and that of the Anglo-Saxon were decidedly different in many respects.

'I've had Irish chaps workin' here for me for years,' I once heard a Bolton farmer say, 'the same family—come over here for the hay they do, an' I hire 'um for the month. You never saw better workers in your life; an' I'll tell you summat, they're not clockwatchers, they're gradely workers—they keep gooin' till the job's done. Now at the end of the month on the Saturday night, when they're being' paid off an' ready for gooin' off, it's always been my custom to tak' 'um to the pub an' stand 'um a pint or two. Sometimes they'll get other Irishmen from other farms about droppin' in, an' a nicer crowd o' chaps you never met—that is, until they begin findin' out they're related, an' they shake hands an' start kissin' one another. Then I'm off. For once the Irish start kissin', you can be sure that soon the fists will start—an' they get agate fightin'. Aye, as soon as I see that first kiss I make for the pub door.'

8

Black Friday, 1921

THE Strike had been on for almost two weeks, when on Friday, 15 April 1921—Black Friday it became to the miners—the leader of the railwaymen, J. H. Thomas, decided against joining in the strike, and the Transport Workers Union sided with him. The miners in that year were left out on their own. 'Jimmy Thomas, the meanest scut unhung,' my father used to say. 'May the divil roast him in hell, the bloody ould renegade.' It was now the real nature of the Strike and all its effects began slowly to emerge, once the novelty of the first week or two had worn off.

The man of the house, the chief and often sole earner, tended to build his life around his work. The family had to accommodate it in their habits, according to whether he worked nights or days, left early or left late, and so on. Among miners and others who did hard manual work the job served as a natural balancing force between work and play. The actual work was a sort of catharsis, during which the man sweated, and with the sweat there was released much pent-up feeling, so that it seemed the impurities of spirit were discharged with those of the body. Then he could relax and do pretty well what he pleased when he was away from work, since one hard shift with pick and spade would pull him back into shape. The miner's main pleasure was rest, and from that might follow drinking and chatting with mates, an evening's fishing at the canal, breeding whippets or flying pigeons, playing cards, and any other pleasure or interest his married or single life might provide. But for five or six turns a week he knew he had to be down the mine, and this work, together with any leisure, provided an equable routine for body and mind. There were few disciplines required beyond the essential one of keeping to one's work. A miner and his wife lived a closer relationship than most married couples. He was more dependent on her, and his hard work seemed to polarize their male and female natures—he was doing a job she could not possibly do. Such a wife needed to be a clever woman not to become subject to male domination; also the physical disparity between such a man and his wife declared itself much more strongly. The wise wife avoided conflict, allowed the man to enjoy his own notion of superiority, and used various female stratagems to even things up.

It was during the third week of the Strike that the idleness became difficult to bear—even for my father. He and Cousin John were in need of some task or other to fill in their time, and Mother was on the go making tea and meals from morning until night. 'God save us,' my father would often say, as he looked at the alarm clock on the mantelshelf, 'is that all the time it is!' In our home, with the small front and back kitchens, the two little bedrooms, and the tiny backyard, there was very little a man could do for recreation. The native Bolton man might have built up some satisfying hobby or pastime of sorts, but not the Irish—they needed the land. Almost every day Uncle William would turn up, usually at noon. Appearances had to be kept up, so that boiled eggs would be served at breakfast, bacon and cabbage or the like for the midday meal, and cold meat at teatime. To put it simply, the Irish had to make out that the only matter of true importance was the relationship between one another. What was going on outside was of little account, except for the troubles at home in Ireland. Things were at their worst during the second quarter of 1921; there was martial law in much of Ireland, the Black and Tans and the Royal Irish Constabulary had got out of hand, were ignoring their officers and the law, and were burning, looting, and murdering in revenge for their own losses.

Father would read the newspaper over and over again, and was grieved at the way things were going. There would be the odd caller, some Irishman from our part of the world, perhaps over for the haymaking, who would turn up

unexpectedly, and he would have fearful tales to tell, and
would be treated to the best. Above all, my mother had to
keep up the cheerful smiling face at all times, and serve as a
sort of confidante to each one. She was now running into
heavier debt, and she had to face the numerous weekly callers.
Mr Leach ceased coming until things would get better; there
were others, such as the rent collector and insurance men,
who were all part of our kind of working-class life, and she
had to hold them off with apologies, promises that when the
Strike was over she would settle up. Money had been borrowed from a moneylender. Things were disappearing into
the pawnshop. My father's gold chain and his silver watch
had gone there, of course, and also Mother's gold watch with
the lovely chain, which she had bought when in America.
Next Father's best suit and tan boots had to go in. And
Cousin Willie could be seen hanging out his second-best blue
serge suit on the line when there were signs of a drizzle,
hoping a little rain might serve to freshen it—his best suit
having gone into pawn.

I would go in home from school some days and find the
house quiet. Mother would have chosen these few minutes—
after late midday dinner, and washing and tidying up—to rest
her corns, as she called it. She would be seated on the big
rocking-chair, her feet resting on another chair. Although I
was as unfeeling as any small boy, I usually had tact enough
not to disturb her at such moments. She may even have had a
cheap little weekly magazine to read, for she was fond of a
story: 'I'll be up and have your tea ready in a minute, agraw,'
she would say. 'Don't worry about me, Mam,' I'd say. Then
there might be a light knock on the front door, the door open,
and in would step Uncle Mick Logan from Wigan.

Mother would almost leap out of the rocking-chair, her
face animated, eyes shining: 'Well the Lord save us—is it
yourself, Michael!' she would exclaim. 'Thanks be to God,
but it's lovely to see you!' 'It's no use tellin' you to sit back
on the chair,' Uncle Mick would say. 'Indeed it's not,' she
would reply, 'for amn't I sittin' half of the day. I was just
gettin' up anyway—to feed this man. Sure aren't you lookin'

great! How's Annie?' Then as the excited talk was getting
going Mother would slip into the kitchen, maybe to put the
kettle on the little gas ring if the big iron kettle on the hob
looked as though it might be slow in boiling. She would give
me a hug and whisper, 'Would you go off to Denton's,
agraw, an' see would he have a nice half-pound or so of
boiled ham—or tongue if he hasn't ham?' Then she would
call in to Uncle Mick, 'Sure you have my dream last night
broken—I dreamt we were all back home in Ireland.' Then
she'd turn to me: 'An' butter, agraw—bring butter—an'
maybe we'd need a loaf too. Will you go an' come by the
back gate.'

She would try to arrange things so that a guest saw no one
going to the shop, and all seemed easy and natural, as though
we had a stacked larder. It was not that she would ever show
off, but simply that there was a guest under the roof, and he
had to be made feel at home and given the best. In a minute
she would have her face washed, a new blouse and pinafore
and her soft leather shoes on, and the talk and greeting would
be overflowing in the little home, as though Uncle Mick was a
visitor from America, in place of a man living only ten miles
away, and as though we hadn't a care in the world.

I went out to Denton's corner shop the back way one
Saturday afternoon, and it was strange to see the deserted
backstreet. Mr Whittle was wandering up and down, picking
up the odd nut of coal that had fallen from a coal lorry. What
a contrast, I thought, to the lively scene of a year before, with
all the young miners around, laughing and talking, and swap-
ping money. It was a desolate sight. When I turned the corner
there they all were at the Big Corner. No money was passing
from hand-to-hand now. Instead there was Gilbert Clegg
passing his cigarette around: 'Let's have a bloody draw,
mate,' called Tommy Burton. 'Aye, tha'rt welcome,' said
Gilbert, 'but don't put it halfway into thy kisser an' leave a
bloody big tripe mark on it.'

9

Idleness and Depression

THE threat to our family as the Strike went on was not the same as that to the poorer families who were our neighbours, or that to other miners' homes, which was mainly one of getting heavily in debt, of the bum-bailiffs calling, of children and others going hungry, or going to the Public Guardians for food vouchers and the like, and perhaps not getting any. We were, or had been, a relatively prosperous working-class family; our men had worked six hard shifts a week down the mines over the war years, and had set up a good standard of living. But the thrift and prudence of most Lancashire mill workers seemed qualities that the Irish were unable to engage in. That sort of behaviour was rather disapproved of—it was not Irish. Getting on in the world—with the exception of having a son a priest—went against peasant tradition, was not the thing, and attracted both suspicion and superstition, as did the saving of money. After all, in a world of want who would be the only one with money! My father was always astonished every annual holiday week when he read out the vast sums that had been saved over the year by workers, for it seemed that the most he could save, even at the best of times, was a pound or two. Scrimping of any kind, but especially over food, appeared to be going against nature, which was either abundant or lean, but always unmeasured. The diet of the Lancashire industrial worker, lacking the daily big meal of boiled bacon with cabbage and potatoes, seemed not inadequate so much as unthinkable to the Irish mind; an Irishman would have considered himself to be starving on the daily food of a well-fed spinner.

What we most feared during the Strike was to lose the respect and family pride built up over the years. Our people had an awful sense of shame with regard to poverty, and of not being able to hold one's head up. To undergo privation and hardship meant nothing providing we could conceal our condition and not suffer a loss of face, especially so amongst our respectable English neighbours. All lack of money, all furtive pawning of possessions, and all borrowing, shortage of food, absence of tobacco or beer—in short the lack of such material comfort that might bring a little ease to life—meant nothing beside the fanatical need to cover up, to let no outsider know, to avoid being classed as some kind of Irish pauper. We would sooner miss a dozen breakfasts than have it known we had missed one. The thing that counted was to preserve dignity, decorum, and self-respect. Sops in the way of free soup—as provided daily by the local brewery of Magee's, and seized upon by some of our neighbours, but mostly avoided by miners' families, who were after justice not hand-outs—or anything that in the least smacked of charity, would have been odious to us. Centuries of subjection had created among the Irish a beggar class, but we belonged to that of the respectable smallholders; not the ones who sought charity but those who felt privileged to exercise it.

The native Bolton people among whom we lived knew what it was to be hard up, but begging as a way of life was almost unknown. They often displayed their plight, called across the street to one another as to how they would manage, even made jokes of their straitened condition, which most of them managed to laugh over. The Irish from Mayo had need to hide it; what little the oppressor had left them had been laid waste by natural disaster during the potato famines. Somehow they had retained their Catholic faith, and also a certain respectability and even pride. Having known and enjoyed in England a kind of working-class emancipation and independence, it was not the old familiar hunger they feared, for they and their breed had known that in a form which had left the corpses of young and old strewn by the side of the road. It was the loss of honour and decency, that was their fear, the menace to the spirit rather than to the body—an experience remote from the good Lancashire people. It is one thing to have lived a life of exploitation by the more privileged and resourceful group of one's own race, but as degrading as that may be it is not to be compared with that subjugation which an alien mind can impose upon helpless people over the centuries.

I can recall many small incidents from those Strike days, and one is of Mother coming into the house one day after visiting a Galway woman, Mrs Thornton, a neighbour who lived in the next street. 'I came down Thomas Rostron Street there,' she said, 'an' do you know I couldn't believe it, the breeze that was there! I stood in the street a minute—the people must have thought me mad—I stood for a full minute, feelin' the way it was blowin' across one's face, and within the eyes, so it seemed. It was just like I was comin' down the little hill back at home.'

'Shure you're never done talkin' of home an' the little hill an' the breeze, woman,' said my father. 'What's on you?'

'There's nothin' on me,' said Mother briskly, as though hiding her emotion, 'but never will I be done talkin' about them, about home an' the hill an' the breeze or even the single blade of Irish grass.' I had never realized before how much she missed Ireland. Then she began to put on the tablecloth, and hum lightly to herself, as though she had revealed too much and would cover it. I didn't look at her face, and my father must have felt something too, for he went silent.

The feast of SS Peter and Paul, celebrated on 29 June, fell midweek in the year 1921. The weather was warm and sunny, yet, despite the cheerful and smiling appearance my mother kept up around the house, and the Irish way of remarking on the bright side, there was an unsettled feeling in our home. Uncle William had decided on the previous Sunday to leave his lodgings at Chequerbent and come to live with us. He had been sorely affected by the Strike, for he was a mild and gentle man, and conflict of any kind upset him. The press was virulent about the striking miners, and the social atmosphere towards them had become bitter; which as a schoolboy of a mining family I did not escape.

Uncle William had achieved his independence by choosing to set rules for himself with regard to work. He had taken scarcely a night off in normal times and, unlike most of his kind, did not feel the need to go out on the occasional spree— or if he did he mostly overcame the urge. He had managed to reconcile the temperament of a provident man to the prodigal ways of the decent drinking Irishman. The one offence the Mayo man had at all costs to avoid committing was that of skulking over paying his round at a bar. Uncle William was always first to pay the round in any company, and, if a friend sent him a drink in from another room or part of a pub, he would return the gesture with drinks for the man and all his party. He accepted nothing that he didn't repay generously. No one could ever have accused him of a mean act. He was generous not only because he had a deep respect for tradition, but because he was a man untouched by avarice, and did not really care for money in the way most careful people do. What he had was an appreciation of the independence money gave him, and the sense of respectability to which it lent substance. In a public house he would be a lavish spender, yet at the same time he preferred a cup of tea to any drink.

He had an unusual savings box, of mirrored glass, with bevelled glass edges, a wide base and lid, secured on to a wood frame by rivets with glass heads. It looked pretty, was nicely jointed, and had a tiny key and lock, but it would scarcely have withstood thieving fingers, it was all so delicate. He must have feared for his savings if the Strike went on, and at the same time experienced an invidious sense of security in that he alone of all our people had money put aside. Now, more than ever, he had to be the one who paid the first round and most of the subsequent ones in the pub. And, as reluctant as he must have been to go drinking during the Strike, it would seem that for appearances' sake he simply had to.

What most depressed him was that he had to give up his weekend work at the farm in Chequerbent. He had worked there for some years, and his help had been valuable during the war years when labour was hard to get, and for a year or so after, by which time he had become a trusted man, working a few hours at weekends and giving a hand in the afternoons when needed. When unemployment began to be a problem someone made a remark in his hearing about one man doing two jobs, and this upset him. Yet Uncle William could hardly keep away from the farm, he enjoyed the work so much, and he was a man who gloried in work. Once the Strike had begun he had to stop work at the farm, for he could not bear to offend against the traditions of his fellow miners, and so he had to cease the work he loved, just when he most needed the deep satisfaction it gave him. No one who has not known what it means to live by simple work of the hands, the joy that gardening or work on the land may bring, can imagine the dejection that comes over a man or woman when such a fulfilment of nature is denied.

The Strike went on throughout April and there was much excitement over it. In May the public feeling against the miners grew stronger, especially in Bolton where many mills closed down or went on short time owing, it was said, to the shortage of coal. There were large imports of cheap coal, mostly as reparations from Germany, a country almost bankrupt after the War. The ordinary homes all around us were for the most part short of coal or without it altogether, and in homes where the fire normally burnt night and day, and was constantly used for cooking, this caused much vexation. The summer of 1921 turned out to be one of the sunniest and warmest, and this took much of the drama out of the Strike. The newspapers began to put it on the back page, and to give prominence to sporting events, the Derby, and news items of an egg being fried on a hot pavement in Piccadilly. 'The bloody newspaper owners are in league with the mineowners,' my father said, 'so that the Strike will die out.'

There was talk of bringing in total martial law all over Ireland in June of 1921, with endless restrictions on the Irish people, the closing of ports and cutting down of trade and exports, and the likelihood of numerous executions of suspected IRA men. My father was in an awful way about what might happen, when suddenly there came the most promising gesture from an unexpected quarter—King George went to Belfast to open the parliament of Northern Ireland, and made a speech that astonished and moved my father to actual tears. The King spoke of all who loved Ireland, as he did with all his heart, and told of the happy times he had spent as a midshipman in Ireland, and of his affection for the Irish people. He suddenly made Ireland seem a real nation, as he spoke of Irishmen stretching out the hand of conciliation; he spoke of parliaments working in common love for Ireland, in justice and respect. My poor father couldn't believe what he read—that the King of England would speak like that of poor old Ireland! There was no threat in it, no sign of coercion, just a sincere longing for peace. It seemed there was now a possibility that the fighting would come to an end.

Apart from the evenings, which were mild and pleasant, bringing people out on the pavement and setting going the street games, the persistent sunshine was wearying. Cobbled streets and narrow backstreets, mills, factories, and work-shops, did not improve with constant sunshine, lacking all those summer smells that grass, flowers, and hedges give off. The pavements got hot, dry, and dusty, the backstreets more smelly, and sunshine instead of cheering seemed to make things worse. Out at Chequerbent where Uncle William had lodged, the haymaking was just starting in that last week in June, and he was most unhappy that he could not be amongst the men out in the hayfield.

My father, being the finicky man he was, may not have cared for Uncle William around, since he preferred to eat alone. The home with its two small bedrooms felt overcrow-ded. Edward, aged fifteen, had to move out of the back bedroom, which he shared with cousin John, to allow Uncle William to move in with him. Edward now slept with May and me, he and I at the top of the bed, and May at the bottom. In the same bedroom was the larger bed in which Father and Mother and five-year-old James slept. Normally, with the men working night shift, the sleeping arrangements would have been easier.

The reason for Uncle William coming to live with us was on account of his being depressed. He had been to visit one of the priests at the church of SS Peter and Paul to seek some comfort and advice. It was an unfortunate chance that the priest who saw him was not the sort to give support to anyone. A prim and fussy man, his confessional was avoided because of his stiff penances—he spoke in petulant tones, and was altogether lacking in the warmth and understanding of any of the other priests. At Mass he would go up into the pulpit to read the notices, name the souls of the dead for which Masses were to be offered, and then, after a violent blowing of his nose, he would pause and survey the congregation with apparent distaste before the sermon. He more than once interrupted his own sermon—and dry and dull they were—to order a mother at the back of the church to remove herself and her bleating infant. Many heads were shaken over such an incident, to shame a mother and her babe, for, as distracting as it might be, it would be the strange Mass in which celebrant and congregation, both so often drawn from the poor and the Irish, could not resignedly accept the wailing of a child, since an infant's cry echoed some innocent human appeal that seemed in the spirit of Mass.

On this feast-day of SS Peter and Paul I had got up with a sense of that quiet withdrawal from the life around me, which the fasting before Communion and the anticipation of the Holy Sacrament induced. I took my knickerbocker trousers from the bedrail and put them on, then knelt beside the bed and whispered my morning prayers. I went downstairs and opened the back-kitchen door, and was making to the closet across the yard when my sister May called out after me: 'Hy Our Bill, you're not half showin' your tea an' sugar!' I put my hand to the seat of my trousers, and to my alarm I felt the tail of my shirt thrusting out through a hole. I hurried into the closet to examine things more closely, recalling that there had been a ragged area the day before. When I got inside and pulled the trousers down to look, I saw there was a gaping hole, with a piece of an old patch hanging down. I was fussy over my clothes, liked every single thing to be just so, and the idea of going to Communion in those trousers was out of the question.

Mother was attending on Uncle William when I went into the back kitchen, chatting away to him in an easygoing manner, and watching for a moment to dart upstairs with the big mug of tea and slice of buttered bread for my father. I greeted them both and waited for the right moment to have a word with her. After a few minutes, with Uncle William drinking tea in the front place, I was able to corner her. 'Mam,' I said, 'I've a great big hole in mi trousers. Look, I won't be able to go to Mass in them. I'll have to put my best suit on.' She looked worried: 'God save us, agraw,' she whispered, 'but I haven't got the suit. I had to give it to Mary Anne to pawn. I'll not be able to get it out till Saturday. Will you take the trousers off, let me see what I could do with them.'

I took the trousers off and stood there in my shirt and stockinged feet whilst she looked at the hole. 'The Lord save us,' she said, ''twould take a month to mend that. But maybe I could fasten it up some way with safety pins.' She had to keep leaving me and hurrying to do one thing and another, and time was going on, so that finally she came to me: 'Musha, I wonder would it be an awful thing altogether if you was to miss Mass on this one holy occasion—the way the world is an' everythin'? I'm sure God would forgive you. You could go up an' slip back into bed, an' when they're all out of the way I'll have a fine breakfast for you with bacon sandwiches. And in between I'll mend the trousers.' I agreed. Secretly I was a bit relieved, for I was always glad of some excuse that would keep me from the hurly-burly of the streets and the noisy behaviour of boys before Mass. But after my hour in bed there came the low spirits that followed a second sleep. When my mother at last patched the old trousers I went off alone on a long walk, almost sick with loneliness, and longing for the company of the mates I somehow felt a need to avoid. And all through the day it seemed that nothing went right for me, and I could not shake off my unhappy feeling. How could any day go right, I reasoned within myself, when I was too cowardly to go to my Holy Communion because of a hole in my trousers!

There was much talk in the evening of what seemed a simple happening that same day. Uncle William and Cousin John had been to Mass, and later in the day, upholding what would be the custom in Ireland, they had gone along with my father to the Ram's Head in Derby Street for a few drinks, a popular pub, kept by an autocratic landlord, Tom Barrow, a man of some authority. Paddy Conboy, a great friend of Uncle's, was seen over in another part of the bar having a drink with friends, for, although he was a navvy and unaffected by the Strike, Paddy was not a man to go to work on a saint's day. Our men did not care to intrude on Paddy's party, but after some time Paddy came over to Uncle William and greeted him and the others and asked what they would all have to drink.

A meeting between Irishmen, particularly of Uncle William's and Paddy Conboy's temperaments, would be no simple matter. They were fond of each other, each had respect for a certain touchiness in the other, and in some way they were not unalike, in that each was proud, generous, and sensitive. The range of feelings involved, the subtlety of exchanges, and the intuitive nuances brought into play would be such that few Englishmen could apprehend, and perhaps even fewer would care to be caught up in. Gestures and looks of the most innocent nature would be significant, and words would need to be well chosen for such an encounter, which took on the tones of a ceremony. And so hypersensitive would each party be, that he could be affronted by some article of dress worn by the other, a new tie or pair of boots, or even a haircut—every tiny thing had some implication, either fitting or unfitting for the occasion.

In reply to Paddy's invitation Uncle William warmly suggested that on the contrary Paddy, and his friends too, should all drink with him. No doubt Uncle William was paying for all the drinks among our group, but never ostentatiously, for it was his way to pass a pound note secretly to one of the others, so as to avoid drawing attention to himself. Paddy could have sensed that this may have been so, and for that reason insisted that he would buy the round. There were many Irishmen short of money at the time, and Paddy would wish to make it clear that he was not one of them. Uncle William may have been offended by Paddy's refusal, or indeed he may have been moved by a generous impulse, and he countered Paddy's offer by saying no, he would pay for the drinks. Finally, neither one paid for a drink for the other, since it happened that Tom Barrow called 'Time', and when he called not another drink would be served. So Paddy Conboy and Uncle William, two old friends from the same part of the country, came out of the public house in the afternoon on a holy day, without having had a drink together, and this simple but inauspicious incident was to prey on the mind of each man.

That evening I heard Uncle William ask Mother did she think that Paddy Conboy intended to slight him by not accepting the drink. Wouldn't Paddy be the last man in the world to do that, said Mother, for weren't they the greatest of friends. It was strange, persisted Uncle William, that Paddy Conboy, a man from a nearby Irish village, would refuse a drink from him. The thing became such an issue with Uncle William that my father suggested they all go up to the Ram's Head, and, as Paddy would probably be there, they could all have a drink together and the whole matter would be settled. Uncle William had no real wish to go, but he was persuaded, and the men went up, but Paddy was not there. Then down home they came after having had a few drinks, my father rather talkative, full of the noisy agreeableness he tended to put on at such times, and Uncle William oddly quiet. There was some talk of the Strike, now likely to be settled after the ballot of the various coalfields, but Mother talked gently to Uncle William about Ireland.

IO

Tragedy in the Home

I SLIPPED off furtively to bed, without saying goodnight or giving the usual kiss all round. The bedroom was gloomy and had a smell of stale sleep, and the beds lacked their usual comforting appeal, for the best blankets had been pawned. I stood behind the rather tattered curtain and looked down on the cobbled street, where the girls were playing. Twilight was falling and they had given up the livelier games and were now singing plaintive songs. I could hear the voice of my own Alice out there among all the other voices, singing, 'And he left his girl behind him, Weeping by the Liverpool Sea'. I was full of yearning to see her, to have her alone and close by me, to hear her sweet English voice and clasp her small firm hand, and to feel myself glow from the tender look of her large gentle eyes. But it had been weeks since we had even exchanged looks; it seemed she may have been avoiding me. And I was too proud and dispirited to push myself to make an effort to meet her—as much as I longed to. I was looking a bit down at heel, for not only did I need new trousers and other things, but there was no way of getting hold of the odd sixpence I would need when I took her out. And both the Irish and the miners were becoming even more unpopular, especially amongst the likes of her family, the father with a regular job at the corporation. And if I couldn't have Alice, it would even be a relief to stand among my mates at the street-corner, to listen to their chattering and arguing, instead of being stuck where I was with my miserable self—and no hope, it seemed for the future. But I hadn't the heart to get up and go out.

The only thing for it, I decided, was to turn to God. I knelt down at the bed, felt a little rested, and began to say my night prayers of Our Fathers and Hail Marys, the cumbersome Apostles' Creed. But it was all no use, I felt, for now they were only words whispered on the tongue, missing that speck of spirit from the heart, which gave them life and opened the vast cloud of the soul, into which one could enter. I tried the Prayer before a Crucifix, and yet even that most touching end did not take hold '. . . the while I contemplate with great love and tender pity Thy five most precious wounds, pondering over them within me whilst I call to mind what the prophet David put in thy mouth concerning Thee, O good and gentle Jesus: "They have dug my hands and my feet; they have numbered all my bones."' There was nothing for it but to take off my clothes and hang them on the bedrail, and get into bed in my shirt, all of which I did, vowing as I did so that no matter if my naked backside was sticking out of the seat of my trousers as I knelt at the altar would I again miss Mass and Holy Communion.

I was woken up next morning by what seemed to be wild voices calling out in alarm. Then I heard heavy footsteps clattering up and down the stairs outside the bedroom. I felt the nervous thudding of my heart, the dryness of tongue and throat that went with it, and the hot sweaty smell that rose up from under my armpits at such times. I was aghast that my father would let such an uproar happen in our home, but then recognized his voice was calling among other voices. I closed my eyes, tried to shut my ears against all the commotion, told myself it must be one of my nightmares, and that if I kept calm I would soon wake up from it, but the pandemonium went on, more voices calling out in alarm, people running about, the bedroom floor shaking from it all. I became aware of the torn wool blanket and knew I was still in my own bed in our front bedroom. What could be the matter? Now I opened my eyes and saw that the morning light was in the room. The voices went on even louder, and I began to feel sick, and started my usual instinctive whispering of Hail Marys for protection. I saw my sister May was still in bed near the wall, and I said, 'What's up, May? What's all the noise?' 'I don't know,' she said. She looked pale and frightened: 'Somethin' must have happened. I've been hearin' it for a bit.'

The next thing I saw our bedroom door being shoved open and to my amazement Mrs Walsh, a neighbour from across the street, came in: 'May love,' she said briskly, 'come on with me—over to our house. I'll come back for you, Willie.' 'Yes, ma'am,' I said. I knew now there was something wrong, but I couldn't bring myself to ask her what it was. She was hurried but concerned as she quickly put a blanket round my sister May, over her flannel nightgown, and led her out of the bedroom. I heard her firmly close the door after her, and I was left all alone in the bedroom. I got out of bed, kept on praying, found my trousers and stockings on the floor, and put them on. I felt terribly frightened, for it seemed that there was some awful panic going on in our little home. It all sounded so close, there in the next bedroom, the voices and the moving about, and I could hear the high excited voice of Tom Walsh: 'Will ye take hold of his hands—hold his wrists,' he cried out, '—whilst I staunch it.' The word *staunch*—I couldn't think what it might mean. And mingled in with the men's voices I could hear Mother's. I thought I should kneel and pray but I was somehow unable to, and was relieved when the door opened again and it was Mrs Walsh.

'Come on, Willie love,' she said.

'What is it, Mrs Walsh?' I said.

'Something's happened, Willie,' she said. 'I'll take you with me to our house—out of the way. Come on love, don't be frightened. You'll be all right.'

She opened the door and we made to go downstairs. But on the small landing at the top of the stairs we had to hold back, for my Cousin John was just hurrying up the stairs. The house seemed to be full of people and alive with voices. The back-bedroom door was open and I looked in and saw that Tom Walsh was stooped down, and had in his hand a piece of white sheet which he was using as some kind of a bandage. My father, white-faced and wearing a singlet, was beside him, looking helpless. They were facing Uncle William who was seated on the floor in his shirt, his back propped up against the side of the bed. I saw that Mother was kneeling down facing him, and she was stroking his forehead and face, and chiding him in a way I had never before heard: 'Oh why would you do this to me, agraw,' I heard her say to Uncle William, 'and me in the strange land with my children—amongst strangers?'

The wailing in mother's voice gave me a feeling of shock. I had a sense of being cut off from her, for I had never heard that voice before or the sorrowing moan that followed it, so wild and desolate it sounded. Then Tom Walsh moved aside and I saw the front of Uncle William, with open shirt, and a red wound at his throat. And yet on his face was that same quiet smile—as though he was apart from all the fuss, just looking on. Mrs Walsh pulled me to her breast to take my gaze from the sight. Then a policeman came upstairs following Cousin John, and they all crowded into the little bedroom.

Mrs Walsh now took my hand and led me quickly downstairs. As we went through the back kitchen I could see the front door open, and was taken aback to see a double line of neighbours, standing there and looking in. It was hard to comprehend that our own neighbours would stand there with such cool curiosity. An ambulance drew up outside, and men in uniform came in with a stretcher and went noisily upstairs. 'I'd rather not go out,' I said to Mrs Walsh, 'with all the people there.' She understood, and I went and stood out of the way in the far corner of the front kitchen.

Then with a calling out of voices and thumping of feet the ambulance men brought Uncle William downstairs on a stretcher, his body covered up to the face with a blanket. I watched them carry him out and put him in the back of the ambulance, close the doors, and drive off. Dear Uncle William, God rest his soul, whom I had so often seen kneeling at the side of the bed praying for a happy death, was to die in the ambulance as it drove through the streets of Bolton on that sunny June morning.

11

The Wake and After

THE death of Uncle William, and above all the shocking way it had occurred—so violent an end for one so gentle—left a sorry mark on our family life. The image I got of his faintly smiling expression—the final one which I caught as I passed the open door of the bedroom, minutes before he died—was to remain with me over the years. I avoided going out in the street or near my mates at the Corner, since I felt I couldn't speak of the happening to anyone outside the family. It was strange and upsetting to have policemen and detectives entering our home and asking questions, and, although they were considerate and kindly, the contrast between the Irish mind and the English official one caused some disquiet. In the early afternoon it was good to see Uncle Mick come in the door: 'Maria,' he said, embracing my mother, 'my heart is with you in your great trouble, may the Lord save us.' There was something impressive about Uncle Mick, a man born and reared among the solitary plains and boglands of Mayo; he appeared to have an inherited faith and honesty, one that endowed him with a strength to give comfort in times of affliction. The atmosphere of the home, orderless and floundering, seemed to steady the moment he entered. My poor father seemed to lack the authority given to the benevolent and big-hearted, men who can be wholly relied upon to do what they believe is right.

There was the inquest on Friday morning: 'Suicide whilst temporarily of unsound mind,' was the coroner's verdict. Money had to be borrowed from a moneylender to get the men's suits out of pawn for the funeral the next day. There was a small amount of insurance money, but it turned out that Uncle William had the sum of three hundred pounds saved in War Loan certificates. It was not only a surprisingly large amount for an Irishman to leave—equivalent to two years' wages—but unique in that no one belonging to us had ever before left any money; since he had made no will it was later divided between my mother and her two elder sisters in Ireland, Margaret and Helen. The Strike, which with its period of enforced idleness was at the root of his depression, was settled that weekend, the miners having to return to work on the terms they might have had much earlier.

The body was brought to our home after the inquest, and laid in an open coffin, set on draped trestles near the window. There was no sign of the injury—the lower part of the shroud was set securely below the chin—and Uncle William lay there in all the magisterial peace of the dead. The high forehead looked even broader, the lower face firmer, and the still and waxen appearance enhanced his look of quiet composure. Mother kept turning to the corpse, whispering about how it was hard to think she would never again see him cross the street on a Saturday evening, or hear him lilting a jig for me to dance to, or indeed ever hear his voice again, as long as she lived. She spoke to him as she might to a child, as though he could hear her every word, and she often stooped and kissed his cheek. She may have detected a reluctance in me to kiss the dead face, and she turned on me reproachfully: 'Is it hesitatin' you are', she said, 'to kiss your dear Uncle, who loved you to distraction!' 'Musha, Maria,' said Uncle Mick, 'would you leave the ladeen to do what is in his heart to do.' I put my lips down to the broad forehead and was shocked by its extreme coldness.

There was a kind of wake that Friday evening in our home, before the funeral fixed for Saturday. The front kitchen was full, mostly of Irish, although a few neighbours called in and seemed reluctant to leave a scene so unusual as that of a wake. The evening was warm, and I was posted near the open door, answering it to callers. The young Irishman would enter, turn at once to the bier, kneel down, bless himself, and whisper a prayer, then rise up and go to my mother, 'I am sorry for ye, Ma'am, in yeer trouble,' he would say, and shake her hand. Tea was being served to the women, and my father was on the go with jugs and bottles from Nancy's, seeing that no one was short of beer. The talk was kept up, but it was too painful an occasion for an Irish wake, since the nature of Uncle William's death did not allow for the levity often arising at such a gathering.

Later in the evening, when only the close friends and relatives were left, Mother's reserve began to weaken and she turned once more to the coffin and whispered endearments. Uncle Mick let her go on for a few minutes, and then put his pipe aside and spoke to her: 'Now Maria—that'll do you,' he said, and I was surprised at the firm tone of voice. 'It wouldn't be right to give yourself up entirely to the grief—'. 'Sure you're right,' she said, 'I know you're right. But it's hard.' 'It'll be hard for many a day to come,' he said, 'an' I'm afraid there's nothin' for it but bear it, since it's God's will. You know that Annie an' myself lost many a fine lovely young child.' 'I do, I do surely, God save us,' she said. 'Remember, Maria,' he went on, 'you have himself there, an' your children, God bless them, but above all, William wouldn't want it—that you'd grieve him too much. For as they say at home—he'll never rest as long as you grieve him in that manner. You must compose yourself to allow peace to his soul.' Mother came away from the coffin, looking more herself, if a little rebuked.

Then Uncle Mick took up his pipe and began to light it: 'Well, God rest you, William,' he said, now using a calm tone, '—you never harmed a soul in all your life.' 'There was no one ever', said another, 'that I heard say a word against him.' 'Arra no one could—he never wronged a one in his life—never said the nasty word.' 'He was the soul of decency,' said Tom McNamara. 'A decenter man never wore shoe-leather.' 'An' a great worker. God save us, but no man ever I knew could keep pace with William in a field of hay.' I sat there beside Willie Kirrane and listened, and it seemed Uncle William was being brought back into life in some way, as though his sick spirit was being given a new airing, a healing as it were, but in death the smile was gone. Willie and

John Kirrane stayed up there all night, for they had the Irish way of never leaving the body unattended.

(Some thirty years later I stayed up all night in that same little room, on a chair beside the body of my dead mother. Seeing her lying there in her coffin, with the kindly dignity of death upon her, I began to wonder how much greater in their going from this world would be those ones who had been wiser than she, who in the conduct of their lives had been more sensible. She had not managed too well—not with the material demands of this life—for often she had been prodigal where it would have paid her to be prudent, lavish when it might have been excusable to stint. For being remiss in this respect she had endured much distress and, often enough, humiliation. She had worked hard all her life, but had made little attempt to garner any fruits from her labours; indeed had asked nothing for herself, and, so quick was she to give, that in her departure she was leaving almost as little of worldly value behind as when she arrived. In her love and consideration for others she had always been most generous, and not only had she avoided bringing pain to others, but she had striven to see that none of us should. And, despite the apparent humbleness of her days, she was and always had been proud and independent.

And as I sat awake there through the night hours, which curiously enough in no way seemed long, I recalled the big meals she enjoyed to make for guests, and the substantial teas she would provide for the poorest caller, and the countless coppers her short fingers never failed to find in her purse for young children, street singers, and others. Not that she ever set the least store on any gracious deed of her own—she was ashamed to have it mentioned, for to her generosity was the most natural of impulses. 'Ee, Willie, the most we've ever got,' one of the neighbours was to remark the next morning when she brought in the wreath after the customary collection, '—an' there's enough over for one of them Masses. Not a single refusal!—first time I've know that. Ee, I never realized your mother was so well thought of—bein' as she were never one to put herself forward.' Yes, she left a legacy of love and respect among those who had known her, and, had she scrimped and saved all her days, it is likely that the most there would have been was a few miserable pounds in the bank.)

A frequent visitor for some weeks after Uncle William's funeral was his old friend Paddy Conboy. The episode in the Ram's Head had preyed on his mind also, and Paddy came not to console my mother but to seek some comfort from her, for he was in a sorry state after Uncle's death. Often I would come in home from school, and Paddy, so unlike his usual gracious self, would give me no more than maybe a nod or a greeting in a distant voice: 'Is that you, Willie!' Then he would turn to Mother and carry on with his talk, repeating himself: 'Maria,' he would say, 'I cannot close my eyes at night in sleep but there is William before me. Last night and every night, God in heaven save us!' Paddy was no longer his spruce and smiling self, for now he went on the drink for a period, did no work, and occasionally looked sleepless and unkempt, in spite of the loving care of his Bolton wife, Lizzie.

'Didn't I ask William, the Lord have mercy on him, to take a drink from me—then didn't he refuse—or at least he asked me in place to take one—the decent man he ever was—an' whatever it was happened there was no drink at all taken between us. No health drank, no drink shared, a sorry thing surely, the Lord between us an' all harm, that two friends so old an' close as himself an' myself did not raise glasses together that day. What terrible things can go on in a poor man's mind—an' no one to know! Wouldn't I sooner the tongue was taken off me than I'd offend William—he was closer to me than a brother.'

Mother and Paddy were Catholic enough in their general outlook, but their faith was more than tinged with ancient beliefs, with what would be called superstitions; death was to them the eternal mystery, one which their everyday minds could not comprehend, so that they would grope out for some spark of guidance from above or beyond all religion. Mother was able to comfort Paddy—she was the only one that could, he used to say—but when he had gone she seemed unable to lift herself out of her own grief. At times she made brisk attempts to shake free from it, and would rise from her knees as though determined to go on courageously, but there was something unreal in such expedients, and mostly she would be sunk in a heavy sorrow.

Then for a time she would go round the house at all hours muttering prayers for the dead, and these were mixed with murmurings in Irish, and in between she would talk to Uncle William as though he were there beside her; it seemed she found ease in abandoning herself to the affliction, and putting aside the concerns of daily life. I would open the front door after hurrying home from school in the afternoon, forgetting for a moment the change in the home, and expecting the smell of hot potato cakes, and the pleasure of sharing these on the sly with Mother, and the freshly brewed tea she was fond of, but instead there would be what seemed to me to be a strange woman and a stranger home. The fire would be almost out, and the room cold and gloomy, and she would be down on her knees saying the Rosary, seeking a touch of comfort from her beads and prayers. And there would be no potato cakes or tea, and above all no jokes. It distressed me that I could make no real contact with my mother in her demented state.

'Mam, what you're doing is a sin,' I told her one day when she was calmer, and I had come quietly into the home from school, and we were having a cup of tea together. 'It's what they call giving way to despair, it's a sin against the Holy Ghost. You're shuttin' your soul off against God.' She looked at me with surprise, 'Musha I am, I am surely,' she said, '—amn't I shut off against everything. And God knows haven't I had enough to shut me off.'

She had a way of glancing up to the ceiling, as though God were there, quietly taking in all she had to say, and, although she didn't care to overstep the mark, it seemed that the odd bold hint was allowed to be drawn out of her. After some months she became easier in mind and manner, but not like her old self. The house was small, and she rarely went out except to Mass; she had to make the bed daily in the little back bedroom where the terrible happening had taken place, so that the memory must have been constantly brought back. And it was the same at weekends, for which it seemed she would try to brighten up and take a lively interest in the home. But when the time approached that Uncle William used to make his usual Saturday evening visit, we could not escape the old sense of expectancy, of the neat and sturdy figure crossing the road, and of the happy ceremony of his coming into the house. 'The only one ever belonging us, agraw, that had the violent death,' she would whisper.

There has always remained in my mind two distinct impressions of my mother: one of the way she was before Uncle William's death, and the other the way she became after it. She remained as gentle and gracious as ever, and quietly eager to help anyone in need. But the proudly erect figure stooped, the light quick step slowed down, and the happy laugh was gone forever. Her grey hair turned white, her fresh skin became lined, the cheerful look was dimmed, and it seemed she became an old woman almost overnight. It was not surprising that some shabby decline affected our home and family life. That special tone which Uncle William effused, one of decency and honour, was missing. I suppose it was then—and probably rightly so—that my father came into his own. The presence of Uncle William had overshadowed him, and forced on him a restraint, a quelling down of his own nature and the impulses and opinions it would give rise to.

12

Poor Prospects

MY own boyish feeling of sorrow and loss over the death of Uncle William was real enough, but compared with the afflicted grief of my mother it seemed hollow and put on, and I felt guilty that I didn't feel more than I did. My cheerful nature found it difficult to adapt to the gloomy domestic atmosphere, for I was inclined to spontaneous bouts of humming and whistling. It was a relief now to get out of the house, and often I would return with a sense of foreboding. What made my home life even less inviting was that I no longer had the moral support of Uncle William, and it seemed that my father took advantage of this. He had been a different man during the three months of the stoppage; just as work answered some need in Uncle William, my father seemed to blossom during a period of rest, especially so when he had less to drink at weekends, so that he escaped the sudden flush of high spirits the drink induced on Saturday evenings and the consequent morose mood of Sunday morning. Now he had to return to work after suffering defeat at the hands of the mineowners, and take a big cut in earnings, a bitter upshot to which he could never reconcile himself.

The manner in which he prepared to go off to the pit every evening, pale and silent, loaded with his huge tea-can and snap-box, and the sombre way he turned to May and me to kiss him goodbye, exchanging anxious looks with my mother before going out of the door and clomping across the cobbled street in his loose pit clogs, was like a man going not to work but to a penal task, a punishment for some crime. There was a feeling that as a family we had not emigrated from Ireland but had been transported, and were in bondage, living a harsh degraded life, alien in every way to our natures, our one hope being that the entire land of Ireland would one day be free from the British yoke, rid of all the soldiery and police, and that we could all go back and live there like lords. And it was not difficult to imagine the reaction of our tolerant English hosts: the sooner the better!—good riddance to the lot of you!

The Troubles in Ireland were over, at least for a time, with a truce operating, yet it was far from peace. In July Catholics in Belfast were attacked, a dozen killed, many more badly injured, and over 150 Catholic homes destroyed. Eamon de Valera went over to Downing Street to discuss a treaty with Lloyd George but refused to accept his terms. Later de Valera sent Arthur Griffith, Michael Collins, and three other members of his government over to negotiate the Anglo-Irish Treaty. In December Lloyd George insisted the Irish delegate sign the Treaty or the hostilities would start all over again in three days. They signed under pressure, and returned to Ireland with a copy of the Treaty, which de Valera rejected, but the Dail accepted by a narrow majority; de Valera resigned, and the Civil War broke out, between the Free State troops of those who had accepted the Treaty, and de Valera's followers, the Irregulars or Republicans.

Few developments could have been more unforeseen to us than that of Irishmen who had fought together now killing each other. And it proved almost as ruthless and brutal as the conflict with the British forces. Apart from the appalling executions on either side, and the woeful destruction such a conflict brought about—it was to go on for a year, until de Valera accepted defeat—it was mortifying that the English could now point out that the Irish were, as they had claimed, an irresponsible people, unfitted to govern themselves. (It would seem that Lloyd George's trickery in dealing with the Irish question was to have bitter consequences in Northern Ireland throughout the century. Nor was his severe treatment of the British miners—to be taken up by Baldwin after the General Strike of 1926—to prove fruitful. Miners became a socially degraded class, and so depleted of manpower did the industry become that young men had to be compelled to work in the mines, the 'Bevin Boys', as an alternative to military service during the Second World War. Above all, the bitterness created among the mining communities was there to stay, and recalcitrant echoes of the injustices and indignities suffered in the 1920s were to continue for decades.)

It now seemed to me that ordeals of one kind or another were to beset me at every turn. School life, with its severely repressive atmosphere, inducing wild behaviour in boys released from it, I had endured but never liked, although a kindly teacher, Miss Conway, had made it less of an ordeal; but she had gone off to get married, and for a year and more I had suffered under the intimidating Miss Newsham. She was a plump-breasted woman in her forties, with a birdlike face, pale blue eyes, and a fierce temper. I was always well behaved, and often came top of the class at exams, but my handwriting was quirky and uneven, and for this I was frequently rebuked. She was expert with the cane, and brought it down on the outstretched palm with astonishing force; for such canings I could always brace myself, and adopt a calm unflinching exterior, no matter how great the pain and agitation underneath, but for the swinging slap from behind, known as 'a winger', I could never prepare myself, and was knocked off poise and felt humiliated. What I most detested was the loss of personal dignity. I had hoped after the summer holiday, moving up a standard, that our class would get another teacher, such as the bumbling Mr Kelly, but no, to my dismay there was Miss Newsham in front of the class—she had moved up with us, and I was in for another year of apprehension and misery.

The Boys' Corner, where all the boys sat and chatted, told tales and made fun, and often played games, had often been my haven of escape from my father's presence, but now I dodged it. It was not only that I disliked being the subject of talk and sympathy, but I also felt that it would be some time before I could let myself be part of the lively leg-pulling mood of the place; so I kept away. I never realized that I would miss it so much. Cornerboys such as myself had a need for each other far beyond what may be imagined. Living a deprived existence—deprivation so bred into most of us that we were unable to grasp it was anything other than what might normally be expected from life—meant that boys had so much more unsatisfied feeling to devote to a friendship. I always fitted in better with boys a year or two older than myself—boys younger seemed too childish to me—so that nearly all my mates were working, either half-time or fulltime. Another vein of my life which had ceased completely was my love affair with Alice. I felt that her coolness had to do with the unpopularity of the Irish, because of the conflict with the British forces there, and also because of the bad name the miners had got after the Strike. I missed her greatly.

Most evenings I found that I made my way to our church of SS Peter and Paul. To kneel and pray seemed to give me peace at once, and I was comforted by the red glow of the companion light on the altar, signalling the Holy Presence in the form of a host of bread within the tabernacle. On Tuesdays and Thursdays there was Benediction, to which I always looked forward. I would choose a seat at the back, close to the wall, where I wouldn't be noticed, for I didn't want to be taken for a Holy Joe. In contrast to the Latin Mass, the droning of which could weary one, I enjoyed the Benediction of the Blessed Sacrament, since I knew what it was about from start to finish. The altar would be radiant with bright candles, and the Host exposed in the setting of the gold monstrance, which seemed to add to the glory and mystery, and the singing of 'O Salutaris' and 'Tantum Ergo' was always spirited. I especially enjoyed the Divine Praises at the end, 'Blessed be God—Blessed be His holy Name . . .', usually followed by a hymn to the Sacred Heart. The congregation at Benediction was nearly all women, gentle women who were there from love and not duty as was the case at Mass, and I let my unhappy feelings be taken up by the words of the hymn, as they raised their plaintive voices all around: 'Thou hast taught me in my sorrow, | Where alone the heart finds rest, | I have learnt 'tis sweet to suffer, | Pillowed on thy Sacred Breast . . .'

On my lonesome wanderings I would think of the future, and although optimistic by temperament it was clear to me that my own expectations when I left school at the age of fourteen would be bleak. I was quick at sums and good at composition, but I tended to be slow on the uptake away from my school desk, a bit dreamy and forgetful. The worst part came when I had to do jobs with my hands, such as fastening a loose heel-iron on my clog, shuffling the cards over a game of pontoon, or playing pitch-and-toss, for it seemed I had an Irish clumsiness and none of that manual dexterity which came naturally to the fingers, stubby and nail-bitten but surprisingly deft, of my street-corner mates. All in all, it seemed I would hardly survive. To get on in the world in which we Irish found ourselves, one of steam, smoke, machinery, and din, you definitely had to belong, since it had its own élite caste, nurtured by generations of skilled industrial toil, and of such rigid exclusiveness that no Hibernian of our breed could hope to be allowed in.

For a start you had both to look right and behave as expected for each and every job, with a proper spinner's face and figure for the cotton mill, for spinners were mostly lean and pale, and although sharp of tongue you hadn't to be too sharp; a certain stolid mechanical look of sorts was needed for a loom-fettler's job in the weaving shed—not a hope for an Irish mug like mine, since it took ages to breed the genuine article. Then it seemed you were expected to know everything about the job before you even started, from what and how much to say—loquacity of any kind was frowned on—down to what kind of clogs and overalls to wear; and all the rest of your gear had to be just so, for traditions were strict and must be observed. Then of course you had to come from a proper neighbourhood, and the right kind of family too, one with a proper Lancashire name, such as Halliwell, Hesketh, Six-smith, Baverstock, or Baxendale—names with a bit of punch behind them and nothing fancy or foreign. On top of that you needed at least one relative whose word carried some weight, a carder or overlooker and like as not a member of the local Conservative Club, so that you had somebody to speak for you, for he could put your name down months ahead for a job, and you needed that bit of influence there all the time to back you up. Then you had to show the gaffer and the others that you had your wits about you—a numskull or slowcoach would end up as an oiler-and-greaser, but not of course if he had folk behind him, for they would somehow pull him through. Allowing all went well, and you attended night school, the best you could expect was to become a spinner or tackler, for the staff posts had to be shared out among the directors' relatives. (If you went after a job down the pit they would always take you on, as long as you could grip a pick or shovel, for the poor pay and arduous work sorted them out, and a man either scraped through and became a miner or sacked himself.)

It was obvious that neither I nor anyone belonging to me qualified for a skilled job, and, as I became more keenly aware of my lowly and alien identity, I turned even more for reassurance to Matthew, 'What doth it profit a man—?' Most of those well-off folk'now having a good time in this world were fools, I decided, for they failed to see that God's grace, bestowed on you for having lived a good and selfless life, would be taken beyond with you—but not money, power, and wordly goods, for they became meaningless once you drew your last breath. Yet it was clear to me that, no matter what the difficulties and miseries that seemed to harass one from rising in the morning to going to bed at night, one's life had to be lived by and to oneself. That was obviously what God intended, and being that circumstances were so clearly against me, the question I asked myself was: *What should I aim for?*

13

Trinity Sunday Procession

ONE Thursday evening I went off to church for Confession, so as to have my soul immaculate for Holy Communion next morning at the early Mass at a quarter-past-six. This Mass was arranged for mill workers who were doing a novena, or the Nine Fridays as it was called—taking Communion on the First Friday of nine consecutive months—and I took advantage of it, for I relished the feeling not only of having my soul spick and span, but also of gaining the plenary indulgence that went with the devotion, which meant a remission of all the punishment still due to sins after they had been forgiven. After Confession I stayed on for the usual Benediction, and then home by a circuitous route to allow time for my father to have gone to his night shift at the pit, at the same time avoiding the Corner and all my mates. Before going to bed I gave my mother strict instructions to see that she wakened me not a moment later than half-past-five next morning, so that I would be sure to be well in time, and could say a Hail Mary or two and sit down and calm myself before Mass began; which, as I explained to her, was the way I liked to hear Mass—not arriving at the Gospel, as was the way with some Irish.

'Yes, my saintly son,' she had promised, 'I'll have you up before the lark.'

I knew that with my religious bent I was a bit of a nuisance around the house. During the week Mother and young James slept in the big bed in the front room—joined by my father at weekends; my sister May and myself had the other bed—she at the top and myself at the bottom—being disturbed by my early rising annoyed her. In the back bedroom slept Cousin John and my brother Edward, who had left school and now

worked in a shop. I was downstairs on this certain morning
just after half-past-five, washing away at the cold tap in the
back kitchen, hoping to scrub my outside self to blend with
what I took to be my soul. Mother and John were chatting as
he ate his breakfast of stirabout before going off to his day
shift at the mine; I enjoyed listening to their talk, since they
spoke in an intimate Irish manner, one never heard when
others were around. This was the form of exchange of their
particular families, the Flemings and the Kirranes, and of
most of the people from the country area of Mayo. It was so
soft and quiet, laced with such humour and innuendo, that it
was like two persons creating something out of nothing. The
gift of speech appeared to be precious to them; each one
spoke with an individual style: every word seemed to be part
of them, so that they did not churn them out rashly, but, by a
pause, a rise or fall in the voice, an extending of a vowel, and
various impulses of enunciation, they instilled their simple
use of language with rich and delicate nuances. It was conversation of a nature quite beyond my father, who was something of a townie Irishman, not given to listening to another;
and it seemed an art wholly lost to us children brought up in
Bolton, who had largely adopted the flat and direct mode of
talk, and whose minds appeared unable either to catch or
hint at such subtleties.

I said goodbye to John, kissed Mother, and set off through
the maze of narrow streets as dawn was breaking, feeling that
certain happy lightness that went with the fasting for Communion. I had the feeling that I was the only child in the
family, so little interest had the others in the next world or in
Ireland and the Irish. It was as I was crossing the open spare
ground near Magee's Brewery—a spot where it seemed that I
was often touched with some fresh idea—that Mother's
expression 'saintly son' came to mind. Why, there as clear as
could be was the one answer to all the doubt and uncertainty
about my future: why bother at all about jobs and getting on
in the world, and all the many useless concerns and worries,
since nothing ever worked out as planned anyway? Why not
keep independent of everybody, go your own way, take

things as they came, breathe not a word to a soul, keep going with only one goal in mind—and with God's help, daily discipline, and a bit of luck you could *end up a saint*!

When I got home with what I took to be a fairly clean soul—the angel's wing, set there inside me over my heart, was difficult to keep white because of selfish feelings that kept bobbing up—I found that being the first at breakfast I was able to grab the last of the barm cakes left from Wednesday's baking. Mother had dipped it in hot bacon fat, and garnished it with scraps of burnt bacon, which I liked, and I was eating it when my sister May came into the front kitchen. She was known for her bad temper and funny moods, and when she saw me with the barm cake, and realized she would have to have bread, she gave a sort of snort: 'Trust you to get in first,' she said, '—*Saintly Billy!*' I don't suppose I should have taken any notice had Mother not spoken to her: 'Never speak that way to anyone,' she said, 'you wouldn't know how you could discourage a person.' I swallowed the last of my barm cake ánd got up and went out of the back door. I'll bet Mam's giving it to her now, I thought.

Although I didn't let myself be put off, I could not escape feeling guilty over nursing such a pious intention, and not for anything would I have had it known. Mother may have suspected something odd, and would occasionally urge me against too much churchgoing, hinting that in Ireland such behaviour was not thought right, and that the priest himself would warn a person to give God a little peace, and not be always pestering Him. I was only too aware that there was something most unsaintly in my nature; I was shrewd and knowing, not to say crafty, and lacked the open frankness of most English lads, since I had the Irish habit of telling people what I imagined they would like to hear. I had not yet dis-covered the sacredness of truth, and would turn to a lie if the situation demanded it. Although drawn to the ideal of charity and giving, I often found it uncomfortable to part with what I had; and, whilst my behaviour could not have been more modest, it was only an act, for I was intensely vain and self-centred. My saintliness, it seemed even to me, was all in the head and not in the heart; I was all knowing and no being, and my observances of the Faith, and any good deed I did, were done with one eye on the reward of 'eternal life of unending joy'.

Above all I was a born sceptic in many respects, and believed only in that which I felt must be true. Satan I only half believed in; my mother, a great Catholic, once said she didn't believe in him at all. As for the one criterion of canonization—that of the person having performed or induced a miracle of some kind—this made little sense to me, since I was undecided about miracles. As much as I loved Easter and rejoiced in it, I tried not to think of Our Lord actually rising from the dead, of the shocking state He would surely be in after the crucifixion, and the night and day in the tomb; what I always asked myself was: Why should God or the Son of God wish to impress *us* with a miracle? Who are we that He should wish to gain our awe? Since He was God He could resurrect every soul that had ever died—not only Jesus. And so I decided not to pursue the question. As for the water being turned into wine, and the miracles of the loaves and the fishes, walking on the water, and others of that kind, I was well aware of a weakness of my own—how I would often tell a whopping fib just to prove more strongly what I believed was true.

Praying for some wish to be granted was another problem of sorts for me. There was one morning at the School Mass when Canon Holmes, a big man with a florid complexion and grey hair parted in the middle, stood in the pulpit and told us that God responded more to children's prayers than to anyone's—which I doubted at once—and so would we all pray for a fine day for our annual Trinity Sunday procession through the town. He is a nice kindly priest, I thought, as I looked up at his boyish English face, but surely a bit simple; when God created the universe he must have set going the processes which would cause the sun to shine and rain to fall. Water, as we all knew, evaporates from the sea and lakes and is carried up in the atmosphere, which water vapour when rising over hills and mountains is condensed by cold air and comes down as rain. Is it feasible, I asked, that because a few hundred boys and girls in a school in Bolton are chanting Hail Marys He is going to step in and alter the laws of nature? No matter how well disposed to Catholics He was known to be, it did not seem likely. And suppose some poor farmer happens to be praying equally sincerely for rain for his crops? What a dilemma to present to God. So, secretly, I withheld my own prayer and decided not to get involved.

On that particular Sunday as we marched in our hundreds from the school, carrying banners of all kinds, to gather at the Town Hall Square together, the entire Catholic community, with all traffic stopped for us, it was being openly whispered that a miracle had indeed happened: the many dark clouds of the morning had simply floated over Bolton, without a speck of rain falling. It was as the same miracle was proceeding, and we were all massed together in our thousands on Victoria Square, many more thousands thronging the pavements watching, and all singing the glorious hymn, 'Faith of Our Fathers'—I was always out of tune so that I only mimed the words with my lips—that I chanced to look heavenwards and saw the blackest cloud above. I watched it creep along and then it seemed suddenly to stop; the next moment there was a clap of thunder, a cloudburst, and such a violent downpour that in moments everyone was soaked, since there was no place to escape. And as I looked upwards again it seemed that God and myself were having a little private exchange: *See what you've done now!* He was saying, *You and your questioning.* I was relieved to feel that at least He couldn't give the show away.

Yet it was the one occasion on which I really enjoyed the procession, for it seemed that Miss Newsham and the other teachers in their drenched finery, and Mr Smith in his top hat, could no longer preserve their usual stern dignity and discipline—a shower of God's rain, I thought to myself, finds them out—and for once I could be happy, striding along through the puddles, carrying my cap, which for that one event each year I had to wear but now making out it was too wet to keep on, and enjoying the soft and cool pinging of the large drops of rain on my head. Above all I delighted in the obvious discomfort of the teachers and the other big nobs, and even sang hymns loudly between cracking jokes and exchanging laughs with my pals, without hearing any of those incessant commands about keeping in line and lifting one's feet. Suddenly, as we got to Moor Lane on our way back, the rain stopped as if by magic and out came warm bright sunshine. Then everybody seemed to look to the sky, and made friends with the weather, and for a few cheerful minutes it seemed that Mr Smith and all the teachers shed their usual air of cold authority, and they too began to smile to each other, and even to smile on us, and I got a feeling of how good it would be to be one of a happy school, where the teachers inspired affection and respect in the boys, instead of dislike and fear, and learning became the interesting work it could be, in place of the hateful grind it was.

14

The Barker Twins

THERE lived opposite us in Unsworth Street a family by the name of Barker who had twin sons, Willie and Harold, about my own age. Mr Barker, a short muscular man with a lean stern face, was a horse-carter for the big haulage firm of Nalls, and over the war years and for a year or two after would leave home for work at five o'clock in the morning to drive his team of horses with the huge load the eleven miles to Manchester Ship Canal, unload, and drive back home for evening. He was unlike other carters in that he didn't drink and was thrifty and industrious. (He kept a few hens in the backyard, and I remember food rationing was very strict in 1918 when my mother sent me across for a couple of eggs for my father's breakfast—I never saw an Irishman sit down to *one* egg—and I paid the sixpence each for them, and how my father when he heard the price burst out: 'Well, the bloody rogue—to think of the thousands of eggs I sold over in Ireland at sixpence a dozen!' 'Thanks be to God', remarked my mother, 'that we have the money to pay for them.' There was truth in her words, for twelve years later, in 1930, ex-service-men had set up poultry holdings all round Bolton, and would bring lovely fresh eggs to the front door for ninepence a dozen, but by that time, after the General Strike of 1926, the miners were down near the bottom of the list in the wage-earners' table, there were eighty other occupations above them, and alas, even at ninepence a dozen we hadn't the ready cash.)

Mrs Barker was out of the ordinary in the way she worked from morning till late evening, and was careful how she spent every penny. (They were saving up to emigrate to Canada, which they did in 1923; but things there proved not as good as they had imagined, and a few years later they were back in Bolton, declaring there was no place on earth to compare to it.) One task which Mrs Barker was capable of—which few housewives in our street would have been up to—was that of taking in washing from two elderly ladies who lived in a posh house in Howcroft Street. She had only the one cold-water tap in the back kitchen, the copper to boil the clothes in, and the backyard or backstreet to dry them in, where there was always the danger of smuts from mill chimneys, and, as there were sheets, towels, tablecloths, dresser covers, antimacassars, ladies' underclothes, and various delicate items, it always struck me as a weekly miracle how she could get them so beautifully laundered, ironed to perfection, with sheets of tissue paper separating certain items. It was not only pleasing to look into that wide clothes-basket into which they were placed for returning, but nice to smell the clean fragrance of starch which clung to the clothes after ironing. The thought used to strike me that they were almost as immaculate as one's soul after Holy Communion.

How I came to know Mrs Barker and her washing so intimately was because of the discord between Willie and Harold—I am going back a year or two to when I was around nine years old. They were unidentical twins, totally unalike in appearance and nature: Willie had a thin, pale face with brown eyes, and Harold a round rosy-cheeked face with blue eyes; Willie was slow, careful, and honest, Harold quick, easygoing, and a bit of a liar. They argued incessantly and fought frequently, and having to live together they hated each other as it would seem only brothers can. It was essential that the basket got carried with a proper balance between the two boys, each grasping a handle, but they bickered about who should carry with the right hand and who with the left, and about rests along the way, and more than once they had actually upset the basket and laundry had fallen on to the pavement. One day in desperation Mrs Barker had asked me would I go with them as a spare carrier, but more to act as a peacemaker between them—a role much to my nature, since I disliked quarrelling of any kind. 'I'll see you right, Billy,' she said, using the common form of a promise to reward without actually being bound to any sum. I decided from the tone of voice that it meant giving me a penny. That then was how I got to know so much about 'the clothes' as they were always carried. 'Whatever you do,' said Mrs Barker, '*don't touch the clothes.*'

My presence and the fact that I took turns in taking hold of a handle on the basket appeared to create a sort of amity between the twins on that first occasion; then as we approached the house they took hold of the basket between them. 'Stick close,' said Harold, 'an' come in wi' us, an' tha'll get a piece of cake. Eh, Willie?' 'Aye,' said Willie, 'but not too close.' I always enjoyed going into an English home, since even the poorest English family revealed a houseproud spirit quite unknown to the Irish—although some Irish would attempt to imitate it, as did my father, but he lacked the true feeling and mistook it for a form of showiness. The variety of knick-knackery and decoration within each home even in our street was of extreme diversity, with a picture or two— although not 'holy' ones of saints, as in our own home, since they preferred samplers, embroidered pieces of needlework with a biblical quotation or the popular, 'What is Home without a Mother!' The dresser was often packed with orna- ments, and what would interest me most would be the framed photograph or two, usually of a young soldier or sailor. Certain items, such as the polished fire-irons or the huge bronze ornaments on the dresser, meant a good Lancashire family, the articles probably handed down; others, such as the collection of items under one of the pair of glass domes on the dresser, which might range from a baby's clog to a sea-shell, had a way of expressing a family singularity.

'This cigarette-case saved my Dad's life in 1916 on the Somme. Canta see that dint where t'bullet struck? This strap were my Uncle Herbert's—he got killed int'Pretoria Pit disas- ter. These were our Philip's first clogs—he died of fever when he were three.' One home I once visited had had a collie dog, Rex, which was killed in an accident, and it was decided to engage a taxidermist to treat the skin. A dog is missed by any family, but in a small and crowded home, where the dog has his secure place in the corner, spends most of his time on the rug in front of the fire and at meal times by the table begging scraps, greets each one of the family as he or she comes down in the morning, sees the adults off to work and the children to school, welcomes them on return, and above all is never moody or in a bad temper, that animal may become a more regarded part of family life than any member of it, with the exception of Mum, and the sense of loss in such a home when he is no longer there is not easy to imagine. A cane frame held Rex's skin, and this was displayed on the wall. Whilst no one would compare it to a lion or leopard skin, of a sort which might grace a more noble home, the skin of Rex had its own homely distinction, and perhaps meant more in that it was not a trophy of some act of slaughter but a token of affectionate memory.

The two Winkworth ladies led us through to a kind of large scullery at the back of the house—Harold having got me to keep a hand on the clothes, which were piled up, as though they needed holding on to—so I didn't actually see very much, but the nice smell of the home told me all. I had the most sensitive sense of smell, and the moment a front door was opened to me something instinctively identified the class of family—the range of smell extending from the warm baking and cooking smell in the best homes to the cold empty smell of poverty in the poorest, the poverty smell always tinged with one of gas and the smell arising from a damp uncovered stone floor. What surprised me most in the Winkworth home was how the two elderly ladies, each wearing a Paisley shawl, seemed so eager to greet Willie and Harold and hear all they had to say—as though they had actually been waiting for them—and how my two mates chatted loudly and freely, not adopting, as I tended to, a voice to suit the listener. They cut a generous piece of cake for each of us. Then one sister picked up four pennies which had been placed at one side on the dresser, and gave Harold and Willie twopence each. 'Billy helped to carry part of the way,' said Harold, giving me a wink. The other sister, however, had anticipated his remark, and already had her purse open and was fingering out two coins for me.

'Tha'rt lucky,' said Willie, '—we get tuppence an' a piece of cake when we tak' t'clean clothes back, but nowt when we collect the dirty clothes on a Monday.' The moment Harold got me on my own he whispered: 'If my mam gives thee a penny, I reckon I deserve a ha'penny of it.' I agreed at once, but as it happened Willie told his mother when we got back of my getting twopence, and she said to me: 'I told you I'd see you right, didn't I!' as much as to say that she was behind my getting twopence.

A mischievous practice at the time among schoolgirls—the work in a cotton mill at thirteen prematurely aged girls so that puberty often passed unnoticed—was that of chalking enigmatic messages on backstreet and gable-end walls, the purpose being to settle some grudge or get even with a rival. Any writing of any kind at once caught my eye, and when I saw, 'HB f.u.c. with EW' I could see that 'HB' was likely to be Harold Barker and that 'EW' was Edna Whittaker, but what 'f.u.c.' was I couldn't think, until a girl told me in a whisper that it meant 'feeling up clothes'. I thought to myself, Mrs Barker did warn us about not messing about with the clothes once they were so neatly laid in the basket, and Harold shouldn't let some girl do that, but surely there's no need to talk about it as though it were a crime. I went around with the impression that there was a lot of that sort of thing going on, with the increasing number of initials chalked up. And one day a girl called Lizzie drew my attention to three different lots of names chalked up in the backstreet. Lizzie was a Catholic, and so I was able to say to her, 'But it can only be a venial sin at the most.' 'A venial sin that!' she exclaimed with a shocked air. I knew that I must be on the wrong track, but I didn't want to give myself away entirely, and I said: 'What does it mean, Lizzie—I'm not sure?'

Lizzie looked around to make sure there was no one watching or listening: 'Are you certain positive you don't know?' she asked. 'I think so,' I said. 'Come 'ere,' she said, and she began to whisper in my ear. 'It means when a boy an' girl go off in the dark an' stand in the backstreet like,' her whisper seemed to tickle something inside my ear, 'an' she lets him put his hand under her frock, feelin' at her bloomers an' that,' she said. Lizzie's little brown eyes looked at me keenly to watch for the effect. It was a revelation to me—to think that I, so smart and clever, had been going around thinking it had to do with the blooming clothes-basket! For once I was speechless. 'You know what I mean,' she went on, 'like say we were to do it now—like you were to come right close up to me and put your hand right up under my dress, right up my leg an' that.' And she put on such a strange face as she spoke; it was odd how the way she said it made me go funny in my throat. 'Feelin' up clothes is a *mortal* sin,' she said. Once I'd got my breath back I agreed at once that such a carry on must be a mortal sin, and she chimed in with me, and we both heartily reviled such a sin, and the tension went.

Then after a time Lizzie said: 'It's not always a mortal sin, you know.' That was a surprise to me. 'How do you mean, Lizzie?' I said. Lizzie had another good look round; it was a light summer evening, and we were the only ones in the backstreet. 'Here,' she said, 'let's go in against the skipyard gate, where folk can't hear us or see us an' I'll tell you when it's a sin an' when it isn't.' I went into the seclusion of the gate with her. Lizzie was as cool as a teacher explaining the cate-chism to a pet pupil: 'It's a sin on a Sunday,' she explained, '—you must never feel up clothes on a Sunday. It would be the worst mortal sin—worse than missin' Mass.' 'Gerroff!' I said. 'Oh yes,' she said. '"Cut my throat if I tell a lie."' She went on thoughtfully: 'It's a sin on a Sat'day as well, but only a venial sin on Sat'days. On Mondays it can be a sin during Lent.' Lizzie had to think things out, but it was astonishing how much she knew about the sin of feeling up clothes. 'A lot depends on how far the boy feels,' she said. 'I mean if his hand goes under the elastic of her bloomers. That is a sin . . . ooh!' I felt her brown eyes on me and off me. 'It can be a sin—let me see—on Tuesdays, an' Wednesdays.' 'What about

Thursdays?' I said. 'Not on Thursdays,' she said, '—there's what they call a dispensation.' I knew what a dispensation was—it was such as when Christmas Day fell on a Friday, then Christmas Eve would be an abstinence day but on the Friday meat could be eaten. 'A boy and girl can play at feeling up clothes as much as they want on a Thursday,' went on Lizzie.

'It's Thursday today, Lizzie,' I said.

'An' to think fool me thought it were Wednesday,' said Lizzie.

She opened her eyes wide, and looked around ever so innocently, drawing closer to me at the same time, and indicating she had done her part and it was now up to me. What can this strange feeling be, I thought, suddenly stirring inside me? It made me feel helpless. This must be what they mean by temptation. My will was gone, and I put aside my hope to become a saint, feeling afraid as those brown eyes looked at me, and something mysterious in her voice seemed to draw me on to do something with my hands which my conscience warned as a mortal sin—no matter what day in the week.

15

George and Bimmy

ONE Saturday morning I went out of our front door and could see at once that the top-and-whip season was giving way to the marble season. This in turn would yield to the button season and the kite season and these to a subsequent round of seasons and passing games and recreations. There were games that could be enjoyed on and off all the year round. Football was one, but to play with a real ball was a rare treat. Any boy lucky enough to get a ball needed some persuasion to risk having it burst in the first five minutes with a misguided kick from the metal strip on a clog-toe. The common substitute for a ball was a tin can, and these were readily available from most middens if one delved amongst the ashes and refuse. A salmon can, not too large, made a good substitute for a ball, and, although the finer points of the game had to be sacrificed, yet there was many a fierce and enjoyable game in the backstreet using a tin can for a ball. True enough it was a bit noisy, and any family with a sick person or someone working on night shift did not care for it. An hour of 'headers' could often be got out of a ha'penny pig's bladder from the slaughteryard, but there was often an argument about who should put his lips on the slimy teat and blow it up.

There were three very popular games—piggy (the game I had played with Ernie Fairclough on the day I broke the window), swing-round-can, and duckstone (even the names are not without a North-country plebeian ring, one not belied, I might add, by their practice). The first thing needed for a game of swing-round-can was the right kind of tin can, which meant a trip down some neighbouring backstreet, kicking open ashpit doors; they were usually secured by a small metal catch in the better backstreets or makeshift wooden pegs in our own. Backstreets such as our own we avoided, since canned goods were luxuries, and the cans that contained the cheaper pineapple chunks were not strong enough or too big for a game of swing-round-can. Lads went up to Maybank Street where there were spinning-room families, folk who could afford John West's middle-cut canned salmon. A backstreet after such an expedition for cans was not a tidy sight, for on opening an ashpit door there would be a flow of ashes on to the pavement, and it was rarely possible to close a door again, so it was a good idea to get away from the scene as quickly as possible and back to your own backstreet.

Once you had your tin can the further requirements were simple: a stout nail was needed to punch a hole in the bottom of the tin; you asked for some *banding*—the word string was never used—and there was no shortage of good strong greasy cord, known as banding, amongst the little-piecers. The banding would be threaded through the hole in the bottom of the can and a knot tied to secure the can from slipping off; then the player who was out would have to stand in the middle of the backstreet holding the string over his head and swinging the can round clockwise. The other players would be gathered in an eager circle around him, standing about eight feet away, armed with sticks, usually boiler sticks or short hammer-shafts, with which they struck the can as it went round. The first player to hit the cord instead of the can had to take over the swinging. An exciting game, for the swift pleasure in giving a good clean swipe to a can travelling through the air was a most unusual one, and there was danger too, for if the swinger was not holding on tightly the can would easily fly into the next player's face.

Duckstone was played on what was known as the Brickfield. You went up Thomas Rostron Street, along Peace Street, crossed Gibbon Street, and there you were: the lower side of the Brickfield met the back of Burnaby Street, the far side Quebec Street, and if you ventured right across you came to a hill called the Spion Kop. Near the top, enclosed by a rough garden and trees, there was a house in which Daddy

Pye lived, a man said during the War to be a German spy, who at nights would plainly be seen with a torch—signalling a code across to Germany, to let them know where to send their Zeppelins—or at least, so it was said.

The lad who was out gathered about five or six duckstones, large round stones, even enough to be built into a pile known as the duck. The other players would stand at the baiting line some twelve yards away, armed with stones. At the call they could start throwing at the pile, and, if one of them knocked it down, the lad who was out had to build it up again and grab one of the players whilst he was retrieving his duck-stone. It was a fast fierce game, and if you didn't look out you often went home hobbling—if no worse.

I was no good at games, being slow of movement, unsure with foot and hand, and lacking the eye and the balance needed for so many games; coming from a peasantry among which such pastimes were unknown I had neither the innate ability nor the interest, and my favourite pastime was standing among my mates at the top corner of our street telling tales.

'There wur this chap ont'stage, makin' out he wur a preacher, see, an' he'd raise his hand an' call out to t'audience, "An' God sent fire down from 'eaven!"—an' he 'ad this lad up int'loft above, an' when he said that the lad 'ud strike a match an' set fire to a bundle of straw an' drop it through t'trap door. An' this neet t'chap called out, "An God sent fire down from 'eaven!"—but nowt 'appened. So he shouted louder, but nowt 'appened. Then he roared at top of his voice, "An' God sent down fire from 'eaven!" an' he looked up. An' t'lad stuck his yed out of t'trap door an' yelled back, "He can't!—cat's pissed on t'matches!"'

After a time the tales would be all told, and on cold nights there was an activity known as 'More Weight'. The smallest boys, and usually the coldest, would huddle and stoop at the street-corner, and the cry would go up from them: 'More weight!' The boys apart from this group, the ones who were most active and the least cold, would draw back across the cobbled street, then take a run and fling themselves, stomach down, on top of the bunch of crouched figures. This thudding action generated warmth, and those crouched against the wall would let out groans and then howl out: 'More weight!' There were no rules, so that the sport could be enjoyed with almost total abandon, but it was inadvisable to peep out, for a clog-toe might catch you in the face.

The evening game that often followed this was known as 'Ride or Kench'. For this game sides were picked by the two captains, after which they would *foot each other* for the side to be in; that is, the two captains would face each at a distance of about ten feet, and take alternate steps in which each one pressed heel against toe, the winner being the one whose final step took his clog-toe over that of his opponent's. Then the side that was *out* had to form a caterpillar line at right angles to the street-corner wall, bodies bent, heads down, whilst the players who were *in* leapt on to their opponents' backs, until either they *kenched* or they guessed which sign was displayed in the air by the opposing captain when he called out: 'Finger, thumb or nowt?' This game was seldom played for long as it brought about much argument and gave opportunity for cheating. (A doctor friend told me of working for a period at Bolton Infirmary some forty years ago: 'I once heard a colleague there use a word—one which I have never heard since, and one which no one has ever been able to explain—it was the word *kench*.' 'It means collapse or give way,' I said. 'Yes,' he said, 'that could be it, for he said "I kenched my ankle this morning."')

On this certain Saturday morning when I had spotted marbles being played, I saw a boy called Georgie come round the street-corner driving his top along the pavement with a whip. Georgie lived in Birkdale Street, the slightly better-off row of houses which backed on to our row of houses, and his dad worked at Magee's Brewery, which made Georgie a cut above us, and, whilst it would have been thought cheeky for one of us to go and play in his street, it was not looked upon as such that he came to ours. There were numerous signs of his being better off; the look on his face for a start was a look that none of my mates had—it could be said to be one of openness and assurance, whereas the look on ours probably indicated doubt, shiftiness, and vulnerability. Georgie had a fresh complexion, as though his bowels were kept regular, and none of my mates had a fresh skin nor, as far as I could judge, healthy bowels. Moreover, Georgie wore spectacles, and spectacles were never worn by any of us, for nobody bothered about a boy's sight much short of his going blind, and also they cost money, and they marked a lad as a softie. If spectacles were forced on one of our lot by the school doctor then the boy managed either to lose or to break them. Further touches marked Georgie as different: the heel-irons of his well-polished clogs were not worn down, his jacket and knickerbocker trousers were carefully patched, he wore a celluloid collar not an old scarf, and, above all, his top-and-whip were not what might be commonly imagined as a top-and-whip. They were old and could have been in the family for years; the whip was a strip of leather well over a yard in length and about half an inch wide, and looked as though it had been carefully oiled before being put away every year, so as to preserve it, and at the end of it was a short piece of plaited cord, and the lash was secured to a short firm handle. Almost every time Georgie hit the top he contrived to make that whip crack with authority in the morning air. As for the top itself, it was so solid and heavy that the pointed steel base on which it spun appeared almost to drill tiny holes in the pavement when it spun in the one spot for long. No family in our street would rate a top-and-whip of that quality.

'Want a go?' said Georgie to me, in an uninviting tone, any display of amiability being suspect.

'Yes—aye,' I said, correcting my Irish. 'I wouldn't mind.' I had learnt that you must avoid giving the impression you were receiving a favour. 'I wouldn't mind at all,' I added, as a touch of Irish got out.

'Then don't stand there skennin',' said Georgie. 'Get hold of t'whip or tha'll have t'bloomin' top stoppin'.'

I grabbed the whip and made a few furious but ineffective lashes at the top, which began to slow down and spin uncertainly, and finally the top fell over.

'Wut did I tell thee!' said Georgie, as I picked up the top and attempted to set it spinning with my hands, which was the usual way with an ordinary top. 'Some bloomin' 'opes tha's got!' he said. Georgie could be seen to be enjoying himself. The top was heavy, solid, symmetrical, about the size of a large Jaffa orange, encircled with three smooth ribbons of perdurable wood, marked by countless lashings from the leather whip but unflawed, with a pivot of tempered steel at the base. Georgie took the top from me, deftly twirled the whip tightly round it, and with an adroit movement dropped the steel point on to the pavement and at the same time pulled the whip in such a fashion that the top was set spinning smoothly and steadily on the pavement. 'Right,' he yelled at me, at the same time throwing me the whip, 'get gooin'!'

A born Boltonian uses words like others might use hammer and chisel, and it seemed to me as though I were not listening so much as having them engraved on the cerebrum, so forceful each vowel, so inflexible each consonant, and so penetrating the delivery. By good fortune I chanced to strike Georgie's top right the first time—with the tough tail-cord, of course, for the purpose of the leather lash was to provide the means of acquiring the essential power and velocity for the tailpiece to drive the master top along and keep it spinning. After conquering the first few difficult and uncertain yards of pavement with a bit of luck, a confidence began to glow in me, yet, when I came to the end of the pavement at the corner and swiftly wiped the sweat from my forehead, I saw there was a good drop at the edge of the sideset, then the rough cobbled roadway had to be crossed, and next a lift of four inches or more to bring the spinning top safely on to the opposite pavement. I was not an unskilled top-whipper, but my tops had had difficulty in getting down off a pavement, let alone getting up; as for those treacherous interstices of soil between the bumpy cobblestones, it seemed that no top could be navigated through those, for the soil offered insufficient support, and the spinning top usually collapsed. What I didn't realize at the time was that all my tops had been shop tops, manufactured to be sold, whereas Georgie's top was one of the various 'foreigners' made by some fitter or mechanic at his bench during moments when the gaffer wasn't watching. These were made with extreme care and skill, not intended for sale but as a gift to some young relative or friend.

Georgie's spinning top weathered the drop from the sideset, the lumpy cobblestones and the niches between them, and at last the pavement at the far side, although it needed some driving along to get it up there, but when it did that top spun as proud and steady as could be. The whacking and steering along of Georgie's top back to the street-corner was one of my earliest experiences of feelings rarely enjoyed by lads such as myself—a discipline and determination in the use of a skill, and a sense of loyalty to the relationship created between myself and the top—and the experience seemed to nudge me into a new world. I was in a lather of sweat when I got back. 'Tha kept it gooin' then,' remarked Georgie, frowning at the same time, which was a tactic used when bestowing lavish praise on anyone. 'Aye,' I said, 'I did that an' all.'

A lad called Bimmy turned up at the street-corner as I got back with Georgie's top-and-whip, and he called to me: 'Art' comin' wi' me tut'coalyard?' I nodded, for, although I was flattered by Georgie's company, there was something about his presence and his top-and-whip that tended to overpower me, so I was not sorry when I got this chance to escape. 'He wouldna let thee 'ave a go wi' 'is top', remarked Bimmy when we got away, 'if the season 'adn't been o'er an' marps comin' in.' I gave a bit of a nod to this but kept my mouth shut. 'His sort', went on Bimmy, 'will give thee owt, providin' it costs 'um nowt. As tha goes through life tha'll find 'um out—they'll only do summat for thee when it suits 'um.'

Bimmy spoke like an old woman, and his careworn face reminded me of one. This womanly trace was not uncommon among boys, for many were brought up with grandmothers, as seemed to happen often when the mother worked in the mill, or, as in Bimmy's case, were chosen by the mother to be the confidant of so many family problems, of Mum's many

fears and worries, and it was as though the experience of so
much elderly female intimacy created a sort of feminine
patina, so that their young boyish faces were toned off with
some trace of womanly concern. I found that this particular
strain in Bimmy suggested the opposite of emasculation,
making him tougher and giving him some strength that I and
other boys lacked. (Anxiety, fear, hunger, and pain—from
which the well-cared-for child is protected—may be almost
as necessary as love for development of character.) He wore a
huge cap, an old one of his father's, with a big neb at the
front, which he kept lifting back as it fell over his eyes, and
his pale hair looked lifeless, giving him a look of premature
baldness. He had a broad nose and large mouth, and on his
left lower jaw was a patch of discoloured skin, which was
said to be a birthmark—a mother's shame, it was called.
Bimmy's light blue eyes missed very little of all that was going
on.

We came upon a bunch of young children near the bottom
of the street, playing a game and laughing loudly. Bimmy
paused for a moment to watch them, and then he turned to
me and said, 'They wouldn't laugh like that if they knew
what life 'ad in store for 'um.' We walked on a bit: 'Perhaps
it's as well they don't,' he added. I nodded, and tried to
imitate Bimmy's wise look. Just near the corner was a group
of small boys gathered round an open grid along the gutter.
The heavy iron-slotted lid had been removed, and beside it
was a pile of black slimy street sewage, made up of soot,
horse-droppings, fag-ends, and the like, all stinking in the
morning air.

'Hy, what's gooin' on 'ere?' Bimmy asked. 'D'you not
know you'll get fever messin' about wi' yon lot!'

'He's lost his Sat'day penny down it,' said one lad who was
down on his stomach.

'Anybody as finds it for me', said the boy who had lost the
coin, 'can 'ave 'alf of it.' 'That's different,' said Bimmy, peel-
ing off his jacket and rolling up his sleeves, displaying arms
that were thin and white and covered with fleabites. He surprised me—as so often happened with Bolton boys—by his

energy, for in a moment he was down on his stomach on the ground, his head disappearing down the black gridhole, as he reached into the sewage, and came up with surprisingly large handfuls.

'I've getten summat,' said Bimmy, as he splotched one handful down, spread it out, and then picked out a small coin.

'Aye, that's mine,' said the boy who had lost the money.

'Nay,' said Bimmy, holding up the coin, 'that's only a ha'penny—so that can't be thine.' A moment later he found the penny. 'Right,' he said, 'yo' can keep that—divide it between you an' you— eh?' indicating the boy who had been down the grid and the owner. 'One of you ask your mam for a bucket of water—we can't leave it like this in a mess.' When the water came Bimmy first delved his arm in and washed off the drying dirt, and then swung his arm in the air to dry it. The slime was swilled back down the hole and the lid replaced, the boys seemed satisfied, and Bimmy and I went off to the coalyard.

At Considine's coalyard a boy was shovelling coal on to the big scales and weighing it; then it was tipped into a low truck with solid iron wheels and an iron handle, which could be pulled by the customer along the pavement, and later returned so that the shilling charged on it could be retrieved. Bimmy had numerous arguments over quality and weight of the coal when he was being served. 'Tha'll find as folk'll walk o'er thee in this life, Billy,' he said to me, 'if tha lets 'um.'

On our way back we came upon a woman with an old baby-carriage, in which she had a half-hundredweight of coal. The carriage was stuck beside the pavement, a wheel having come off. Bimmy got the carriage hauled safely on to the pavement, whilst the woman kept repeating: 'Oh, what'll I do!' 'I mun find a nail,' said Bimmy, 'an I'll fettle your wheel. So don't fret yourself.' He spoke to her not as a boy to a woman, but as woman to woman. I had spotted a shop window with some new marbles in it, and during Bimmy's repair of the carriage, in which he used his clog-heel as a hammer, I slipped into the shop and bought a pennyworth of glossy marbles. Bimmy was just getting the woman on her way when I got back. 'Ee, I dunno 'ow to thank you, luv,' she said. Bimmy said to her, 'Don't you worry, missis—Lancasheer helps Lancasheer.'

When I proudly showed Bimmy the marbles, his face wrinkled up with regret: 'Nay, nay,' he said, 'tha's never spent good money on them!' 'Why,' I said, 'what's wrong?' 'Her musta seen thee comin',' said Bimmy. 'Them's not proper marps—them's war marps—made outa plaster an' gilded o'er to look real.' As Bimmy spoke the glossy gleam of my marbles was reduced to a sham. 'Look, I can almost squeeze 'em to bits wi' my fingers. Proper marps should be of stone, an' bounce—let's try one.' Bimmy took one of my marbles in his hand, flung it down on the pavement, where it broke up in bits. 'What did I tell thee!' he said, as he got hold of the heavy iron handle of the truck and we set off for home. 'Why, wi' that penny tha coulda bought a penn'orth of Wiggawagga toffee from Old Daddy Addison woulda lasted for hours, or I'd 'ave taken thee to Miss Wells's shop, got thee a penn'orth of broken choc'lut—oh, Billy, why didn't tha ask me first!' The sweat was on Bimmy's nose as he pulled the coal bogie along the street, and I made a pretence of helping him, and trying to sweat a bit out of sympathy.

16

Friday Dinnertime

FEW boys, I should imagine, were brought up with more inhibitory warnings of one kind and another than myself. When my father was around I seemed to go through daily life bristling with things to be remembered and others to be shut firmly out of mind. In most families something of this subterfuge may go on, but in our home it was often carried to such a depth of whispering deceit, all of an innocent enough nature but taking on a guilty character merely from being trafficked in an underhand way, that I developed a sort of husky whisper. And so much did secrecy become a part of my life in those days that for long after I never allowed anyone to see my true feelings, but put on a cheerful smiling front to everyone, no matter how I felt.

One thing I had to keep in mind was that when opening the front door at the dinnertime break on Fridays I must do so quietly. This was not difficult to remember, since Friday dinnertime was different from all others. Boys were let out as usual at noon—oh but what a different emergence! There was a sudden bright active mood on this day as the boys raced through the yard towards the gate. If it was a sunny day they yelled with joy, and hopped and skipped along the streets in a hurry to get home, especially the poorer boys; if it was raining they ran heads down, jacket or jersey collars turned up, cap pulled over the face (almost no boy but myself went to school with a bare head). Mothers from poor homes often worked in the mill and got paid at Friday dinnertime, and most lads knew that, no matter how scrimping Mum had been during the week, once she got hold of money she became vulnerable to the pressure of their cadging: 'I can get owt out of her once she's drawn her wages,' they would boast.

It was not only the mood of the playground that told me it was Friday, for had I been dropped down blindfold by parachute into the Bolton of that period, the early 1920s, on a Friday dinnertime, I should have identified the day and the time by the sounds and smells—the swift clattering of loose clogs on shawled women hurrying past, and the smells from the baskets of freshly wrapped fish-and-chips, with the vinegar soaked into the paper giving off the most appetizing aroma (to the native that is). Standing among the customers ranged three or four deep at the counter, I used to make a judgement of a woman's standing by the basins she took to the fish-and-chip shop. The poor took none, for they had none to spare. A housewife who had three or four basins to take to Bibby's shop was of a family that had these basins at one side, on the shelf or in the cupboard doing nothing; in a poor home almost every article was in constant use, and no hard up housewife thought of buying anything that was not urgently needed. Even in our home I would sometimes empty the sugar out of a rather nice china bowl, wash the bowl in warm water, and take it for fish-and-chips. Basins— the Irish called them bowls—came in various qualities and sizes, and much could be deduced from a study of them. There would be the lad or woman who turned up with a large basin of cheap thick pottery, not very good for keeping fish-and-chips warm, and in such cases Mrs Bibby would very often serve the fish-and-chips on the usual white paper and then slide it inside the basin; otherwise, if she served straight from the big metal pan with the scoop, a pennyworth or even twopennyworth of chips into such a basin would look skimpy.

There would be the better-off housewife, wearing an old coat and shoes in place of a shawl and clogs, with a large basket of various basins of fish-and-chips: Dad's special basin of cod, chips, and beans; Mum's plaice, chips, and peas; and working down with various degrees of discrimination amongst the wage-earners, according to how much they were bringing in, to the youngest schoolboy's pennyworth of wet chips and a batter cake—he would hope to cadge bits of fish from the others. Fish-and-chips kept much nicer in basins, of course, for the basin protected them better, allowing the vapour to escape so that the contents didn't become too soggy, or see too much of each other as when huddled together in paper; also, as they were eaten straight from the basin, the lower layers tended to become soaked with delicious vinegar, and sometimes needed sopping up with bread; and there was none of that brutal separation of fish from paper, when skin and batter might get stripped off. Also it was reckoned you got more for your money if you took a basin, especially a large one, for Mrs Bibby would often pause during the serving, take a look, and add a few more. Some maintained that they preferred to eat their fish-and-chips from a paper, but this was considered common, a weakness, for the smell of newsprint mingled with food. The one disadvantage of basins was that you had nothing new to read over your dinner. Apart from such distinctions, it could be said that there was about fish-and-chips a sound democratic touch that no other food possessed; the poorest person could shop alongside the poshest, for nobody asked for fish-and-chips on the strap. It was money down on the counter with every purchase. Protestants, who enjoyed freedom of choice, queued alongside the Catholics, who had to observe an abstinence from meat on Fridays. You were all one in the kingdom of fish-and-chips.

There were other smells around, those of succulent meat pies, steak-and-kidney pies, pork pies, meat-and-potato pies, and pasties, but although such odours were appetizing they could not compete with those of fish-and-chips on a Friday. Foundry workers usually went in for the meat—men who could stick a meat pie straight into the mouth and bite half off at one go; also labouring types, such as oilers and greasers in the factory, who may have seen and handled enough grease and oil during the morning to prefer the crispier crusted meat pies to fish-and-chips, which tended to become flabby if left wrapped up.

Friday treats were not exhausted at dinnertime, since in numerous corner shops there would be roast pork, roast heart, and brawn being prepared for teatime serving. The pork was sold mostly in two-ounce portions, with a bit of stuffing added, if the money would run to such; otherwise a sliced banana with tinned milk poured over it was considered nice, or banana butties, or perhaps sliced orange with sugar sprinkled, often eaten between slices of bread-and-butter. Fish-and-chips were again a favourite on Friday evening—the feasting would go on whilst the money lasted—and many an old-age pensioner, who had that day drawn the pension, would indulge to the extent of a gill of draught stout; although others might prefer to call at Vose's tripe shop for twopennyworth of tripe bits, and enjoy these with a gill of ale.

It was not simply this dominance of savoury smells around the street that told one it was Friday dinnertime—it was the unmistakable feeling about the place that wages had been or were about to be paid out, so that the magical words, *wages* and *money*, were being bandied about together with expressions from working mothers such as, 'I'd a good week in—so I thought I'd treat 'em.' Through the mill gates poured the various mill workers, the little-piecers, side-piecers, cross-piecers, minders, slubber-tenters, doffers, carders, weavers, winders, machine-fettlers, tacklers, and various others. On Friday dinnertimes everyone looked so different, and even the spinner, who preferred to mask his feelings, could not wholly suppress the glow that money in the pocket brings to the face.

In our own home on Friday dinnertime there was an excitement of an associated kind—and this was why I had to learn to open the front door gently, enter quietly, close the door softly behind me, tread carefully in my clogged feet over the oilcloth on the stone floor, and then settle down standing up on the peg-rug—made by Uncle William using pegs and pieces of old cloth—in front of the fire. The reason for all this caution was that my father had to be woken up around noon every Friday to go off and draw his wages, and it was more than likely that when I arrived home from school he would be thrust up against the cracked looking-glass hung over the slopstone in the back kitchen, with his lower jaw submerged

in lather, his gaze fastened upon the reflection of his unsmiling face, and a German Solingen hollow-ground razor in his
hand, hovering shakily around the mound of swiftly drying
lather. The least distraction of a sudden nature—the howl of
a rag-and-bone man out in the backstreet, the dropping of a
knife on to the floor, or the sudden noise of the door opening—could startle him and cause him to cut himself: 'May the
devil roast and melt that one in hell,' he would swear sav-
agely, '—I have myself cut!'

He would leave off shaving for a minute or so to calm
down, during which break he would stride nervously from
the back kitchen to the front kitchen, look at the alarm clock
ticking loudly on the mantelpiece, take a look at his face in
the mirror on the dresser, and stare closely at the wild face
with the dried lather on the cheekbones and the flapping bits
of newspaper clinging to his skin—the absurd measure he
took to staunch the blood—and the moment he pulled the
papers off the dried blood would be plucked from his face
and blood would begin to flow again. 'That flamin' English
soap', he would say, talking of the household soap he used
for shaving, 'would skin the hide off a bloody horse.' And
when he came to wash his face after shaving, he would put
his hands under the running cold tap, and without using soap
rinse his face with water and rub his skin, especially round his
forehead, with his hard calloused palms, making a loud rubbing noise, which he supported with some kind of blowing
out of his mouth—a trait quite out of keeping with the
fastidious streak in his nature.

It was customary to dress up when you went to draw your
wages, should you have been off ill or on short time or
possibly on night work. Employers kept a full week's wages
in hand, and after a week off, either because of illness or
short-time working, workers would turn up on a Friday
afternoon to draw the wages due for the previous week's
work. The majority returned to work after an illness before
they were fit; this was only partly an economic consideration:
in homes where a person seldom read, and radio and tele-
vision were unknown, men who were used to work soon

became depressed, and would return to escape the boredom. A man or woman didn't go to draw his or her wages in Sunday best, but in Saturday night gear, for the right note of casual elegance had to be struck. The Lancashire coal-miner would wear a good serge suit, sporty cap, a muffler or a coloured silk neckerchief tied at the throat with a fancy knot, and often the incongruous touch of pit clogs. The clogs made it clear that he was not out to impress, to pretend he was other than a coal-miner; it also hinted that, if anybody fancied a clog fight, he was ready to give a good account of himself.

At the time my father had become one of a group of three who were dirt contractors; they had contracted to clear the coalface for the day shift, for which they received so much a ton. It was exceptionally hard work, but was double the pay of the ordinary dataller. Having neither the breed nor the temperament of a Lancashire man, and yet fussy over his appearance, my father had trouble getting himself to look what he considered to be just right. He would never go in his pit clogs, nor was he a neckerchief man, for he mostly wore a stiff collar, and if he turned up to draw his wages in his best suit, with collar and boots, he would look as though he were showing off. He would wear his second-best suit, but just to show he wasn't short of a bob or two, and also that it wasn't in pawn, he would sometimes wear his gold watch-chain, not swung across the middle of his waistcoat but at one side only, where it could be spotted but was not on display. He had regard for almost every item of dress, and could reel off the weight of the cloth of any good suit—twenty-two or twenty-four-ounce serge—and the exact date he first put it on: 'I will have had that suit five years next Trinity Sunday, if God spares me—and the boots I got Easter the following year.' Shoes, low-down shoes, as they were called, were considered effeminate and never worn by workingmen. And not only was my father careful over the brushing of clothes, always using a light touch to avoid wear by brushing; he wouldn't even brush his boots too hard, although he liked a good shine. The same sense of ownership engaged him even down to his spectacles: 'Them's the finest pair of glasses ever was known,' he would often remark of his old wire spectacles, '—I bought them in Woolworth's three years ago—the day Uncle Mick was here—an' they never gave me a minute's trouble; but the pair I paid fifteen flamin' shillings for from the bloody ould optisheen wouldn't compare with them—the bloody robbers them optisheens are.'

He might finally cool down after shaving, sufficient to eat his usual meal of two boiled duck eggs, two or three cups of strong tea, and a single piece of bread-and-butter. He would not be calm enough to sit down at the table, but would eat his food standing, moving around in an edgy fashion, looking for collar studs and the like, with Mother quietly in attendance, between getting her own jobs done. Often Mary Anne would pop in with a cup of sugar under her shawl: 'There's your sugar I borrowed,' she would call out. 'Pay back an' you can come again is what I always say. How's the mester?—going off to draw your wages are you?' It was refreshing to hear a normal voice; then, as Mary Anne handed Mother the sugar, she would give her a wink—for tucked under the cup would be a ten-shilling note. Mr Haworth, who got paid at Friday dinnertime, would have given her the housekeeping money, and she would lend Mother ten shillings until the evening, so that our fish-and-chips could be bought. Not that there was any question of our eating until my father was gone, for his presence took the pleasure out of any meal. And now I would sit on the sofa, well out of the way, and, whilst not actually looking at him, would mark every movement of his performance.

17

Father the Miner

DESPITE the tension in the home as my father prepared to go off, there would come a point at which I felt a satisfaction from sitting there, watching his antics as he moved around and kept looking at his face in the big mirror over the dresser. He had sported a large moustache when we first came over to England, and over the years he began to trim it—perhaps to give him a younger appearance or to fit in with a changing fashion—and I remember one Friday when he went rather too close with the razor and left himself with what was called a 'toothbrush 'tache'. This, for some reason I could not understand at the time, annoyed my mother intensely: 'What have you done to your moustache!' she called out, '—what do you call that thing!—the Lord save us, but you're going out looking like a floorwalker!' It was only later, aided by a cunning suspicion, that I was able to piece together the fact that the pub the miners went to after drawing their wages was kept by a widow, and this had been brought up more than once. Was my father doing some kind of a line with the widow in the pub? (I wouldn't have put it beyond him, knowing what I do of those of his blood that came after him, myself not excluded.) And I would watch him as he stood by the dresser, unsure as to whether he would wear his gold watch-chain or not, chain in hand, dangling it with a bogus air of introspection, as though thinking of something else—and that watch-chain would impress any widow.

The gold watch-chain, I should point out, had been acquired in the first place by the purchase of a pawn-ticket from a man in the Pike View pub. It was a not uncommon way of getting watches and chains and the like in those days, to buy a pawn-ticket in a pub, since it was in the pub that a man's need for money became most pressing, and the atmosphere was right, as a certain persuasiveness was required. It was a transaction that would have been eschewed by Uncle William, who would sooner have given money than be involved in anything the least squalid. How had the man in the pub got possession of the watch?—by buying a pawn-ticket for it in the first place, then redeeming the pledge, as it was called, and pawning it again when he was hard up. There was a custom among workingmen—that is the largely unskilled worker, such as labourer or miner, but not engineer or spinner—men who because of working shifts and social habits made no contact with a savings bank, that when one got hold of some extra money the thing to do was to buy a good watch or chain, usually silver, although gold was even better. A man who had acquired a few pounds would plan days ahead to go off on such a buying mission, and then choose a quiet Saturday morning or afternoon, and having screwed up the necessary willpower, since it took resolution to part with actual money, he would set off to scour around a few pawnshops, to weigh up the 'unredeemed pledges', as they were called, on display in the window. He would never consider buying a new watch—he was not concerned about knowing the time—since not only would a new watch be too expensive, but it lost considerable value the moment it left the shop, which was not so with a second-hand one. A good watch or watch-chain was looked upon as a standby for when times became bad, and also it allowed the owner a measure of regard, if mainly self-regard. The purchase ensured that a man would not fritter away the money, and there was the ulterior advantage that he could not be approached for borrowing purposes, from either wife or friend, having invested his cash. If you had money to lend you were not expected to refuse, but for only a very close mate, and his an urgent need, were you obliged to pawn a possession so as to procure the money he needed. It was assumed that an article of solid gold or silver would not decrease in value, ensuring that when in need of money a man had something that could be pawned or sold: *Gold always holds its value*, was a common saying of that period.

My father arrived home in an excited state one Saturday night and produced the soiled and creased pawn-ticket he had bought, with the date and amount pledged clearly legible ('It has another month afore it runs out,'—an essential proviso, that the pledge had not expired). The grubby ticket was said to represent an unseen article of almost fabulous value, for as in most of such cases there was a story attached to it, and my father, with considerable relish, told it as it had been told to him. The watch-chain had not been manufactured to sell, he explained, it was that most rare of articles, a bespoke watch-chain. It had been wrought by a London goldsmith to the instructions of a wealthy client, so the story went, who, due to some misfortune, was subsequently unable to take purchase of it. In the first instance it had been sold at much below its actual value, for the design was unusual; then through a series of owners it had finally reached Chris Hart's pawnshop in Bolton. The holder of the ticket could by law, it was said, view the goods in pledge on the payment of a nominal sum to the pawnbroker, but this privilege was scarcely ever availed of, for the pledgee's story mostly did the trick, reinforced by the statement: 'I only asked for a fiver— he gave it to me at once—I could have got more, but it was all I wanted at the time,'—together with the understanding that it was pawnbroking practice to pay out only one-third the value on goods pawned.

So great was the awe built up in our home by my father over the splendour of the as yet unseen chain that the ticket itself might easily have been left on the dresser under a glass vase, and passing by one would have been tempted to genuflect, so convincingly did it represent an object of reverence. Such a gold watch-chain was one that no one in Bolton could ever afford to purchase new, and few indeed could ever hope to own second-hand. And indeed, when my father actually redeemed the pledge—it was a month later before he could get the full amount together—and brought home the chain, it proved to be of such appearance and weight that it certainly struck me as most impressive. It was a broad flat chain, made up of small square links, four of which made the width of the chain, with the hallmark of a tiny crown on each one, and an 18, apparently signifying 18-carat gold. Somehow I never liked the chain, for it was not pleasant to handle like the silver Albert chain which Uncle William had, nor was it so pleasing to the eye, and I had a feeling that Mother thought it did not exactly suit an Irishman. Possibly my father himself did not really like it, except that having bought it he had little choice, and of course our humble impressions were swamped by my father's repetition of the remark of Chris Hart, the pawnbroker: 'I never in all my puff saw a gold chain to compare with it!' (Since then I have seen women with so-called antique bracelets that might have been cut from it. Alas, however, for the vanity of possessions— when the 1926 Coal Strike came my father had to pawn his gold chain and later sell his pawn-ticket to a greengrocer he met in a pub, for a sum much smaller than he gave for it, for by then the slump had arrived and money was so scarce that even the pawn-ticket of a gold chain failed to keep its value around Bolton.)

Friday dinnertime, my father almost ready to leave, and now he stands before the big mirror on the dresser, rubs his cheeks and forehead nervously with the palm of his hand, as though wishing to rub off one face and find a more suitable one underneath, or perhaps it is to give his skin a little colour, for a certain drawn pale look has begun to take hold of him, as it did with so many miners working very hard. My father's Friday face shows far more strain than his face of earlier in the week, and he seems to be searching for a suitable look or expression with which to face the world, but the right one is slow in coming. After adjusting his cap three or four times he says: 'I think I'll be off.' 'Go careful now, sir,' Mother tells him, in a sort of waggish manner, perhaps as a comment on all his attentions to himself; 'Godspeed!' He makes for the door, and walks nervously across the cobbled street. Mother opens a piece of curtain and gives him the expected wave of the hand as he turns the corner.

It would seem that my father never got over the upset to his nerves that must have struck him on his first experience of the harsh work needed in the mines, after a lifetime of the Irish peasant way, 'Shure what we don't do today we'll do tomorrow.' Hard and demanding physical labour can have a deep shock effect on one not used to it. Yet it was not the work alone in his case, but the sense of a painful uprooting that must have taken place: there was scarcely a sight, sound, or smell in this new life, one which he had been forced to take up at the age of forty, that was not strange—and he was a man with no heart for change and dearly loved the familiar. In those early years he seemed always to be on the look-out for an Irish flavour: the English potato and cabbage did not taste the same as the Irish, he used to say, and the bacon lacked Irish flavour; the tea sold in the poor areas was inferior to that which he had been used to in Ireland, for the poorer Irish always bought the best tea. When we got the Irish geese sent to us at Christmas, the tin of Mick M'Quaid tobacco, and the bottle of Jameson whiskey, they would not only draw the most intense praise from him, but would touch some deep chord of feeling, for he had only to lift the lid and smell the tobacco, and he might turn away to wipe his eyes with his handkerchief.

At the end of his night's stint at the coalface, coming up in the cage with his mates, he would try to get used to and fit in with the English talk—to which in fact he never became used. Paddy Conboy told of meeting him in 1914, when he had been working in the pit only a few months: 'How is the work goin', Tom?' asked Paddy. 'Shure divil a one of me knows how it's goin' or isn't goin',' replied my father, 'for amn't I eatin' coal an' drinkin' bloody sweat the night long—an' what sweat doesn't go into my mouth goes into my two eyes an' damn near blinds me—an' between that an' all the coal you'd swallow in a night 'tis little else a man would need.'

My poor mother must have been sorely aware of the con-

strained atmosphere in the home; I took it for granted, feeling
that if you had a father like mine there was nothing you could
do about it. The moment he was away off beyond the street-
corner, she would dance and jump around, boxing with me,
and would give me or my sister May the basins to go for our
fish-and-chips: 'Bring what you want for yourselves,' she
would say, handing us the ten-shilling note lent by the neighbour Mary Anne, 'an' bring me a nice fish an' a few chips.'
Getting on for one o'clock, after the long and busy queues,
the shop would be nearly empty, and it seemed that fat Mr
Bibby—about the best fish-and-chip fryer in the British
Isles—would have relaxed, and now be allowed to return to
his artistry, give the chips more time to become not merely
good but perfect, and the fish that extra minute or two, which
made all the difference to the crisp coating of fried batter in
which they were dipped.

As for my sorry and distracted father, I would often be
home from school to take in his behaviour after his having
drawn the week's wages and enjoyed his usual drink with his
workmates. Now he would be flushed in the face, caught up
in that garrulity of the man who has something on his mind
but is set on keeping it hidden and so jumps edgily from one
subject to another, hoping by luck to strike some vein that
will produce natural talk. Is it the question of wages he has
on his mind and is trying to keep out of the conversation until
the right moment—or is it the widow woman at the pub?
Finally, he goes out to the backyard privy closet to start
sorting out his wages, making the decision on how much he
will give to my mother and how much he will hold back and
what fibs he will make up about the work being done but not
booked in until the week after. The drink has broken down
the clarity of mind brought about the week's work, and, with
the bets he has put on the horses and the money spent, he
isn't quite sure of how much he should have left, and he
comes into the back kitchen: 'I think I'll be off to bed,' he
says, and then with a transparent air of forgetfulness he
abruptly hands over the housekeeping money to Mother,
thrusting it into her hands with an air of brusque generosity,

like a toff tipping a railway porter, and turning away at once.

Mother would rarely complain, except when he had given her much too little, and then, and only quietly, would she say: 'I'll never manage to run the house on this.' Not only was she too dignified to argue with him, but she was one who had no interest in money itself—and strived only to be able to pay her way. It is one of the truly unbecoming situations in life where a person of a noble nature is forced into commerce with one less so. Ah well, maybe she'll be able to whip something out of his pocket later when he is lost in sleep. She'll have to do something. I used to sense almost everything that was going on—and to me this was one of the squalid aspects of working-class life—the male greed of the man beside the motherly concern of the woman for the home and family.

18

The Corduroy Suit

ON rare occasions during which my father was earning big money, he and I would be egged on by Mother to go out to do a bit of shopping together—meaning that he should buy me something. He needed tactful persuasion, and to my alarm Mother would begin to wheedle him by talking of father and son, and how it would be the decent thing for a father to go out and buy the son something he needed, for wasn't it a strange thing altogether that a man wouldn't take his own child out now and again, and the poor ladeen sorely in need of a decent pair of trousers in which to go to Mass. Has she gone off her head, I would start to think, going on about father and son, for I never saw a man I'd less like to be my father; yet after a time her sentiments would take hold of me and I'd get a lump in my throat, for I had one weakness which I could never overcome, and that was a tendency to tears if anyone showed sympathy.

It happened on no more than a few occasions, but it was always an embarrassing experience for me, since not only was it an ordeal to be seen out and about with him, but the reason for my going had to be the humiliating one of my being in need of a new suit or a pair of boots or of my school trousers having got beyond repair. On his part it had to coincide with some bit of good fortune, such as a win from backing horses on Friday, coming together with having had a good week at work and drawing large wages. The genial feelings aroused by having money in the pocket and a sense of things going well could often—when primed by a pint or two of beer, not too much—blossom into a seeming benevolence, when promises were made of the good things he was prepared to do. The display was extravagant but the mood brief, and the right moment had to be taken advantage of at once. He might promise anything late on a Saturday evening, but such a promise was hollow. The only time when it had the least chance of being given fulfilment was early on a Saturday afternoon when the shops were open, and the effects of the midday pints had not worn off nor driven him to bed to sleep them off. Once he had closed his eyes in sleep, if only for five minutes, it was all over; the expansive mood dispersed and a sort of crafty sanity replaced it, one in which I would have been lucky to get a penny out of him, let alone a suit.

Mother used to work this cajolery on him, and she had also to coax me to take advantage of the promises, for, as bad as it was going out with tattered trousers, it was worse going out with my father. 'He won't buy me owt, Mam,' I used to whisper, as she pressed me to hurry, wash, and tidy myself up. 'I can guarantee you that—he's promised before. I know him an' his bloomin' promises—they're like last year's snow.' And indeed well did I know them, for more than once he had taken me out to buy me a suit, and before the money was handed over and the suit bought the mood on him had worn thin—I could often see it fading away as we came in sight of the shops—and it only needed a negative response from the shop assistant to my father's Irish bargaining tactics for the whole thing to be blown into the air. He was skilful at seizing the first opportunity to escape his obligation—and the most I could expect then was to be dismissed and given twopence, which did not compensate me, I felt, for an unpleasant afternoon, let alone my dashed hopes. If only I'd had the guts to tell him to go to hell at the start, I would think wistfully to myself when it was over—now that would have been worth it. And I had a feeling that he would have liked me better for it.

Crossing the street with my father I keep thinking what an odd couple we make, for, after the drink, and with the money in his pocket, he is inclined to swagger, and to turn a bold front to number 5, where the Walshes live—no doubt he has some private feud going on with the father, Tom Walsh. I feel encased in that strict conformity of the Bolton way of life, so that the more my father puts on a swing the more I shrink within myself—yet strive to put on an air of it all being natural and myself at ease, and in the act of doing so I cannot escape a feeling that I am making us appear an even more ludicrous pair. 'That's a decent maneen,' remarks my father of a greengrocer in Derby Street; 'I once got the finest cabbage in Bolton from him for tuppence.' He nods to this one and the other as we walk towards town, about seven feet of pavement between us, and many of the people he nods to he doesn't appear to know. Whether they smile, nod, or greet him back does not affect him, since he is the sort of man that, when the last word has left his tongue, or the nod or smile has been given, the communication so far as he is concerned has been cut off and he is back with himself and his own thoughts.

'Yur walkin' like yur ont'front at Blackpoo',' calls Mary Anne as we pass her. My father touches his cap: 'It's a great day, ma'am,' he says, '—thanks be to God but a great day.' In fact it is a grey and misty day, but he will never fault a day in the English manner; to speak of a rotten day, as some do, would be sacrilegious to him. 'What did that one say?' he asks me, for he still can't grasp the dialect when spoken fast. 'Somethin' about bein' at Blackpool,' I say, resorting to the Irish way of not telling a thing explicitly in case it might offend. And indeed my father has a sort of holiday walk when he is going about with money in his pocket. I'm wishing I had some of it. There is a male habit of walking hands in trouser pockets, jingling money in an almost tantalizing manner, and, although he is not such a one, for his swinging walk needs the balance of his hands, he gives a reassuring grab rather than a jingle to the money in his pocket. I think, if only he'd give me a half-a-crown I'd shake his hand, tell him that all his responsibilities are over and we might part company forever.

He stops to admire the pieces of leather displayed in the leather-and-grindery shop, and seems undecided as to whether he should buy a fourpenny bundle of leather pieces—old pieces of leather from disused pulley belts out of the cotton mills—which he uses to fasten on to the bottom of our clogs in place of clog-irons; he decides he might take a look in later. He proceeds in this way, stopping outside various shops to look in the window, at the Maypole Dairy and the Meadow Dairy shops: 'Shure them are two awfully clean shops,' he remarks. Then he pauses at a shop known as 66a, where cotton and linen goods are sold cheaply, and he exchanges a nod and a word with the proprietor, a short dark man of unsmiling appearance. 'Shure now that's an honest shopkeeper, Willyeen,' he remarks to me, '—I once came out without a handkerchief and he gave me a great one for a sixpence-ha'penny—I never knew the like of it. I have it to this day.'

We go round by the Wheat Sheaf corner and along New-port Street and he stops at The Shop with the Man at the Door—at the entrance of which there is a sort of plaster figure of a man in a boiler suit—and there are overalls, jackets, and other things hanging inside, which my father tests between his fingers: 'That cloth', he snorts, half-smiling to himself, '—wouldn't hould a bloody mouse.' I can feel the prospect of the new suit becoming remoter, for he is already off on to his usual tack of praise and finding fault, which indicates some change of mood. Any minute now he will remember he has somewhere to call and will pay me off with twopence—maybe only a penny or nothing at all if that mood takes him. He is not a man to be bound down by either promises or precedent if neither happens to suit him at the moment, More than once I have said to Mother: 'Why can't he be like any other man—why does he have to be like he is!'

Finally, on this certain occasion, we call at a shop called Dewhursts in Deansgate, his eye having been caught by a light brown corduroy suit in the window. If there is one suit I don't want to be seen out in, I think, it's a suit that colour. When we get inside I am made to try it on; the colour is awful, but the pungent smell of the corduroy is even worse. I wouldn't be seen dead in this thing, I think as I obediently try it on. What I particularly hate is that there are lapels but no

collar, nothing to turn up to keep out the rain from the back
of one's neck. It looks like a workhouse suit—folk will take it
that I've been let out for the day. The suit fits me, but my
father makes the man bring a suit two sizes larger, to allow
for my growing into it. I stand there before the big mirror, the
sleeves over the tips of my fingers, the jacket seemingly down
to my knees, and I feel I could cry for myself. 'I'll give you a
guinea for it,' says my father. The man who is serving
remarks quietly, 'It's twenty-six an' elevenpence, and twenty-
six an' elevenpence it has to be.' The haggling goes on, all
on my father's side, but of no avail. Finally, and in a bad
temper, my father buys me the knickerbocker suit. 'The
bloody English shopkeepers,' he says as we leave the shop,
'—wouldn't give a man the price of a drink if he spent a
hundred pounds with them. Over in Ireland I'd have been
handed a fine half-a-crown back or maybe five shillings. The
divil roast that one.'

I have agreed to take the suit mostly to escape the embarrassing scene between the shopman and my father, and
perhaps at the same time working in a bit of revenge against
him that I am getting him to spend money, even though I
don't want what he was buying me. I am expected to wear it
next day, and, under duress from Mother at what himself
would think if I didn't, I go off to the nine o'clock Mass
wearing it, and ashamed of the spectacle I imagine I am
presenting to the world. I make up my mind to slip into one
of the narrow side pews, up by the wall, out of the way. And
just as I am sneaking in Sister Hyacinth calls me, and asks me
to go and assist the girls at pumping the organ up in the choir
loft. Up I go, and I flush and blush that much that I half
expect my skin to be wholly changed. At Communion I feel
so conspicuous at the altar rail that I find I can't swallow the
Host.

It seemed that corduroy suit went a long way towards
changing my character. In the early days I walked many miles
alone, especially in the dark, up the Middle Brook and even
as far as Barrow Bridge, to avoid being seen in it, to get used
to wearing it, and in a vain hope of wearing off the corduroy

smell. When I went to the street-corner there would be a sniffing among the boys and they would put their fingers to the nose, making mock signs of shutting out the smell or of being suffocated by it. Even Ernie Fairclough, one of my best mates, made some comic jibes about the smell and the colour, when he was supposed to be sticking up for me.

Then suddenly, one Monday evening, the worst day in the week, something changed inside me, and in an instant I shed all my shame about the corduroy suit. I've had enough, I thought, and, to make up for all that I had suffered, I went stalking up to the street-corner, chose the most crowded spot, and plopped myself into it, backside first, forcing my way between those who had made most fun of me. 'Poo, what a bloody stink!' said Teddy Fairclough. 'Who's bloody talkin'!' I said, 'I'd sooner that than my breeches arse all ripped.' Teddy was bigger than I was, and for a minute it looked as though there might be a fight. Then I looked round challengingly at the others. Nobody spoke. It seemed that after that I began to set about annoying different ones, deliberately easing myself down, right up to a lad's face. And once I'd grown into it fully, I almost went to bed in that corduroy suit. In time I grew really fond of it.

Today I almost love the memory of it, for, had my father bought me some nondescript suit in which I should have happily passed unnoticed, I would have forgotten it long ago, whereas now, half a century and more later, as I write these words, not being able to get the memories down fast enough, I almost feel as though I were wearing the corduroy suit once more. Perhaps in that little anecdote of the suit, together with the larger one of my father, there is some simple parable of life for me—namely, that, if we place ourselves with patience, and a will to love, and some hopeful acceptance before those little trials and adversities, be they either conditions or people, in our life, then over the years they seem to turn to blessings. Of course it's a long time to wait—but a writer needs his memories to brew.

19

The Diaries.

'THERE is nothing more mysterious', wrote Charles Péguy, 'than those dim periods of preparation which every man encounters on the threshold of life. The whole stage is set before we are twelve years old.' I did not grasp the personal significance of those words on the first reading, but early in the year 1951 I suddenly perceived the truth they revealed for me. I was tying up in bundles the small black journal books which I had written in the previous year, 1950, and out of curiosity I decided to make a rough calculation of how much I had written—an idea which I had never before considered. Each page averaged one hundred words, and each book one hundred pages, which at ten thousand words a book made the task a simple one. There were eighty complete books, making the total some eight hundred thousand words in one year. That seems an awful lot of writing to hand down to posterity, I thought—since the journals were so detailed and intimate I had accepted that they could not be published in my lifetime. I might occasionally read the odd few pages, but seldom more, for a journal of that nature can bring up some painful memories. The fact was, I couldn't understand my own motive in writing such a comprehensive document—one, I might add, in which I did not appear to come out too well.

Then I recalled a Christmas time in Bolton when I was twelve, and there came back to me a memory of a wistful longing I had nursed about what Christmas present I hoped to buy for myself—should I get hold of enough money. It was for something no other boy I knew would even consider, let alone value. And yet, day in day out, that hankering persisted. It was only then, as I was stacking away those journal notebooks, among piles of others in an iron trunk, that I realized that what I had been doing in writing those millions of words was fulfilling a childhood predilection.

Toys were largely absent from the Irish home such as ours, and the idea of providing something to play with was not even considered, apart from the games which took place between the children themselves, perhaps with a piece of string passed in patterns from hand to hand, or the asking of riddles and the like. Thoughts, talk, the odd prayers, and the daily flow of life itself was taken to be enough to occupy a child. At school when I was seven we were asked to write a composition about our favourite hobby. The others got down to it at once, whilst I remained mystified by the word itself. Is it some kind of hobby-horse they have on the fairground, I thought, or has it to do with the hob in the fireplace, or what? What can it mean—a hobby? Slowly I grasped what was meant, and, whilst all around me the pens were scratching away, I had to think up a hobby or two other than those of reading comics and telling tales at the street-corner.

The toys of my schoolmates stirred little interest and no envy in me. What satisfaction is there in playing with things, I used to think, surely that's for infants; no wonder they're not too bright in the head—messing around with bits of metal on wheels, when they could be talking, reading, or going about the streets watching and listening to all that was going on. The posher the people the more they kept themselves to themselves, and the more need for toys it seemed they had. 'Our Leslie', I heard one mother boast, 'can go into that room with all his toy soldiers an' keep hisself amused for hours!' Why play with toy soldiers, I thought, when you've got all your mates at the corner? It was the make-believe nature of it that seemed so childish and put me off; I had a much more real world of the imagination in the Catholic faith. A boy who was mad about toys, I learned, seldom made a good mate. 'He's in the back kitchen,' a mother would tell me, 'playin' with the Meccano he got for Christmas. Go in to him.' All alone, away from the warmth of the fire in the front, away from all the chat of the home, the boy would be down on his knees on the cold stone floor of the kitchen, attempting, often futilely it seemed, to construct a toy of sorts from strips of metal lined with holes, by aid of tiny nuts and bolts. In place of the usual eager response I would get a cool nod, indicating that my presence was welcome only as a spectator. Often the father would turn up and join in the playing, especially if the toy happened to be a train set. I'll have to get back to my old mates at the corner, I would think to myself. But to return to that Christmas.

'Yu' know Boots' chemist in Derby Street,' I said to my brother Edward, 'yu' know what I'm goin' to do—I'm goin' to go in there to Boots' and see if I can get mysel' a dairy.' 'A *dairy*,' he said, '—what kind of a dairy?' 'Yu' know,' I said, 'a *dairy* that you write things in every day an' keep a track on everythin'.' 'Oh,' he grinned, 'you mean a *diary*.' I felt a pang of shame. Of course it was *diary*—but that I should have been so ignorant as not to have known it! And to give him the chance to lord it over me!

I passed Boots' chemist shop every day on my way to and from school, and it was seldom during the diary season—from November until around early March—that I did not pause to look in the side window at the display of diaries. They had every conceivable diary, from foolscap size down to the small pocket edition. The side window, a magnificent plate-glass rectangle, looked out of place, facing as it did into Rothwell Street, a poor area leading off Derby Street, where it seemed—apart from my own interest—the exhibits were wasted. Along that street there would usually be seen some old woman hurrying along in her clogs, mostly with a bundle concealed furtively under her shawl, and on her face that look of anxiety which it seemed all such women wore, appearing to blind them to the visual world, for they would bump into you if you didn't dodge out of their way. Such a one, I had the feeling, if she could even comprehend what diary-keeping was, would not only regard such an activity as superfluous, but the record as further punishment; so desperate was life that she didn't care even to register it as it happened, let alone recollect.

Often there would be one of the huge old-fashioned baby-carriages in sight, a throw-out from some better-off family, but now antiquated and rickety, and in it would be some pale unwashed baby, a girl wheeling the carriage, with a bunch of younger members of the family clinging on, and a hanger-on or two as well. They might stop and stare at me gazing in the window, even sidle up and, challengingly, survey the display themselves, as though considering a purchase or two. Cripples were common, a boy or girl with irons on a leg, or using crutches, moving along with a certain distinctive air, and the odd ex-soldier with a wooden leg. At dinnertime there would be a noisy clattering of mill workers going by, and I used to press close to the window to avoid being bowled over. 'Get fru' under t'feet!' would be the call to anyone in the way. They moved swiftly, and always had some lively chat going on, and, as it was the custom for the leading characters to walk abreast holding the centre of the pavement, the younger supporting members, striving to get a word in, and hoping to remain part of the scene, would have to spurt along, dodging lamp-posts and pillar-boxes, and hopping off and on the kerb. The stray mongrel dog would be sure to make an appearance, its clacking feet betraying distemper and hard pad, its unhappy eyes appealing for a gesture of kindness; not too much of that around for a stray dog, but maybe a little.

Behind the window a selection of diaries would be placed on open show, some folded fully back with pages temptingly disclosed, revealing a titbit or two of the feast of information within. I would peer closely at these pages, often stooping and twisting my head to one side to make out the recto page, which was often placed vertically sideways. I would take in every item revealed of the Church year, from Septuagesima (I liked to savour such a word, with both mind and tongue, as though I were sampling a succulent scrap of mental marzipan, one with a rich Latin flavour, exotically remote from Rothwell Street) Sunday up to and beyond the First Sunday in Advent, with any of the fixed and the movable feasts; if lucky I might widen my interest and get a glimpse of when to expect the Jewish Passover and Day of Atonement, and along the route would absorb some secular details, such as when grouse shooting would begin and the Oxford Michaelmas Term end.

The ecclesiastical year, as I recall it, gave colour and significance to the calendar year; to the Catholic child it offered an annual string of feast-days and celebrations which brought an excitement and purpose to a life lacking incentives. It was said to begin with Advent, at the end of November, the four Sundays of which would take us to Christmas Eve. I always thought of it starting at Hallowe'en, the evening on which we actually played games in the home, the eve of the feast of All Saints', on which day we had a holiday. I liked the sombre mood of the feast, and also that of All Souls' Day following, for I took a deep interest in death, and liked the feel of my prayers having effect on the souls that had gone on to purgatory. Advent created a promising anticipatory feeling of Christmas being on its way. Next came the happy Christmas cycle, the celebration of the birth of Our Lord, the Circumcision on 1 January, and the Epiphany a week later. A dull stretch followed, up to Shrove Tuesday with its welcome feed of pancakes, followed by Ash Wednesday—'The holy fasts of Lent, wherein we fight against the spirits of evil with the weapon of abstinence.' Each feast-day had its own particular mood and colour, Ash Wednesday, being solemn, with its vestige of 'sackcloth and ashes', was dark grey, Corpus Christi poignant and red, the Assumption of Our Lady into heaven a happy feast-day of bright blue. Saint Patrick's Day was always handy—it was bright and emerald green—dropping as it did on 17 March, and allowing a holiday and a bit of a celebration. Nothing much then until Passion Sunday and Passion Week—indulgences galore to be picked up around this time for anyone who studied the Missal—then Palm Sunday: 'Fools! for I also had my hour; | One far fierce hour and sweet; | There was a shout about my ears, | And palms before my feet.' Holy Week was an intense period, Confession on Wednesday, Communion on Holy Thursday, Stations of the Cross on Friday, the Twelve Prophecies on Holy Saturday. Then came the glory of Easter Sunday morning. The ordinary pleasures, such as hot cross buns and a walk on Good Friday, could be enjoyed more, it seemed, because of their religious meaning. We Catholics felt most privileged compared with Protestants, for it seemed we got more out of all the festivals.

The diaries in Boots' window gave an anticipatory hint of the feast-days, and also contained many tasty facts on which to feed a mind desirous of some knowledge of an incontrovertible character. No matter what one was informed of by word of mouth, it seemed likely to turn out fallacious if not wholly false; and also this was intelligence of a nature, or so it seemed to me, that any right-minded person would need to have ready at the fingertips, just for self-satisfaction or in case an argument broke out. I longed to have one foot inside the window—standing within that temple of enlightenment—since it seemed that that was the world I would feel most at home in, a quiet world of knowledge in place of one of noise and work. Those diaries appeared to represent a scholarly effort to bring a measure of understanding to time and events—the rising and setting times of the sun, accurate to a minute, the phases of the moon, the times of high water and low water at London Bridge, and much other information that was utterly reliable—whilst out here in the dusty street, where it seemed all my days were destined to be spent, the mindless mob went clattering by on their way home for midday dinner, some of whom would hardly know the day of the week were it not for the signs and smells about them: the slaughterhouse was a hundred yards away, always busy on Mondays, Magee Marshall's Brewery brewed up on Thursdays, and so on. Most of them if accosted would certainly not know the date, some looked as if they might not even know the year—although the spry ones always knew exactly how many weeks it was to the next June Holiday—and as for not knowing Quinquagesima Sunday from Quadragesima Sunday, which ignorance one could forgive, they cared even less; they just went milling by like hordes of noisy and good-humoured barbarians.

I vaguely considered myself above some of these workers—

not above the skilled man, of course—and yet when I forced myself away from the window, and reflected on the multitude and myself, it seemed that they might be getting along in this life rather better than I was. They were more themselves, more lively, more useful and at home, more cheerful in the way they called out to one another, and, it seemed, going about the world far more sensibly than I seemed to be. Unlike me they didn't nurse illusions about some remote and lofty world, a world clearly denied us all; they were making the best of their allotted station in life and getting the work done that had to be done. My discontent did not appear to be taking me far, and, if there was anything divine around, it seemed it could be their whole-hearted involvement in the life open to them. I half envied them—but only half, for I had a way of keeping half of myself to myself.

Standing looking into shop windows was a common pastime of the day, and often two or three of us would set out from the street-corner to do just that. It was Skinny Nancy's sports shop in Derby Street that my mates always made for, and they would gaze into the grimy window, pointing out footballs, football boots, cricket bats, boxing gloves, Indian clubs, fishing tackle, and many games, all faintly coated with dust, and the odd cobweb. No matter how I led them on, it seemed they could not so much as spare a glance at Boots' wonderful side window of diaries; and if they did it was always bedpans and appliances that caught their interest. I never disclosed mine, for I had learnt that one's enthusiasms were best kept to oneself, to flower naturally within, and perhaps to die in like fashion. Once others got to know of them they could be discouraging or, worse still, take up the enthusiasm on one's behalf, which often meant you weren't allowed to drop it when it no longer engaged you.

I did not get my diary that certain Christmas, but I did pluck up courage to go in and ask at the counter about the various prices. It was really a bit of an act in the hope that some kind assistant would perhaps be impressed and let me have one on the cheap, but it failed, and I came out of the shop flushed and rather ashamed of myself for trying it on. I kept a watch on the window in February for the first reductions in price, but now I had spent my Christmas money and even the most reduced diary was beyond me. In early March the diaries were down to half-price, but I could not afford one, and also my hankering was on the wane. By the end of the month the display was abruptly withdrawn, giving way to the thermos flasks, elastic stockings, packets of corn-pads, hair-dyes, and various rubber rings and medical gadgets.

For me this same pattern of window-watching went on year after year, and, although I made attempts to get the money, handy jobs to earn it by were not easy to get, and so I always ended up standing gazing into that side window at the open pages, striving to glean information on the cheap. I was not disheartened by my failure to acquire a diary, for it seemed that in the order of things hopes had to be dashed, and in time disappointment became its own rancid form of fulfilment. Early on in life I had learnt not to allow fancy to grow to expectation, nor did my feelings die off, but rose again every November when the diaries reappeared. I seemed to be the only one that ever looked at them, and it was as though they never sold a single one. Who in Bolton would want a diary, I used to think, except me? What do they do with them, I used to ask myself, when it comes to the end of the season and they haven't sold them? I shouldn't have minded giving a few coppers for a last year's diary. I had an idea as I stood at the window that, if I could get hold of one of those diaries and keep it in my own drawer, the one which was allotted to me for my personal use in the back-kitchen chest of drawers, and took up my pen every night, I could somehow bring an order to this unwieldy flow of life that went on day in day out, year in year out, and was then mostly forgotten.

No one, it appeared to me, was taking a proper record of things, with interesting events taking place every day. There was the fog which had engulfed the town one dinnertime, a black fog, quite different from the usual fogs, one which had turned day into night. I had heard Mrs Langstaff say that it could herald the Second Coming. Then there was that fearful story of the young girl from Astley Bridge—it was going round amongst grown-ups—who had gone to Blackpool on her holidays with her young man and when swimming in the sea had somehow got impregnated—at least that was the word they said the doctors used—with octopus spawn; they had come home after a good holiday, but as the weeks went by she couldn't understand why she was getting bigger and bigger round the stomach; she went to the doctor's and was told she was pregnant. She couldn't believe it for she insisted she was a virgin. Her young man packed her in when he heard—swore he had never touched her; then her dad turned the poor girl out of the home, and finally she gave birth to a monster in Bolton infirmary, one with more than one head—nobody could say for certain how many—and it took three doctors ten minutes to smother the thing with pillows. Such events as good as happening on your doorstep and nothing being done about it. Moreover, I had a feeling that with a diary I could secure a neat picture of each single day of my life, so that it would all be put down in writing in a book, rather like the way some boys put stamps in a stamp album, all nice and neat, and over the years in place of the messy and half-forgotten impression on the memory there would be a record, an account which one could almost hand over to St Peter at heaven's gate to save any argument.

20

James and Sylvan

SEATED next to me in school when I was in my thirteenth year was a boy called James. Boys who failed to make an impression of one kind or another on their classmates did not emerge from the identity of the full Christian name which the teacher read out twice daily when calling the register, so that James was not known as Jim, nor did he have a nickname. Yet in his quiet but individual way James had more character than almost any boy I knew, and during the year in which I had sat next to him in Miss Newsham's class, in the new desks which seated only two boys instead of six, there had grown in me a warm affectionate respect for him. We were not matey outside the classroom, since James was not a marble player, did not go to play on swings in the park, nor join in with any group; poverty of the kind he knew did not attract companions.

James was from a poor home in Isabel Street, a few streets from our own; his clothing was of the shabbiest, with holes in his cheap old jersey and often in the seat of his trousers, and his clogs were down at heel and in need of irons, to all of which he appeared happily unaware. His neck was a mass of fleabites, almost merging with his abundant freckles; he had a strong body odour, a stench which no boy from a bug-infested home could hope to escape. His face, however, was always so well washed that the the skin seemed to glow; he was cross-eyed, and seemed blessed with a most innocent and sunny nature, so that when he smiled his brown squinting eyes became bright and lively. This smile seemed at its brightest on those mornings—and in Bolton they were not rare—when the rain in the streets was heavy and unceasing, and James, whom I never saw hurrying, would arrive in a soaked state. Unlike other boys he would be quite unfussed, and would stand calmly beside me before prayers, beads of rain trickling down the back of his neck—he had no jacket and raincoats were unknown among our sort. He would then join hands and close his eyes, and begin to pray. Glancing at him, with the raindrops glistening about his high forehead, his tousled brown hair above, often with glimpses of a steamy vapour rising from him, it was not hard to imagine him as a saint of sorts, cheerfully serving his time in this vale of tears until called to his reward. He was surprisingly well spoken, and he had a bright mind, but he held this in restraint, never proffering the correct answer to a question at the expense of a boy who couldn't answer or had given a wrong one. At such moments he would bring his head backward and tend to gaze towards the ceiling to avoid catching Miss Newsham's eye. He was remarkably cool, his writing was much better than my own, and his exercise books clean and unsmudged. Somehow it would have been an affront to cane him, and I must say that I never saw Miss Newsham ever threaten him in any way. Over a period I had grown used to his smell, although it was an ordeal for the first half-hour or so every morning, particularly so on Mondays, but I took care to avoid any sign of reluctance in my sitting close to him.

At the end of the summer holiday, which spanned the month of July, I returned to school in Miss Newsham's class—the third year she had taught the same forty boys—to find that James had not yet turned up at school, having had to attend Flash Street clinic to have his ringworm treated. As much as I liked James, it was with a certain relief that I sat down at the desk after class prayers, knowing I would enjoy an hour free of the dear lad's smell. Mr Smith, the headmaster, came into the classroom as the register was about to be called, with a boy of my own age behind him, whom he introduced to Miss Newsham, who was perched on the raised chair at her desk. The instant's distraction was enough to allow boys to exchange looks and whispers. Seated alone I was able to take in what was obviously a new boy—who stood self-consciously before the gaze of the class. He was about my own height, an inch or two above average, had a fresh clean English look, and was obviously from a good home. The moment I saw him various details combined to give me my usual instant impression of character—whether tough, soft or in between, a show-off or a dark horse; he was a nice lad, I decided, not a fighter, not clever, but from a posh home.

Miss Newsham stood up surveying the class as she was deciding where to put the new boy. It was plain to see from her welcoming manner to him, and the way in which Mr Smith was attending to the issue, that this boy was a cut above the average, socially at least. She hesitated about where to place him, and I saw Mr Smith look at James's vacant place beside me, then whisper a word to her, and after a moment or two of discussion, presumably about James, the new boy was directed to the place beside me. I stood up and gave him a grin of greeting, feeling rather sorry for him, and at the same time I felt ashamed of the flush of relief as he sat down clumsily beside me, for in place of the rancid smell of the poverty which clung to James there was almost a fragrance. Not merely the smell of a well-cared-for boy from a good clean home, but the aura of a boy from a better class, one who has known nothing of poverty or hunger, and precious little of fear or anxiety, a boy secure in his ignorance of the seamy side of life. Such boys, I found, usually had a pleasant smell.

By chance on that certain Monday morning I happened to be aware of a glow of self-assurance. The reason was that at the end of the month's holiday my usual old school suit had become worn out beyond repair, and, although good enough for the street-corner, was not up to the image of myself I had been able to present at school. By frequently drawing my mother's attention to this, I had extracted a promise from her that my Sunday suit of blue serge with knickerbocker breeches would be available for regular school wear on that Monday. It was not that Mother was in any way concerned over such matters, carefulness of that kind being alien to her nature, but she had become a victim to the habit of pawning that particular suit on Monday mornings. She would never have been seen taking a bundle to a pawnshop—we were a respectable family, above that sort of thing, which, if it were known, incurred a severe loss of face among neighbours. Mary Anne, a little woman with a goitre neck, who took snuff, backed horses, and was frequently on the borrow for a cup of sugar or a brewing or two of tea, always dropped in on Monday mornings when my father had gone to bed after his night's work down the coal-mine, and asked Mother had she anything she wanted taking to 'Uncle's'.

Pawnshops were used regularly by only about one in ten of the Bolton families, and these were from the poorer neighbourhoods, since working people were generally canny and frugal, and would not resort to such wasteful expenditure of money even in emergencies. The mother in the fairly prosperous working home usually dealt at the co-operative society—the paying out of the 'divi' proved handy at holiday time—and had no need of pawnbrokers; the very poor, who were constantly in need of money, seldom had anything to pawn; any article of value, such as a watch or suit which they may have acquired by some unusual turn of fortune, would often be pawned and never redeemed. It was the wife and mother who had regular workers, usually the father and teenage children, but who was a poor manager, as the phrase went, who had need to frequent the pawnshop.

Early on a Monday morning, usually before seven o'clock, the odd woman, shawled and wearing clogs, could be seen sneaking up the backstreets to the local pawnshop, to join the queue of women waiting outside the back entrance for the premises to open. Pawnbrokers knew their regulars well, and seldom opened the wrapped-up bundles. 'Same as last week please—' was the usual request, and the man behind the counter would hand over the regular few shillings, less coppers for the ticket, and stick the bundle on the shelf. Certain women were driven to pawning the working clogs of one or other of the family on Saturday, when getting the weekend clothes out of pawn, and then had to be there with the Sunday suit the first thing on Monday to get the few shillings needed to run the home until Friday, out of which they would hand back a couple of shillings to get the clogs out of pawn.

To be in debt was considered a discreditable thing in the Bolton of the day, and it seemed that almost any disgrace could be lived down except that one; buying on hire purchase was considered a bad sign. Clothing-club cheques issued by the co-operative society, with which one could buy furniture, clothes, or even coal, were acceptable, since they had to be paid up in twenty weeks. The deep sense of shame that attached itself to the wife in debt—it was always the poor woman of course—had grown from long experience of the misfortune and tragedy that debt so often brought about. (I was to know personally three women who committed suicide because of debts hidden from the husband, and of course I heard of many more.) Such women were most often the kind and indulgent mother, the ones who took too literally the admonition, 'Take therefore no thought for the morrow; for the morrow shall take thought for the things of itself.' My own dear mother, alas, was inclined to a weakness, if such it be, of giving to everyone, never letting a beggar go singing down the street without finding him a copper; but on that certain Monday she had had my suit all brushed and ready for me for school, with Sunday boots instead of clogs, which to me was always a luxury. The boots I had polished the night before; the celluloid collar and collar-stud were on hand on the dresser—and, although such a collar allowed little freedom to the neck, you got used to its constant grip; then of course it was as well to feel some restraint, for if a boy felt too free he began to run and yell and make fun and give way to impulses, and giving way to impulses was sure to get you into trouble. So that on the morning when the new boy sat down beside me I was free of any feeling of inferiority, since I was a degree or two superior to most of the class.

Before the first lesson of catechism got going I was told by Miss Newsham to help the new boy to get from the cupboard the exercise books he would need for sums, composition, drawing, and practical work; I then explained to him how he would need to get his mother to make a school bag of cotton material with two tapes, for keeping the books in—the bag to be taken home and washed at weekends. He was an attractive boy with dark hair—not as black as my own—which came off the back of his spotless neck in short curls. His eyes were blue, eyebrows curled a little, and he had long dark eyelashes—although not nearly as long as those of Joe Oddie, who sat in the seat in front of us, who had eyelashes so heavy that it seemed an effort to open his eyes. The new boy had a nose which puckered at the corners when he was puzzled—which was to be often—and a mouth that turned up at each side that went with the puzzled look; he looked bright but not brainy. He had what would be taken to be a posh voice by our standards, but it came off his tongue effortlessly, with no sign of swank, nor had he the usual look that so often went with that tone of voice, which was known as mard—meaning marred or spoilt. The unusual thing, which I spotted at once, was that he used the same voice all the time, when speaking to Miss Newsham as to me, whereas every other boy had a special voice he put on when addressing a teacher. He told me that his name was Sylvan; and, although the woodland allusion was but vaguely familiar and that of the woodland spirit not at all, yet the name, a shortening of Sylvanus, I gathered, made an agreeable change from the various Alfs, Joes, and Berts.

James himself turned up before playtime, and an odd sight he looked, for they had cropped his hair so close to the scalp that it had a shaven appearance, leaving him a single bunch of hair protruding over the forehead, known as a cowlick; the unsightly circles of ringworm could be seen, covered with ointment about his head. His looked across to his place at my desk, now occupied by Sylvan, and I gave him a look of sympathy and made a gesture, as much as to say, I couldn't help it. He grinned understandingly. Then Miss Newsham looked at his ringworm and said it might be as well if he took a day or two off school, and he agreed and went off in his cheery and composed manner.

On Mondays, after the weekend break, and especially so after the summer holiday, it seemed that Miss Newsham—

and so far as I could make out most of the other teachers—turned up at school cherishing some intention of preserving an amicable understanding with the class of boys before her. The manner with which she chose to bring it about was one of firm reasonableness, the threatening tone being avoided in her voice, and her hands not held in that manner from which she could abruptly deliver one of her swinging slaps across the head to some offender; to reinforce this conciliatory attitude the cane would be left in the cupboard and not displayed warningly across the wooden pegs on the easel which supported the blackboard, as was the practice most mornings. Such peaceful intentions, it seemed, were always to be disappointed, since they failed to take into account the capricious nature of schoolboys, and this morning was to prove no exception.

Pat Carol, a tall sandy-haired lad who also had a peculiar squint—the poorer boys appeared to suffer strabismus of various kinds—had slipped his mate, John Bryan, a piece of Wiggawagga, a cheap black toffee made by Daddy Addison who kept a sweet shop. In the relaxed atmosphere of that morning John had rashly given way to a temptation to have a taste before playtime, which he might have got away with had he not then risked a quick chew—it was an insipid concoction and needed chewing to surrender a morsel of taste—but rarely could a boy in Miss Newsham's class get away with such a liberty, no matter how much he stooped his head over the desk.

'Bryan!' she called, 'what're you chewing?'

Every head in the class took on an attitude of alert apprehension at the sudden change of voice. Judging by the wild activity of his jaws, as seen by myself from the side, I assumed John was attempting a few hasty champs in the hope that he could bring the lump of toffee down to a swallowable consistency and size. If so his efforts were to miscarry, for as he replied, '—Yes—*gug*—Miss—what—*gug*—, Miss—?' the presence of the Wiggawagga in his mouth clearly betrayed itself in his voice. Judging by the way his left hand went up to his face, as though covering up a sudden bout of sneezing, with his right hand going under it and, as I imagined, a finger cunningly slipping in it to dislodge the toffee, it would seem that John was in some difficulty.

Sylvan looked alarmed as he heard Miss Newsham bark out: 'Bryan! come out here—out in front of the class!' Her placid appearance of early morning now changed with start-ling suddenness as a flush of red appeared at the top of her blouse, just above her ample breast, and seemed to flow upwards, enveloping her throat, face, and forehead, but not her ears, which remained normal. She turned and swiftly made for the cupboard to get her cane. John seized his chance to stumble, slip over, and, with head hidden, apparently dis-lodge the lump of Wiggawagga and fling it aside (Pat Carol was to pick it up and conceal it down the side of his clog until playtime, when it would be eaten). With a smack of his tongue John was able to swallow the remainder. Now, with a posture of boyish innocence, which he was an adept at assuming, and a certain triumphant gleam in the eye, which he turned to the class, John reluctantly approached Miss Newsham, who was brandishing the cane. Sylvan, beside me, watched the proceedings with what I took to be consternation.

John Bryan was a short lad, under five feet tall, with black hair and dark brown eyes; he came from Reservoir Street, a rough district near Bobby Heywood's park. He was an expert dribbler—such lads seldom made the grade as adult foot-ballers, since they could never overcome a desire to hold on to the ball and would not pass—and a tough lad around the school, leader of a gang of some half-dozen lads from the same area. I was always disquieted at scenes of punishment being meted out, although I knew that John, in the conflict with Miss Newsham, would be less concerned about the caning he knew he was in for than the need he had to keep his reputation up among his mates and the class in general. John now put on an attitude of such dread, so exaggerated that it was clear to us all that he was only putting it on; it may also have served to mask any real fear. And he dodged the first stroke of the cane, which put him a point ahead. When Miss

Newsham managed to get one in, he let out a wild cry of pain and began dancing about on his toes, hugging his hand. This was all good stuff. Miss Newsham's face now went pale and her ears went red.

The few minutes which all this took up, with John backing away from Miss Newsham and her cane, loudly protesting that he was being caned because of a gumboil he had, disconcerted Sylvan, who appeared never to have witnessed such a scene before. The next lesson was sums, long division in decimals, of which it was clear he had but the haziest notion. Yet his bewildered look, as he turned to me for guidance, was free of the fear of the consequences, as would be the case with us; it was simply a look of almost comic bafflement. I gazed at that boyish expression and wondered how anyone could reach the advanced age of twelve, be so ignorant of the painful nature of life, and remain so apparently unconcerned about it. Miss Newsham took care not to bring her attention to our area, for it was an understood thing among the teaching staff that so far as possible the caning of boys from the better-class homes should be avoided, since it incurred the disapproval of the parents; whereas the parents of the poor had no influence, and seldom objected. By the stealthy use of a scrap of paper and a whisper or two I was able to get Sylvan to put down the correct answers.

21

A Musical Occasion

SCHOOLBOYS do not mix easily, and at playtime, as Sylvan had little in common with the other boys, he clung to my side. The small L-shaped schoolyard was crowded, with boys yelling and rushing around as though mad, others less active clinging to a safe place against railings or wall so as to attempt to chat, and a few boys encircling Francis Mundy as he walked round the yard on his hands, going up and over any obstruction. John Bryan and his gang went about the yard with John in the lead, the others making way for them. John was chewing a Roocroft's nut-milk cube, a kind of nougat, which, when well chewed, yielded a milky fluid; this John accumulated around his lower gums, until he spotted some monitor or teacher's pet, when suddenly he would press his tongue under the two large front teeth, and expectorate through the narrow slit between them, forcing a jet of what appeared to be milk at the victim's face, and never missing the mark. I was not a boy to envy the feats of others, but that accomplishment of John's I did, if only for its theatricality. Boys from the poorer and tougher areas, who almost never shone in the classroom, seemed to dominate the playground; fighting spirit proved more decisive than size when it came to fisticuffs. I had many other pals around, for I was an easy mixer and a lively talker, but I missed my usual chats, since Sylvan's close presence did not allow me my normal freedom.

The final morning lesson was practical geometry, a subject for which I had little liking and less aptitude. Large squares of paper, coloured on one side and gummed on the other, were passed round to each boy, together with pairs of small scissors, to be shared by the two boys at each desk; triangles of various kinds had to be drawn—right-angled, equilateral, and isosceles—then cut out and pasted into the exercise books, with various principles supposedly demonstrated, such as that of Pythagoras' theorem, that the square on the hypotenuse of a right-angled triangle is equal to the sum of the squares on the other two sides.

It was a lesson at which I was a duffer, and despite caning and vocal castigation I had been unable to make any improvement. My hand was shaky, my grip unsteady, and I could not draw a straight line even alongside a ruler. The triangles I made were seldom true, my fingers were too clumsy to handle the scissors, and I never succeeded in pasting down the cut-out figures evenly. My spirits sank at the thought of guiding Sylvan through the lesson. To my surprise he needed no guidance, and turned out to be a dab hand with ruler and pencil, and also scissors. Since we were allowed to share one pair, and as Miss Newsham was not looking in our direction, collaboration of a dodgy sort proved easy, and so good were the triangles that Sylvan cut out for me with his sure fingers, and later pasted down, that all I had to do was mess them around a bit so as to make them nearer my own mark.

This saved me from the mortification I always felt over being unable to perform what I took to be a childish activity with scissors and paper, and also served to balance our obligation towards each other, and enrich our friendship. Freehand drawing, an afternoon lesson, was another that created difficult problems for me. Miss Newsham had a thing about flowers, and so intense had been my efforts to reproduce the tulip, daffodil, and even the rose she set before the class that my fingers trembled and sweated, and the pencil became moist and slipped out of my hand. How, I would ask myself, could one even attempt to convey the flowerness of a flower with pencil and paper! Sylvan, however, could do it in moments; just a few lines, without effort it seemed, and there was the flower on paper. One could almost smell it.

Our friendship became more intimate but remained tied solely to school life, for he lived up Deane, in a select district away from the mills and factories. Elswick Avenue, although short, was a genuine avenue with trees—I went to look one day, and with unusual temerity actually walked down past his very home—abutting the pleasant hilly Haslam Park, adjacent to Deane Clough, with the golf course nearby; this meant that he had to hurry off to catch the tram home at dinnertime—as we called the midday break—and he hurried off home again on his own after school, whilst I joined Sandy Fallows and Joe Harrison, two good mates, for an hour in Heywood's Park, where Sandy, a born acrobat, was an expert on swings and parallel bars. Mostly I made ineffectual attempts to swing and hang like Sandy, but more than once fell on my head on the cinder-covered ground, always shaken but unhurt.

Sylvan's surname was Anderton, and the family, cousins included, were prominent in the musical life of Bolton; he had an elder cousin who attended SS Peter and Paul's School, Sylvester Anderton, a noted pianist. Sylvan was not an exciting companion, he never told of any fights or arguments, or came to school with a new dirty tale he had heard. Not that I minded, for in the crowded life of school and street-corner there was abundant chat, argument, and the telling of tales and no end of talkers—what was rare was the listener. I had another pal at school called Desmond Emmet, whose mother bought and sold second-hand clothes, and chatting to Desmond—or rather listening to him—I would hear more during one dinnertime than in a year with Sylvan. The thing I felt charmed by—not without a secret spasm of shame when I looked across at my old mate James in his tatters of clothes and ringworm—and was most sensitively aware of, but could not identify at the time, was Sylvan's middle-class aura. All my other pals, every boy I knew in fact, had an industrial working-class stamp of some kind or other—in expression, manner, voice, general appearance, and, unmistakably, smell—the one from the home of a skilled worker distinct from that of a labourer. Boys from the homes of spinners, miners, foundry workers, leather tanners, and a dozen other jobs tended to carry around with them a family odour and manner indicating such. A boy whose father was a coal-miner walked with a certain swing—one probably adopted by Dad after being confined down a mine and unconsciously assumed by the son. Also, there were numerous other signs, such as the raised voice: noisy workplaces fostered such in a parent and it was taken up by the family.

There were, however, even more obvious signs of Sylvan's difference; for instance, he came to school wearing a fresh shirt every other day, or sometimes a fresh one daily, but one shirt was reckoned to last a full week for most of us. Apart from the quality and neatness of his clothes, what I really envied were the dark-blue wool jerseys he wore, hand-knitted, soft to the eye and touch, with an attractive ring of red around the collar; I would often find my eye caught by the wool socks, grey, and knitted by hand. I was much concerned about clothes and appearance, and felt I would have given anything to possess such wool garments, so different from the shop ones I wore, made of a cheap mixture of wool and cotton. And to my sensitive nose there was the fragrance of some kind of toilet soap they used in the home—I judged it to be Pear's soap, a tablet of which my brother Edward had once bought for himself; carbolic soap, used in the majority of homes, it was certainly not; and I could even detect the faint fresh whiff of Gibbs' Dentifrice. There were a few other boys in the class who came from good homes in Great Lever area, such as Charnock, Carter, and Connor, to mention but three, and, although they had quieter voices and accents less broad than most of us, there was always a sense of conscious modulation when they spoke, but Sylvan's voice was natural and pleasant to the ear. I learnt after some questioning that his previous school had been one where fees were paid. That I found almost incomprehensible, outside the *Magnet* and other magazines which had stories of boys' boarding schools. How, I asked myself, could a father and mother actually think of *paying* for education as though it were a privilege instead of a punishment for being young?

Two simple events in my friendship with him remain clearly in mind—and I shall tell of the unhappy one first. One day, when Miss Newsham was out of class, Sylvan took out of his pocket a golf ball, one which he had found when walking near the golf course. It had hardly been used, and the moment I took that hard white ball in my hand to examine it, and read the name *Star Challenger*, I felt I must get it for myself. A boy's possessions took on a special significance when they were few, and could be carried around in the pocket; you could feel them occasionally, boast about them quietly, and then watch the envy of the other boys when they were allowed a hold—be it of a new knife, a collection of cigarette cards, a glass marble, or a foreign coin. There was a tactic of going about getting possession of what another boy had and you coveted: first you expressed admiration, then you turned it off and became critical, even contemptuous, next you showed him some article of your own, and then a swap of some kind would be suggested, and after some haggling a penny might be added to the inferior item to make up the difference. A golf ball was a rare possession, and at the street-corner a new one such as this would be prized. Because of its lively bouncing properties it could be used for various games, and was known to be dangerous because of all the windows, so one had to be careful. It was no good for football which was an advantage, since this meant you could keep it to yourself. And finally, when badly worn it could be cut open, skinned, and lengths of elastic got from it, which made catapults.

I allowed a day to go by and then offered Sylvan twopence for it. He said he'd rather not part with it, if I didn't mind. I said I didn't mind; later, however, I raised the offer to threepence, then finally to fourpence. I could see I had made him uncomfortable, and felt uneasy that I should have done so, but he didn't sell it. That's the end of it, I thought, but the next morning, when we sat down side-by-side at our desk, he turned to me and got the ball out of his pocket. 'Here you are,' he said, as he handed it to me. 'Oh ta,' I said, 'but I've spent a penny—I can only give you threepence now.' He shook his head and smiled: 'No, thanks,' he said, 'I don't want any money—I'm *giving* it to you.' I could hardly believe it—*he didn't want any money*! He was *giving* it. A boy actu-

ally refusing threepence in ready money and a penny to come!
I had never known anything like it; well not among schoolboys, and certainly not at the street-corner. I looked at him a
bit closer to see if there were any signs of his having gone off
his nut, but no, it was the same Sylvan.

It was an exciting feeling to pocket that golf ball, and to
feel at it once or twice. Yet it seemed that I hadn't had it there
in my left-hand trouser pocket for much more than five
minutes when all the attraction began to pall. What had
made me so madly eager to get hold of it—it was only a golf
ball! Golfers were swiping them all over the place on the golf
links—so what was so special about my *Star Challenger*? I
suggested to Sylvan that he take the threepence, but he
refused; he said that the night before in bed he had been
thinking it over and had decided to give it to me, to mark our
friendship. I couldn't bear to feel so obligated to him, and to
ease my conscience I began to press comic papers and school
magazines on him, and, although he accepted them, he
wasn't a keen reader; I even bought Mackintosh's toffee
delight, and shared it with him, but it seemed nothing would
erase my sense of shame. I had offended against my mother's
code of decency by being grasping, and he, an English lad,
had more than observed it, and shown me how to behave. I
had sold my Irish pride for a rotten golf ball.

Right to the very end that golf ball proved a source of
keenest disillusion. The second weekend I decided to cut it
open and at least get the elastic out of it. This proved a most
difficult job, and I had to go out in the backyard and use a
small axe to cut through the cover. In doing so I chopped
right through the elastic that bound the inner ball, so that it
was all in useless fragments. I then took out the small hard
rubber ball in the centre, and I was playing with it when it
burst in my face, splashing me with horrible white stuff. I
could not have had a more telling lesson regarding the vanity
of possessions.

There was a happier outcome to the second episode. Sylvan
told me that his parents had invited me to come along with
them and Sylvan to a concert at the Victoria Hall in town one

future Wednesday evening, and they had a ticket for me if my mother and father would let me go. The invitation at once filled me with alarm, as did any social entanglement of that kind, since there were so many uncertainties: would my Sunday suit be out of pawn, a nice clean shirt on hand, my boots not in need of mending? One had to be perfect on such occasions, for it seemed that the least slip, such as a thread-bare sleeve to a shirt, could give one away. Mother thought it would be a nice thing for me to go out, and said that surely she would have everything ready for me.

She was as good as her word, and had everything prepared on the evening; she deliberately delayed the time of calling my father for his night's work—she wasn't beyond tampering with the alarm clock, turning it back a quarter of an hour or so, and putting it on again when he was out of the front place—so that I could wash and get ready in the kitchen before he got up. My Sunday suit was brushed and clean; I polished my boots, Mother gave my celluloid school collar an extra wipe, and she had sixpence to thrust into my hand as I was going off and kissing her goodbye. Pleasure of any kind was the last thing on my mind, for all I wanted was to get the evening over without shame or making a fool of myself. And I had to take another way out of the street so as to dodge all my mates at the street-corner, for I should have been ashamed to say I was going to a concert.

I was outside the Victoria Hall well in time, and was surprised to see the throng of people going in. Then along came Sylvan with his mother and father; they were of a better class than anyone I knew, had what I took to be a comfortably off look, of a sort never seen in our neighbourhood, but were older than I had imagined, and Sylvan, it appeared, was very much the youngest son. I was introduced and in we went, and at once I was struck by the vibrant atmosphere of the concert hall; it seemed not unlike that of the Derby Picture Palace before the safety curtain was rolled up, but of a more refined character. Mr Anderton bought four programmes, one for each of us; I perused mine with a knowing air, and the evening opened with the overture, Mendelssohn's 'Fingal's

Cave'. It was new to me, and I didn't think much of it, but assumed what I took to be the right expression, and later joined in the clapping. Then a cellist called Ernest Thorley played what was on the programme as 'The Londonderry Air', which turned out to be one of my favourites, 'Danny Boy', and that I greatly enjoyed. Slowly I found myself getting into the mood of the place, people, and music, and almost regretted it when the interval came. Sylvan and myself went off and got ourselves lemonade, paid for by his father. After the interval there were a number of vocal items, including excerpts from operas. There was a young man with a rich baritone voice—a sound I was most susceptible to during the 'Agnus Dei' at sung Mass—and he sang Valentine's aria from Gounod's *Faust*, 'All Hail thou Dwelling . . .'. I forgot Sylvan, his parents, and all the rest of them, the song so moved me. And to think I could be standing at the street-corner telling tales in place of hearing this lovely music!

The Andertons saw me to the starting-place of the Daubhill tram beside the wholesale fruit market, then they got on the Deane tram, which was just ahead and which left earlier. I reckoned I had just scraped through so far as approval went: they couldn't say much for me or against me. Then I decided to get off and walk home and save a penny; also, I felt too excited to sit on a tram. So I set off. It was a clear starry night, and as I went up Derby Street I kept thinking how strange it was, the different lives people led. My father down pit and all those others at a concert. And I thought too of how privileged such a family as the Andertons were—especially Sylvan. But somehow I didn't envy him, for in that vast interior of my boyhood imagination I felt I was not unblessed, being glad that I was myself and no other; also I was aware of the existence of God, and it seemed to me that the mere breath of that feeling was worth a world of concerts, wool jerseys, and homes in posh avenues. Finally, all those would prove of no matter at all, since I believed that 'God, only, suffices'.

It was after the Easter holiday, when Sylvan had been attending our school for less than nine months, that he did not return on the Monday morning, and the place beside me was empty. He had not mentioned the change to me, but I learnt that his parents had chosen a new school for him, a private one at which they again paid fees. For a time I missed him, and felt rather upset that he had not got in touch with me, but I was rapidly moving into puberty, and had many strange problems to cope with.

I was to see Sylvan but once again. One Saturday in the autumn of 1944—the V1 flying-bomb period was over and the V2 rocket attacks had begun—I was going off duty from my civil defence driving job in South London when three men wearing NFS (National Fire Service) overcoats walked by me on Belmont Hill. At once I recognized the nearest one: 'Excuse me,' I said, 'but are you Sylvan Anderton?' 'No,' he replied quickly, 'my name's Bill Anderton.' It was Sylvan, with the same blue eyes and the boyish expression; but I understood his need to shed Sylvan for Bill. To convince him of who I was I quickly told him many details—of what he wore at school, of the golf ball he gave me, the concert we went to, anything to prick his memory, to all of which he replied with a puzzled look. But he agreed, yes, as a boy he had lived at 33 Elswick Avenue, Bolton, and vaguely recalled SS Peter and Pauls' School, but said he had gone there for only a very short time. My old schoolmate, I thought, who sat beside me in Miss Newsham's class, whose sums I did, who outlined drawings for me, and who clearly can't remember a thing of those eventful days! I had often seen my Irish relatives, big men from Mayo, miners or navvies, embrace warmly on meeting after a long separation, and kiss each other tenderly on the cheek, and truth to tell I should have been happy to respond to such a gesture, for not only was he an old friend from schooldays, and dear to me, but it was a Bolton face, which face and look always touched deeper feelings in me here in the alien South. But instead of my greeting becoming warmer, I began to feel some misgivings at having thrust such memories at him, and so disconcerted him by our encounter. He was clearly taken aback that an apparent stranger in London should buttonhole him in the street, and tell him so much about himself that he had quite forgotten. And as he betrayed signs of wishing to get away to join his mates, who by this time had walked on, I let him go. But I found myself smarting a little, and wondering how it was that I could recollect so much from my boyhood and feel the warm rush of nostalgia that went with memory, while many of those I met could recall so little.

22

The Big Corner

I FOUND I was detaching myself from our own street-corner, since I had been able to wangle myself in among the younger lads of the Big Corner at the end of Birkdale Street beside Can Row. It was ideally situated for a gathering corner, with a flow of pedestrians which added to its character; it had a lively mixture of men and youths, spinning-mill workers mostly, but colliers, foundry workers, ex-soldiers, an out-of-work or two, and younger lads on the fringe. On a summer evening there would often be as many as thirty gathered there, but it had a respectable tone for a street-corner.

Spinning-room workers were the best sort to have at a street-corner; they were unaggressive physically, yet witty and given to argumentative talk. They never figured in the newspaper reports of youths fighting, nor did they engage in juvenile or other crime. When a youth moved into his late teens, and had a job such as coal-mining, navvying, or demolition work, using pick, spade, or sledgehammer, or any other tool that exercised his body without asking much control from his mind, it seemed that he began to experience a surge of virility coursing through him, and with that came a desire for physical contest, an inclination to challenge and pit his strength against another. The opportunities to do so in sport hardly existed, and the feeling remained unsatisfied, so that there was a tendency among such types to turn to fighting. But the work in the spinning mill did not promote a robust sense of well-being, and when a boy had been put to a job demanding delicate manual skill and quiet controlled behaviour, it seemed to inhibit the more violent side of his nature. Older spinners might get a bit drunk on Saturday afternoons, and they would go to the baths and swim it off—

not fight it off. Mechanics and skilled men generally did not get involved in street fighting.

I will not describe in detail my mates at the Big Corner, each one wearing a baggy cap with a large neb at the front, since to do so accurately would convey a false impression, leaving out the vividness of their personalities, the liveliness of their exchanges, and their spirited humanity. The coal-miners were mostly decent and peaceful youths, since the social atmosphere, laced with Methodism, discouraged violence of any kind (and no intelligent man would be unaware of the social tone of his neighbours or wish to live outside it); those who congregated at corners rarely drank, for it seemed one had to be a pub man or a corner man. Yet it was expected of miners to assume a pugnacious manner, and with their big clogs and hardy appearance they gave that impression. They would get down on their hunkers in the usual manner of miners, trunk fairly erect, knees apart, possibly one leg thrust out, and would rest on the back of a clog. It was a posture difficult to achieve for others not used to the squatting posture demanded when working down a coal-mine, and also it needed a good sense of balance, and, although I often attempted it, a few minutes in that stance tired me.

A street-corner could acquire its own special character and tone over the years and after the Great War this developed at the Big Corner. There were so many members that folk could hardly pass by, with young coal-miners hutched up beside each other, the lads from the spinning room actually sitting on each others' knees, and you had to arrive there early on in the evening to get a look in. The best sitting-down place, for the privileged ones—made up of chaps like Jud Burns, Louis Arpino, Jimmy Fish, Tommy Winstanley, Tommy Jones, and others, a mixed bunch from the pit, mill, and foundry—was up against the wall, and if one of them turned up somebody else less important would be eased out to make room. Also, miners did not care to be crowded in, so that, with a little sharp movement of their hefty clogs, a breathing space could be cleared. Young men who had been in the War returned home—well, some of them did—one or two with a limb missing, and these men were glad of a spot where they could stand or sit, and enjoy a chat and the company of mates. The ex-soldier, or one on leave—many a lad with his mate would decide to join up together after the War was over just for the need of a change—was welcome at the Corner, for such a one could usually tap a new and interesting subject. A silent fellow would be considered 'not much bon', but if he had a good job that might lend weight to his presence. Out-of-works, however, although they had to be accepted, tended to lower the tone, and if there were too many around they kept the steady workers away. The fact was, unemployment had a way of eroding a man's character and making him less desirable to have around. A new character might emerge, one less responsible, often more lively and fluid, not as easy to pin down. But you certainly didn't want a corner made up of chaps 'on the bolsheviks'.

It was always a heartening sight approaching the Corner, especially on a summer evening. I could not get there early enough, and I might even get a seat on the pavement for the first half-hour, but would move to the outside when the young men arrived. One had to approach the Corner warily, since the least sign of anything unusual would be made fun of. A haircut always invited 'pow slaps', which could be unpleasant when a few hard hands began to slap one's newly cropped head. To anyone not handy with repartee the badinage could be something of a trial, and the slow-witted had to cultivate a bellicose manner: 'Shut up afore I bloody shut thee up!' For the average lad the street-corner generated fun and laughter of a sort that enlivened the evenings, and made him more alert than he otherwise might have been, so that he was always on the watch-out for being taken in. Swank or side would be put down at once, for there was an almost obsessional spirit of modesty, which seemed to preclude an advancement of any kind in this world.

There used to visit the Big Corner a man in his late twenties, with pale lean face, striking blue eyes, and an intensely searching gaze. He came from a neighbourhood some streets away where there was no corner gathering, and was known as John Eadie—Eadie being a nickname, on account of a bicycle of that name he had with him. John would sit there silent until the mood came over him to tell one of his many stories. There were a number of war adventures, one of how he fell five hundred feet from an aeroplane, landing with his head on a cannon, and how when he came round someone was offering him a drink of water and John said, 'Never mind me—give it to my officer.' What I liked best were recent ones, about his cat, and also his escapades on his bicycle.

'I wur comin' fru' Leigh on mi Eadie machine last neet,' I recall John once telling us, when a silence had been provided for him, 'when I spotted they were after me.' 'Who—who were after thee?' Once he had got going John did not care for interruptions, but accepted an interested enquiry. 'Who! t'coppers—who else! They've been after me ever since I got the machine. My bike wur the last the firm made afore they went bankrupt. They say King George ordered it for t'Prince of Wales, but somehow the order wur never delivered, so I wur right lucky to get it. Anyway, the coppers wur on their motorbikes after me. I musta been doin' about thirty, so I pedalled up a bit and put my speed up to forty. They drew a bit closer, so I went into top gear an' my speed went up to fifty. They put speed on—so I came down on t'pedals and went up to sixty. I musta been doin' about sixty-five miles an hour when I came through Four Lane Ends—I'd to cut between a wagon an' a car there—you shoulda seen the drivers—bloody eyes poppin' out of their heads! Anyway, by this time I'd shook off the police on their motorbikes, or thought I had, till I cum to Daubhill Station—I wur doin' seventy there—an' I saw a line of coppers across the road—arms joined, see, to stop me. They musta' been on the buzzer, see, fru' Four Lane Ends. Anyway, I weren't goin' to stop—so I puts my head down an' goes right through—' 'Get off, John!—tha didn't!' 'I did. I bloody did. Scattered the lot. They all jumped outa the way,' said John. 'An' then I put on speed proper. I knew I were for it if they copped me. But when I were comin' down Derby Street—I saw it from the Pike View—they'd got t'barriers across the road at Bamber

Street. Musta buzzed through again, dusta see. I'm not sayin' wut speed I wur doin' now—it coulda been anythin' up to or beyond ninety miles an hour.' John looked round for contradiction, but there was none. So he went on: 'I could see wi' the state of the roads it wur no use brakin'. But the road barriers were ten feet high. Solid steel. No bike could crash through them.'

'What didt'do, John?' asked Jud Burns.

'Said his bloody prayers,' said Joney.

John hesitated, decided not to take offence, and went on with his story: 'There wur only one thing to do,' said John. 'Turn left by Sam Yick's laundry an' down Bamber Street.'

'What—turnin' at that speed! Didt'not skid?'

'No. I daresay I woulda done, only I ran up Sam Yick's wall. Tha knows, t'gable-end.'

'Up t'bloody wall on thy bike, John!'

'What else could a man do—goin' at ninety! Bike wur keeled right o'er—wheels wur hardly touchin' t'floor—an' there wur nothin' for it but run up t'bloody wall. So's I went along t'wall, down t'backyard wall, an' bang on t'sideset an' away . . .'

John always spoke with a serious air, and his gaze would occasionally be turned scrutinizingly upon us; if he caught the least glimmer of a grin on any face he would shut up at once. I was never one to be caught, for those stern blue eyes put all thought of levity out of my mind. The offender would have to apologize and explain that it was nothing to do with John's recountal that brought to his face what could be mistaken for a grin. John did not accept excuses and with winks and nods the guilty party would be made to sit a few feet away, so that John could get on with one of his favourite stories about Henry, his tomcat.

'I chanced one time to say to Frank Sixsmith—you all know Frank, so's you can ask him if you doubt my word— that our Henry had never messed in t'house—never—an' that he'd as lief die than mess inside, an' Sixsmith bet me half a dollar as Henry would wet t'place if I didn't let him out, an' I took him on, so Sixsmith said he'd come int'ouse to make sure. But I'd stipulated no time limit, see, that wur my mistake—an' owd Sixsmith stayed on three bloody days an' nights. Kept brewin' up tea, an' never took his eyes off old Henry. Any one of you can go an' knock on his door an' ask him, an' he'll tell you every word is gospel. It wur breakin' my heart it wur, the way Henry was hoppin' fro' toe to toe against door, pullin' at mi pants, fair cryin' out to be let out. He even tried to run up t'chimney once. Scorched hissel' he did. But he never made a mess. Till at last came the third day, an' he could stand it no longer, he ran into the kitchen an' we both followed him, poor Henry fair wailing he were—I should never have let him go on that long, I shoulda called off the bet t'first night—an' he jumped up into t'slopstone an' peed down t'sinkhole. By gum, but he went on for some time—musta been a good five minutes. So Sixsmith turned to me an' says: "I reckon I've won mi bet." I had the half-crown in mi pocket, but then what does Henry do but get his front claws up on the tap, an' he starts pullin' away at it with all his might. Owd Sixsmith couldn't tak' his eyes off him. At last he just managed to turn it, an' he stood perched there ont'edge of t'slopstone with watter runnin' until it were all washed away. "Nay," says owd Sixsmith, as I wur handin' him the money, "I won't tak' thy half a dollar—not after seeing that."'

John told us that every evening after tea, when the *Evening News* had been delivered, he would make himself comfortable in his rocking-chair with the newspaper, and Henry would jump up and start reading with him. 'But how dusta know for certain thy cat's readin', John?' Joney once asked him. 'I don't know for *certain* he is,' said John, 'but if tha sees a chap with a newspaper in front of him, starin' at it, startin' at the top where the headline is, and his gaze comin' down as he reads each line, tha takes it that he's readin'—an' since that's exactly what our Henry does I tak' it that he's readin'. Then I might be mista'en, he might only be coddin' me, but here's another sign; in some ways he seems a quicker reader, an' when he gets through a page down goes his paw, an' he wants to turn over but I don't. Henry's not interested in the

racin' results or owt like that—although he'll read about
football an' the Wanderers, but the one thing that does interest him, and he can't get enough of it, is the Prince of Wales.
As soon as he sees yon chap's physog' in a picture he can't
tak' his eyes off 'im, he seems to stare at it hypnotized, an'
he'll keep reading all the news about him—sometimes twice
o'er. Now last night—or was it the night before—I wouldn't
be certain—anyway, some of you musta seen it—there wur
this picture of the Prince of Wales opening a new college or
summat at Oxford. Anyway, Henry is there on my lap, but
kind of standing up, reading all about it, an' lookin' at t'picture when the next thing the gas starts goin' out, needed a
penny, dusta see, so I pretends I don't notice, just to see what
Henry 'ud do. So he looks up at me, then tugs my sleeve, an' I
feels in my pocket an' gets a penny. So Henry puts his mouth
t'ord me, opens it, picks up the penny between his teeth, then
jumps down, goes straight across to the gas meter, opens
door, turns his head to get penny int'slot, and turns th'andle
so's penny drops—and t'light comes up and he comes
boundin' back on my knee—'

  There were some gasps of apparent astonishment. 'But
howd on a minute, John,' said Jud Burns, '—Henry needn't
have bothered need he—I mean I always understood as cats
can see in the dark? Eh chaps?' Murmurs of agreement as we
all turned to see how John would handle this. 'Aye,' agreed
John, never a flicker of doubt or a smile, 'of course a cat can
see in the dark. Any fool knows that. A cat might *see* but it
can't *read* in the dark. Listen, Jud, thee write up to any
newspaper or ask any doctor an' I'll bet thee all the money
tha likes they'll all tell thee the same—that no cat can read in
the dark.'

A one-time outsider who became a colourful figure at our
Corner was Joney, whose family lived in Maybank Street and
could have passed as rather posh, for he had a sister who was
a teacher. Joney had worked in the spinning room up to the
age of twenty, and at that time had all the social signs that
distinguished him from a street-corner youth—the clean look

and quiet voice and manner, unargumentative and civil; but he had got fed up with the spinning and had gone working down the mine. He was one that survived the ordeal, and his personality took on some substance. He worked with Louis Arpino, who introduced him to the Corner, where Tommy, or Joney as he was called, was fairly soon accepted. There may have been a touch of snobbery that someone of a better class—whose houses had a front parlour, used only at weekends—should wish to join the Big Corner. Joney was a lively talker but no show-off and, although he wore an old navy-blue serge suit—which could have passed as a weekend suit—he toned his appearance down by wearing pit clogs with it; apart from knowing a few tales, he could play the mouth-organ brilliantly, was said to be a star pianist, and could compose songs. He had had one published—by a vanity publisher, I gather, who had told him it would make a fortune—'Will you be my Girl?' It was in impressive music folios, which stated clearly on the front: 'Words and Music by Thomas Jones.' I recall staring at it with admiration and reading the lyric he had written: 'Your eyes are just like diamonds, | Your teeth are just like pearl, | I want to ask you a little question, | Will you be my girl?'

Another odd chap who was fully accepted was Bobby, who lived up Higher Swan Lane and was said to 'have letters behind his name'. He was a bachelor in his thirties, who drank but was quiet and unobtrusive, and it seemed he only sought out the male street-corner company after having had a few drinks; because of his superior education, voice, and manner he was welcomed as an adjudicator, for wrangling of a sort was the main form of exchange. There was a fierce eschatological argument raging late one summer evening, on which Bobby was asked to give his opinion: was there life after death? Bobby hesitated for a time: 'I don't wish to offend anyone,' he said, in his cultured manner, 'or speak against anyone's religious beliefs.'

'Carry on—out wi' it,' Joney said. 'Tha can't offend any of us—for where there's no sense there's no bloody feelin'.' Jud Burns said: 'Say what you've a mind Bobby, so long as it's the truth.' Bobby looked round at us apologetically: 'Er, I remember I once played Hamlet at—'

'Never mind what tha bloody played,' said Joney, 'give us th'answer: is there life after death?'

'I—I believe Shakespeare may have it,' said Bobby, as he closed his eyes for a moment, and then began to recite dreamily to the half-dozen of us who were left there around ten o'clock: '"To die, to sleep; | To sleep: perchance to dream: ay, there's the rub; | For in that sleep of death what dreams may come | When we have shuffled off this mortal coil | Must give us pause."' As Bobby pauses I feel inside me gurgles of reverent joy at the simple poetry of the English language. '"There's the respect | That makes calamity of so long life: | For who would bear—"'

'Come on, Bobby—out wi' it,' cuts in Joney, '—do we bloody live after we bloody die? Is there a 'eaven or 'ell—or are we bloody done with?'

'Now, Joney, don't thee interrupt the man,' says Jud Burns. 'Right, Bobby, thee carry on—in thy own time.'

Bobby gives his gentle smile, and begins once more: '"For who would bear the whips and scorns of time, | The oppressor's wrong, the proud man's contumely, | The pangs of dispriz'd love, the law's delay—"' I try to stem up the beautiful flow in my mind, fearful I might lose a word of it.

'Oh bloody 'ell,' sighs Joney, '—all we want to know is there life after—'

'Will tha shut thy kisser,' says Jud Burns. 'He wur just gettin' goin' when tha 'ad to interrupt. Right, Bobby.'

Bobby looks round, and begins once more: '"The insolence of office, and the spurns | That patient merit of the unworthy takes, | When he himself might his quietus make | With a bare bodkin?"'

'His bloody what make with a bare bodkin?' cuts in Joney.

'Aye,' says Jud, 'I were a bit fogged mysel' theer—'

'Quietus,' explains Bobby, 'means "he is quit" or discharged. From life in this instance.'

'Aye, he's kicked the soddin' bucket,' says Jud. 'I see. We've got thee.'

'With a bloody bare bodkin?' asks Joney.

'It's a sharp instrument used for making holes in cloth,' says Bobby.

'A bodkin's like a heavy needle', says Ned Garstang, 'for making hems.'

'Does he mean that if a chap feels that way inclined he sticks it in his bloody self,' says Joney, 'to do hisself in?'

Bobby nods: 'Exactly.'

'Then why the hell doesn't he just say so,' says Joney, 'instead of beatin' about the bloody bush!'

'Do you mind,' says Jud to Joney. 'Right, Bobby, off we go again—we're learnin'.'

Bobby is thrown by the interruption for the moment, and his eye happens to light on mine. I cue him at once: '"When he himself might his quietus make,"' I speak out, '"With a bare bodkin?"'

'Good lad, Bill,' says Jud Burns.

Bobby smiles: 'Thank you.' And goes on, '"Who would fardels bear —"'

'Fardels!' interrupts Joney once more, '—what's a bloody fardel?'

Jud Burns gives Joney a look, and I give a supporting glance, although secretly I'm obliged for I have no idea what a fardel is, but it seems that with Shakespeare you don't have to know the meaning, the feeling is enough.

'A fardel,' says Bobby, 'I believe a fardel is a burden or a bundle or some kind.'

'Aye, summat as weighs a chap down,' says Jud Burns, making out he already knew. 'Carry on, Bobby.'

'"Who would fardels bear,"' Bobby begins one more, '"To grunt and sweat under a weary life, | But that dread of something after death—"'

'Bloody Norah—' sighs Joney, 'how much bloody longer!' He lets out a groan: 'I can't bloody stand much more o' this.'

'Then sling thy soddin' hook,' says Jud Burns. 'But, Bobby, not to hurry thee, mate, tha knows what I mean—but if tha could come more to the point like—'

'I'm almost at it,' says Bobby, and drones on in his

melancholy voice: '"The undiscover'd country from whose bourn—"'

'From whose bloody what?' interrupts Joney

'Whose *bourn*,' says Bobby, getting a bit huffy, 'whose bourn means whose bounds or limits.'

'Why the—' begins Joney, but Jud Burns cuts him off again with a look and raises a hand for him to be quiet: 'Right, Bobby,' he says. Bobby looks at me and I respond, '"But that dread of something after death—"' I speak out in a clear voice. This and the interruptions seem to put Bobby on his mettle, to prompt him into the role of Hamlet, for now he straightens up, pauses, fixes us all, and especially Joney, with his eye, and then declaims in slow and sonorous tones, '"*The undiscover'd country from whose bourn* | *No traveller returns*—"'

For moments there is silence. Bobby, Jud, and all of us, even Joney, seem to be thinking of death. 'That's how Shakespeare put it,' adds Bobby, '"The undiscovered country from whose bourn | No traveller returns." What more can one say?'

I am deeply moved by the poetry, but believe I could give them the true answer from the teaching of the Holy Catholic Church: 'Eternal rest give to them, O Lord: and let perpetual light shine upon them.' However, I feel that the language makes up for the error in faith. I go over in my mind the words of Shakespeare as I walk slowly home, seemingly aware of new vistas of the imagination, reaching out beyond the rows of small houses and the nearby cotton mills, and I am still whispering them to myself before I go to sleep, 'The undiscover'd country from whose bourn—No traveller returns.' Why should he, it strikes me, if he is in God's care in heaven?

23

The Secret Aspiration

I KEPT up my secret nursing of the sainthood aspiration, and the more I thought it over the harder it was to imagine how anyone in his right mind would wish to become anything but a saint. What was up with everybody—*Eternal life*, wasn't that the only goal worth striving for! What was the use of worldly riches and honours—since the moment you drew your last breath they were like a soap bubble that had burst. 'Rejoice,' our Lord had told us, 'for a great reward is prepared for you in heaven.' The lowliest saint in heaven, I figured, was surely in a standing utterly beyond that of king, emperor, or even pope. In place of aiming to become a railway clerk or getting a job at the Co-op or trying to get taken on at the loco' yard and working up to being an engine-driver—none of which one was likely to achieve anyway—why not go all out for the top prize! To become a saint you had no need to learn how to talk posh, or suck up to folk above you, or join the boy scouts or boys' brigade, or any of that sort of carry on, since sainthood was free of worldly influence. Everyone toed the same mark, began at the same starting-point of original sin—Catholics had an advantage here, through the sacrament of Baptism, but then more would be expected by God of us—so that the prince in his palace had no better chance of succeeding than some poor old tramp down in a hedge ('What each man is in God's sight, that he is and no more'); nor did you need to keep nagging yourself to get a move on or be in any way spry or clever to become a saint, for saints were known to be simple—that was going to be a problem for me but I would work at it—and in the saintly vocation you need have no fear of getting the sack, for sin, the one impediment to heaven, could—apart from the

wonderful sacrament of Penance—be forgiven by a short Act
of Contrition: 'O my God, because Thou art so good, I am
very sorry that I have sinned against Thee, and I will not sin
again.'

Sainthood was something you could accomplish all on
your own (with the aid of God's love, of course, which, it was
known, He bestowed in abundance), if you were so minded,
which I definitely was. I might not be able to stand pain like
my noble St Francis but could I emulate the saint of my native
land—'I am Patrick a poor sinner'—and I became eager to get
going. What was needed were faith, hope, and charity (and
who but a right scallywag would be without them), these
three spragged up, as it were, by numerous good works ('She
hath opened her hand to the needy, stretched out her hands
to the poor, and hath not eaten her bread idle'). Pride—
Lucifer's sin and a stumbling block for many aspirants—was
no problem for me, since I felt free of sanctimony, had little
desire to impress or appear pious, no wish to become a priest,
monk, or even an altar boy, nor the least hankering for
recognition after death, beatification or canonization or that
sort of thing. The world could forget me after my receiving
the Last Sacrament and departing. My wish was to slip into
heaven unnoticed—to escape from the almost incessant din
of Bolton into any quiet little corner of God's kingdom would
suit me perfectly—and become one of God's lowly saints,
untalked of and unsung ('Grant that I may love Thee always,'
was the supplication, uttered during the Stations of the Cross,
which most moved my heart, 'and then do with me what
Thou wilt').

I wouldn't mind, of course, if God discovered me and, like
Ben Adhem, Bill Naughton's name led all the rest, but that
was up to Him. I'd be content to end up as one who had set
out to fight the good fight, and despite a falter and scratch or
two along the way had somehow ended up on the right side.
It seemed a far likelier bet than that of becoming a skilled
man. Also, whilst I was useless with a spanner or file, I had
got the odd sense of some deeper or rather different seam of
reality, a glimpse of which might break in at Communion,

making it obvious that the daily round, although it had to be got through, was but a kind of playacting compared with it. The way to go about it, I told myself, would be to carry on outwardly like an ordinary lad, go about whistling and kicking tin cans around as though I hadn't a care in the world, and perhaps even listen to tales at the street-corner—I didn't wish to become conspicuous—but maybe not tell as many, stand up and fight if forced to, so that no one would ever suspect. At the same time, I decided, I would keep some little spot of soul pure and white, to surrender up to God and His holy angels on Judgement Day—and stand meekly aside for my celestial reward: if not eternal bliss at least infinite peace and quiet.

The more I thought it over the less exacting it appeared for one such as I took myself to me, a lad with his head screwed on, as they said (the tricky thing was keeping it all secret). Being Irish could for once prove a help, since the Irish child was reared with an innate sense of being one of the family, was expected to behave sensibly without being told, and mostly he responded to his obligations, at the worst being ashamed not to do so: 'Aren't you ashamed of yourself—' was one of the most cutting remarks that could be made to me. No matter how much I might dislike my father's cranky presence around the house, I never for a moment forgot that he was my father, and also that his bad temper had to do with the kind of man he was and the hard work he did, and it would not occur to me deliberately to annoy him or neglect to go and kiss him when he was going off to the pit in the evening, even when I was out and had to go and kiss him in the street, which embarrassed both of us (the English did not kiss nearly as often as the Irish and boys stared at me with surprise when I left some game to do so, although no one remarked on it). Neither would I have criticized him to anyone except Mother; to do so outside the home would be unthinkable. Irish children such as myself were rarely mischievous—in fact the word itself was never used among the Irish (it seemed enough trouble would come one's way without having to go out and seek it). I could not understand the mentality of those who got pleasure from taking a rise out of others, nor the motive behind the boys' games intended to annoy some householder, such as that of the tying together of two front door-handles, and then knocking on each door; instead of seeing any fun in it, I would always imagine the elderly couple—for such were usually the victims—going about their domestic tasks, and being disturbed in this absurd fashion. In time I grew almost ashamed of my Irish response to every grown-up person, which was one of friendly respect, and especially so to the old, for many of my street-corner pals regarded such behaviour as weakness—being nice when you had no need to be. The sight of a boy tugging the legs off a spider, removing wings from a flying insect, or any of the wanton acts of cruelty that certain boys seemed to be drawn to, distressed me. The breaking of windows in empty houses or the throwing of stones at the four glass panels at the top of the lamp-post which protected the gas mantle— in which some boys took a savage pleasure—seemed to be a violation of some law-abiding instinct, and I kept away from such activities, considering them a kind of boyish lunacy.

It was rare that an impulse of actual dishonesty came to me, and even if hungry I could safely be left in charge of piles of sweets, chocolates, or delicacies of any kind. Indeed, the demarcation of what was mine and what not was so marked in the matter of money that, if I found a penny or a sixpence in the roadway, I at once set out to find the owner; so cumbersome were the effects of conscience on me after such a find that in time I almost preferred to walk past some coin I might spot in the gutter rather than go through the agonies of worry as to whose coin it was I had in my pocket. In the home I made the very rare pilfering—never money but sometimes an orange or the like. (Recently I was awake during the night and, thinking of the past, recalled having stolen a large juicy pear, intended for my father to take to pit with him; I found myself, sixty years later, suffused with shame at the memory of being found out, for I had denied having done it.) Also, I found myself to be more mature than most boys. There was some notion, which I gathered from reading magazine stories, that normal healthy lads detested water and liked to go about unwashed; since I enjoyed getting rid of grime and sweat, and delighted in being fresh and clean, I decided that any lad who lived in Bolton and did not relish such a feeling must be a bit soft in the head.

What I couldn't quite make out was why I should be the only one around that seemed to be going in for sainthood. Often at the midday break I would sneak into the church to say a prayer and have a whispered chat with Our Lord, or His Holy Mother, or Saint Anthony or Saint Francis, and I would be the only one in the vast church. I wonder could they all be like me, I thought; they don't want to give the game away, or perhaps get too many runners spoiling the field. Nor was this mission toward the blessed state all anticipatory, something to look forward to far away in the future, as so many mistakenly imagined, for twice a week I banked on getting a smack of celestial joy. That was the thing nobody ever seemed to understand—how after a time it really wasn't the promised reward one was after, not even the resurrection of the body on doomsday, nor heaven itself, as wonderful as all this was going to be, but that most simple stab of delight which entered the heart on sensing God's presence there.

The fresh savour of it would often be on Friday evenings, when one emerged with a cool sweet flush from the confessional box, all sins having been recounted in a clear voice, forgiven and mostly forgotten, and then, modestly avoiding the gaze of other penitents stained with sin and waiting to confess and be absolved, go tripping across the aisle to the big long main pews, kneel and carefully say one's penance, usually throwing in an extra couple out of generosity. (It seemed I was getting a right good bargain from God, His forgiving all my sins for the usual penance of three Hail Marys and three Our Fathers. I had a suspicion that maybe He was just that bit simple-minded, as was the case with so many nice folk, so that I didn't want to take advantage and drive too close a deal with Him.)

Then up and off, feeling wonderfully light, the great load of sin banished, the soul beautifully white once more, the heart full of thanks. Pausing at the holy water font, dipping the right hand in and taking a generous wetting with which to bless myself on the forehead ('The water that flows over the tips of our fingers', says St Augustine, 'washes away the last trace of our impurities'), I would step lightly out of the porch and into the world of Bolton, almost regretting that there were no lions or other wild beasts of Nero's to tackle, just to let them see that the spirit of the glorious Christian martyrs was not entirely dead, and then I would pull up my slack stockings to the knee, and endeavour to look like a mundane mortal, which was perhaps not too hard, in spite of my seraphic glow.

The second experience was on Sunday morning at receiving Holy Eucharist. There was the long Saturday night of expectancy—unless I kept myself to myself it seemed that at such devout periods I was inclined to get into rows with my sister May and others not so inwardly exalted, for in a pursuit so serious as that of everlasting bliss I learnt that it was not easy to suffer fools gladly—followed by the early morning fast. I seemed to sense the true feeling only at that moment when I knelt at the communion rail, the background filled with the congregation of voices singing 'Sweet Sacrament Divine', inside me the involuntary whispering of the familiar morning prayers which seemed to fit every occasion: 'Jesus, Mary, an' Joseph, I give you my heart and my soul | Jesus, Mary, an' Joseph, assist me in my last agony | Jesus, Mary an' Joseph, may I breathe forth my soul in peace with you.' Then the priest drawing closer with the chalice, and now he is serving the communicant next to me, so head back, eyes closed, mouth open wide, tongue thrust forward to receive the Sacred Host, and the swift comforting drone as the peaceful wafer is place firmly on my tongue: 'Corpus Domini nostri Jesu Christi custodiat animam tuam in vitam aeternam, Amen.' And I am filled with a special intimate happiness as Christ enters, body and soul, and I become one with God and God becomes one with me in a brief rapture. It is a magical sensation, like a heavenly dream, and I try to hold off that moment when ordinary awareness edges in and brings me back into the common world. As in a dream, once the senses break in the spirit must evaporate—perhaps flow upwards from whence it came.

I would often roam about the neighbourhood—I was interested in everything and everybody I saw—and size up this, that, and the other one, and consider their chances of getting to heaven. There were, for instance, the various rag-and-bone men, wheeling their handcarts along the narrow back streets, proclaiming their calling with loud unearthly wails: 'Ee, ragabone ... donkey stone, yellow stone an' rubbin' stone, ee, ragabone ...!' Some of them employed a form of plainsong for greater effect, leading off with a distinct labionasal note on the opening 'Ee'—the sound intensified by the two huge and horny hands employed as a megaphone round the mouth—and the bizarre ululation would issue forth from between the lines of privy closets (there was one woman totter who could be heard miles away on Rivington Pike—or so they reckoned), to be followed by a nimble articulation of 'donkey stone, rubbin' stone an' yellow stone!' This latter part was often pitched to create an antiphonal effect, as though there were two callers, one giving the response to the other—which mournful appeal would take on the intonation of a Gregorian chant, bestirring housewives, who would scutter forth bearing armfuls of old pit clothes, worn-out skirts, and the like, with the odd one humping a burst mattress or broken bedstead. There was one certain ragman, so eloquent of voice and at times producing such rich floating tones, that one would imagine a fragment of High Mass had escaped into the backstreet. Mother would grab some old clothes and thrust them at me the moment she heard him, but somehow I almost never caught up with this fugitive character. It seemed that once he had made his final invocation he would be off, and either he was stone deaf or just came out for the chant itself, for no matter how loud I and some of the neighbours called out after him he would not stop, but would hurriedly disappear round the top of the backstreet with his rag cart.

'Poor chap,' some woman would say, 'he musta run out of rubbin' stones.'

In the front streets I'd be watching the hawkers with their pony carts, and these men went in for an honest bawling, 'Finest King Edward's—five poun' for thri'pence!—who's for King Edward's whilst they last?' There was also the washing-liquor man, with a homemade box-trolley which he trundled along the sideset, and at the same time let out his shrill cry: 'Washin' liquor, ladies! finest washin' liquor—who wants washin' liquor?' There was the black-pea seller, with an old baby-carriage in which he kept a huge pan hot; it gave off a rich enticing aroma on the cool evening air when he removed the lid to ladle out a penn'orth and he used to yell: 'Peas all 'ot—peas all 'ot!—bring your money an' you'll get a good lot!'

The crumpet man also came early evening, with his bell and husky murmur, basket balanced on his head: 'Crumpets!—now, ladies, who says for a nice fresh crumpet? Muffins!—who says for a good fresh muffin? Anybody fancy an oatcake—five for tuppence!' There were many more: Sabini's, with the lively pony in the ice-cream cart, came all through the summer, and there was a knife-sharpener, also the organ-grinder, numerous street singers and others. I might even wander abroad a little on my ruminations and take in navvies and roadmenders at work, or groups of black-faced coal-miners jumping off the Four Lane Ends tram with a noisy clatter of clogs, or see the hordes of mill workers come flooding out of the mill gates, and always it would come round to the same question: Now why don't they all just give up this mad struggle and set their sights on the next world and heavenly bliss! Have they never considered eternity, perpetuity, *in saecula saeculorum* (he'd be a mind-less Catholic child who failed to take in the odd scrap of Latin)? They moved speedily along the streets, each one it seemed had some purpose in mind: how is it, I would ask myself, that these people seem so occupied they haven't time to give a thought to their own Creator! Can it be that I am the only one in this town to have seen the Light? Maybe it's true that poor old Ireland is not only *Tir nan Og*—Land of the Young—but also the Land of Saints and Scholars, for their like seems rare enough in Bolton.

24

Temptations of the Flesh

COUSIN JOHN, my mother's nephew, who lived with us, went over to work in the Yorkshire coalfields in 1923; he had friends there and the pay was better. I missed his Irish presence about the house, and also the pleasure I got from being around when he and Mother were having a chat. However Cousin Willie, his elder brother, made a visit to our home every week—always the Irish way of coming just when he felt like it. Mother seemed to prefer this, since she could usually sense when he would turn up, although it varied. He was happily married to a Lancashire woman called Sarah, from the mining village of Daisy Hill, a few miles away, but it seemed that he had need to have an Irish chat with my mother now and again.

Now that John had left us, I moved from sleeping at the foot of the bed which I shared with my sister May to the back bedroom to sleep with my brother Edward. He was seventeen, four years older than I, and we were unalike in our tastes and interests, except for music. He was a shop assistant at the Maypole Dairy, and unlike me had never stood at a street-corner or mixed with mill workers. Nor did he figure much in our family life since he worked until eight o'clock, after which he usually had some girlfriend to meet, and came home late. He was what would be called a bit of a masher in those days, for he gave considerable attention to his clothes. When he went out on Sunday afternoons, carrying his violin case—he was a member of the PSA orchestra (Pleasant Sunday Afternoon)—he wore a smart suit, dark overcoat, trilby hat, patent leather shoes, and fawn spats. He looked such a toff that I always avoided being at the Big Corner when he passed by.

Edward wasn't a bad fiddle-player—'violinist' was the word he always used—but had a mannerism of pulling his mouth to one side as he played, in a way of indicating the skills he was putting into the performance, and this rather put one off. Our most intimate moments were at weekends, when he had to be home by ten o'clock or so, since my father was not at work, and he got annoyed if any of us came in late; Mother never bothered. Then Edward and I would retire together, and, after playing a tune on his violin, he would come to bed and in the darkness start humming, whistling, and lilting his favourite pieces. He was fond of marches, such as 'Old Comrades,' but 'Coppelia,' 'Souvenir', and 'Les Millions d'Arlequin' were the ones I liked best. He might go on for half an hour or so, before he tired and we said 'Good-night—God bless' to each other, and turned back to back.

I was glad to have the bedroom to myself for an hour or two every evening, which meant I could do my exercises. I had become enthusiastic about physical culture, as it was called. I had come to realize that if you were one who did not enjoy fighting—and I did not—and were not prepared to submit—which I wasn't—you had better develop the strength to scare off opponents, for not a day passed without some challenge or other. The respective fighting prowess of yourself and any boy you encountered had to be tacitly taken into account at once, and that understanding would form a key factor in your relationship. When I found myself in a mock wrestle with another boy, I would face him and get a grip on the nape of his neck with my left hand; then, when I saw the opportunity, I would pull his head towards me, and at the same time put my right arm round his head, and with a twist of my body to the left pull his head down against my right side, holding it thrust hard against my hip, my hands clasped in the 'sailor's grip'. Almost no boy could escape from that. But I never actually made a boy submit, preferring to give him what might persuade him was only a taste of what I was capable of.

Most evenings I did half an hour of press-ups and leg and abdominal exercises on the floor—which I had picked up from reading a magazine, *Health and Strength*—before kneeling, saying my prayers, and getting into bed. Out in the backyard I had made a punch-ball from an old stocking, which I had packed tight with newspaper and hung on a piece of rope from the clothes-line. Mother had bought a fourpenny disk of what looked like camphor from a pedlar at the door—she refused no one if she had the coppers—but the paper it was wrapped in stated that it was concentrated ozone, identical to that of the Swiss alps or the ocean, so that for fourpence the purchaser would inhale this health-giving oxygen which others paid huge sums to enjoy. 'Ta, Mam,' I said to her, 'it was very good of you, but why didn't you buy half a dozen?' I had it hanging from the back window, and would do my deep-breathing exercises in front of it. I was always on the look-out for high horizontal surfaces of any kind, which I could grip with my hands and muscle myself up. In the front kitchen—the room in which we lived, sat, ate, and cooked—there was a very old-fashioned clothes-airing rack. This was not the usual kind seen in most homes, which had three or four wooden rails, and could be conveniently let down from below the ceiling by a pulley rope, secured whilst the housewife placed the ironed shirts and tablecloths on it, then pulled up in place to allow them to air. Ours consisted of a pair of iron fixtures, set into the ceiling about nine feet apart, each with a central bar opening into three appendages; at the bottom of each was a slot, into which were fitted three stout wooden rails. It was immovable—or so I imagined— and my mother had to stand on a chair to reach it; after she had carefully wiped each wooden rail—because of the coal-fire in the range they got dusty—I would hand up to her the various laundered articles.

One evening when the lines were empty, and my father had gone off to the mine, I got on a stool, gripped the lowest rail, and started muscling myself up. It was an ideal cross-bar, so to speak, for the exercise. Then, as I was pulling myself up, there was a wrenching sound, and the next moment the entire line, fixtures, plaster, and all, came crashing down from the ceiling. I got a nasty knock on the head, but never felt any

pain, so aghast was I at the shocking mess I had made. 'The
Lord save us,' called my mother, 'are you hurt at all?' I said I
wasn't, although I felt a bruise on my head. 'Don't worry,'
she said, for she would never scold if she saw any one of us
upset, 'I'll think of something.' 'One of these fine days', said
my sister May, 'he'll have the flamin' house down on top of
us all.' I dreaded what my father would say when he came
home from work next day, but Mother handled the situation:
'I was just hanging up a few clothes,' she said, 'when it came
crashin' down.' 'It was a lucky thing altogether', remarked
my father, 'that you weren't killed—God be thanked.' She
never hesitated to trot out a white lie to shield one of us from
my father's temper; and now she gave me a quick wink and
smile, for like any woman who has to butter up a man she
seemed to regard my father as being a bit wet behind the ears.

There was an old swivel looking-glass in the bedroom—
brother Edward had need of it when dressing—and one evening after my exercises, when I had rubbed myself down with a
towel, I went and looked into it. I could hardly believe what I
saw, as I expanded my chest, flexed my arm muscles, and
gazed with satisfaction at myself: by gum, I thought, I'm not
only on the right track for heaven, but if this goes on I'm
going to be a real muscle man on earth. I could feel the male
nature stirring to life in my veins. And I was secretly delighted
at the sudden increase in strength that went with it; boys I
had once had difficulties with when wrestling I could now put
on the ground in a trice. Along beside this burst of virility,
with the black silky hairs sprouting on either side of my
upper lip, and curly hair appearing around the secret organs
of my body, there arose in me new and alarming sensations,
feelings, and thoughts.

It seemed that I suddenly became obsessed by what had up
to then been a word of little significance—*sex*. Apart from the
rare encounter with such girls as Lizzie, mostly it had been
associated with telling tales at the Corner, but now, as soon
as those three letters caught my eye, I at once became fascinated; I searched the library for books on the human body,
and the one chapter I looked for first was that about sex.

Certain words began to suggest a new meaning and imagery; *concupiscence* took on a meatier stamp than merely impure thoughts—which was what we had been taught for Confession—and with it *prurience, debauchery,* and *lasciviousness,* words which fairly reeked of sex and sinfulness. They seemed to be taking over in my mind from the good words I had liked, such as *chaste, pure, stoical,* and *devout.*

There were the oddest sexual antics going on all over the place. Billy Taylor and his mate Roland, two quiet lads, had two girls, Hilda and Doris, in Billy's home on a Saturday night, and they had actually spanked the girls' bottoms with baking tins. But why baking tins? I asked. Well, Billy explained, his mam had been baking that day, and had left the tins over the oven, so they were handy. All the lads laughed, but I couldn't get the picture out of my mind— especially when I saw Hilda and Doris on their way to work.

There was a married man called Wilfred, living at the top end of our street, with a wife, Amy, a weaver, crippled in the left leg; since they have no family, and the two of them are working, they are quite well off and seemed very respectable, but to my surprise I hear that for some time Wilfred has been 'doing that there', as they put it, with more than one young mill girl, and he has actually got one into trouble—and she a Catholic girl I know well. I can't imagine any girl fancying a fellow like Wilfred, a tall pale man with a weak friendly grin, cross-eyed but hiding it by wearing fancy specs with a little spring that clips across the bridge of his nose. Now how can a chap like that get such nice girls, I ask, and always young ones? I'm told it's because he's got a funny little *cooing* sound in his voice that the wenches can't resist. There are all manner of tricks going on in dark backstreets and behind closed doors, of a kind I could never have imagined. Just below the surface of what had seemed an ordinary world of folk going backwards and forwards to work there was a vast stewpot of sex simmering away. And, from what I could judge, it was the nice quiet sort of chaps with pale faces who were the worst of the lot.

Then there's Joe Hilton, a young coal-miner who lives with

his widowed mother in our street, and who works on the day
shift, and around three o'clock any afternoon can be seen and
heard plonking home from pit in his heavy clogs, his face as
black as can be except for his lips, just like any other miner.
But at six o'clock most evenings a different Joe emerges,
wearing his indigo serge suit, smart cap, tan shoes, and a
greenish shirt. His eyelashes are dark, but this, I am told, is
not from coal-dust but mascara; he has a rosy spot on either
cheek of the pale face of the miner, and his lips are red—
rouge and lipstick, they tell me. I have known Joe for years,
of course, and I like him, a smiling man, who always smells
nice as he is going by. I now learn he is going to join a
company of friends, all men, who congregate beside the
market hall, and never bother with girls. Young boys often
call after him, 'Paint an' powder!' But such ones are
quietened by the men who are miners: 'Shut thi gob, lad,'
says Jud Burns. 'Sarves thee reet if he comes back an' dings
thy earhole for thee!'

It seems that Joe is only one of a number of such men who
prefer men to women. There's Samson's son from the
draper's shop, and his tall slim pal from the Co-op tailors,
and there's plump Billy from Can Row, with his large lower
jaw, big teeth with gold fillings, and high happy laugh, which
he lets out and at the same time hugs himself and lisps, 'Oh
my Christ!' Billy likes to join the lads at the Corner for a spell
before going in home, dressing up, and going out with his
particular man friend. One evening I heard Jimmy Fish
remark: 'I wonder what they get up to—all bloody men on
their own!' And Jud Burns said, 'They aren't playin' soddin'
tiddleywinks all neet—tha can bet thy life on that.'

I soon became aware that I was not to be allowed the fun
and enjoyment of tales and titillations of sex without getting
caught up in the mire myself. Images of plump female figures,
mostly half-naked, began to infest my imagination. They
came so close up to me, images so real that I could almost feel
and smell them, that they became more substantial than
women around the street. I had always regarded myself as
clean-living and clean-limbed, or that way on, but now felt

myself to be a dirty little tick, itching to know all there was to know about sex. I tried to shut out of my mind the sixth beatitude, 'Blessed are the clean of heart, for they shall see God,' for it seemed that I couldn't keep my eyes, let alone my mind, off women. Not young girls but big busty women—those were the exciting ones.

On my way to school every weekday morning there was always one woman down on her knees mopping the doorstep and front of the surgery of Mr Wood the dental surgeon in Derby Street. She was not typical of the Bolton woman cleaner, a respectable figure, often a widow, wearing a long dark skirt coming down to her clog tops, scrubbing and stoning steps and flags as though born for that very task. My temptress was a bulging woman of around thirty, with reddish, uncombed hair; she wore an old shrunken wool dress, short at the bottom and loose at the top, which, when she was leaning forward from within the doorway to mop beyond the step, opened wide, revealing a dark cavern of naked bosom. Women's breasts, the large loose ones, were a fount of imagery for me. I had the notion that their size and swing betokened the sexual pleasure the woman had enjoyed. Clearly she wallowed in it if her breasts were anything to go by. After that swift absorbing look I would walk on to school, lost in a feast of fantasy of myself lying beside her and she snuggling my face down between her paps: *a sin*! my conscience would suddenly cry out—even silently mouthing such a vulgar word.

On other mornings she would kneel on the area beyond the step, with her backside facing the street, revealing her fleshy legs, and the slack garters slipping down below the knee—in Ireland she would be known as a strooleen. She always had the same sleepy look, as though she had struggled out of bed and dressed in the dark, and as I went by it seemed I could smell the sleep on her. She never scrubbed like other cleaners, never took up a rubbing-stone, but mopped in a languid and grudging manner. It often seemed that she was lurking there on her fat knees waiting for me passing by. That was the moment for her to stretch forward as far as she could, displaying her legs, right up to the skimpy bloomers she wore, which were partly torn. I had a feeling that such a sloppy and seemingly heedless woman knew far more than would appear, and that secretly, although her back was turned to me, she knew exactly what was going on in my mind and all the rest of me. Front or back, it was a shameless display for an adolescent Catholic boy to get an eyeful of on his way to school of a morning. The sight I took in as my footsteps faltered when passing by was one that imprinted itself on my mind, and brought about a spasmodic jerking up of my member. She had holes in the heel of her stockings, and, as her feet left the old shoes, the manner in which she sported those two round bare woman's heels seemed provocative beyond belief. I would continue on my way to school, feeling flushed, shaken, and disturbed. So this is it, I would think to myself, what the holy men had in mind when they spoke of the 'temptations of the flesh'. Who'd have thought it!

25

The Captain of my Soul

EVERY morning I began the day by following the Christian's daily exercise in the catechism—a copy of which every boy was expected to have: 'I should begin the day by making the sign of the cross as soon as I awake in the morning, and by saying some short prayer, such as "O my God, I offer my heart and soul to Thee".' I could also 'rise diligently' and 'dress myself modestly'—the trouble began when I went out into the world. The catechism warned not only against sin, but the need to avoid 'occasions of sin'. On certain mornings I would force myself to shun Derby Street and the strooleen— I always felt a certain misgiving when I did, as though I were being unfaithful to her, and possibly to some part of myself— and go to school by the way of Magee's Brewery and Parrot Street, set on keeping out of mind that sinful image of her ample round behind stuck out, the short tight dress around it, and, above all, the two areas of bare white flesh of her fat legs, and the torn bloomer. What must it be like for the man who was married to her, I used to think, to sleep beside her all night, and maybe see her rising and dressing in the morning! I felt I would almost have given my soul to swap places with him; well, at least for an hour or two. But only in the bedroom, for a woman like that would be no use around a house. But then you couldn't expect everything. So resolved was I on certain mornings not to picture that lewd image, to shut it out of mind, that it fastened itself before my inner gaze, keeping up with me at every step. On one occasion I pretended I had forgotten something, and hurried back, so that I could turn down Derby Street and catch her. I was a minute or two late, and she was just picking up her bucket, but I thought she gave me a grin and a wink and a toss of her behind as she went in—although I might only have imagined it, so besotted by that woman had I become.

In what I took to be saner moments I began to regard this erotic excitation as something foul and beastly, a visitation of the devil—it had to be the devil as it was so pleasurable—to plague me, and me alone, since so far as I could see no other boy seemed troubled. One never read of lads in books being concerned with sex. And as for the boys at the famous board-ing schools, of whom I read every week, it seemed sex of any kind never entered their lives. How lucky they were if only they knew it! What has got into me? I asked myself, since up to a month or two before I had passed that way every morn-ing, seen that same woman stretched out over her mopping, and hardly noticed her beyond the mild feeling of distaste her untidy appearance stirred in me—and now I could hardly get my feet to carry me by, so strong was the desire to stop and stare. And it was made all the more difficult for me by the physical upset in my private parts, one of frightening tumescent discomfort, which embarrassed and shamed me, and at the same time was strangely exciting. The best thing to do, I learnt, was to give a squirm, and then furtively direct one's person upwards against the stomach, to obtain a sense of relief. With this dodge I cultivated an immediate reaction of prayer; first I whispered, 'Lord save me or I perish', then went on to the Blessed Virgin whom I felt was all-understand-ing: 'Hail, Holy Queen, Mother of Mercy, hail, our life, our sweetness, and our hope!' I would pour the prayer out without a stop: 'To thee do we cry, poor banished children of Eve: to thee do we send up our sighs, mourning and weeping in this vale of tears.' The invocation seemed made for me, the appeal proved an instant help, and I could nearly always rely on it to ease my unwieldy problem.

But later there was to come a cunning recoil. It was my custom after school, on occasions when I was on my own, to turn up along Pilkington Street and step into church for a few minutes' prayer. It was not piety alone that drew me there, although I found comfort in worship, but a need I had for a moment or two of solitude, peace, and quiet. Again the fingertips dipped into the holy-water font, the blessing of oneself, the seemingly vast silence of the empty church— apart from the odd shawled and humped figure of an old woman down near the alter rails, who kept up a constant praying vigil; this atmosphere brought immediate relief. The feeling of happy composure was given substance once my knees made contact with the hard wooden kneeling board, the moment of prayer, and the gazing towards the altar, with its steady companion light, assuring one of the presence of the Sacred Host. To my consternation this now switched the process, by conjuring up the thoughts and images which the Virgin Mother had once banished. The association became so keen I could no longer pray but there began to enter into me what I took to be a sinful imagery. Even as I went into the porch of the empty church and dipped my fingertips in the holy water, I became aware of sexual stirrings against which I was powerless. What is the imagination, I pondered, that a smart one such as myself had so little control over it? It had always been such a happy state, that of daydreaming, when I could walk for long distances without noticing a thing, so absorbed was I in reverie, but now it seemed that Satan could instil himself there, for the drift was always to carnal fantasy and the pleasures of such. Right then, I would make a fight of it, put all such fanciful indulgence aside, and stride along, shoulders back in military style. Apart from the unspoken understanding that no decent and upright lad ever touched his person, I was determined not to give way to temptation, since the temptation was itself a guilty pleasure, one that was almost unbearable at times. Anything beyond, I felt, would knock me right out.

Sin was not my sole concern. I found I was constantly engaged in a clash of *desire* and *will* within myself. I enjoyed chewing caramel toffee, but sometimes, if I felt I was glut-tonous, I'd order myself to fling it away. I might stand irresolute for a moment or two, and sometimes would per-suade myself that it didn't matter, but most often I would put a hand to my mouth, take the large chewed chunk of toffee out, and throw it away. It was what I regarded as training the will. Then, puffed with a feeling of superiority, I would recite to myself the last stirring stanza of W. E. Henley's 'Invictus': 'It matters not how to strait the gate, | How charged with punishments the scroll, | I am the master of my fate: | I am captain of my soul.' I was much drawn to the image of 'captain', and would firm my lips, grit my teeth slightly, dilate my nostrils, and narrow my eyes into what I took to be the stern gaze of my favourite actor, William Farnum.

I set myself to become master in the conflict between the desires of the flesh and my determination not to give way to them. As difficult as such feelings were to control during the day, I could often escape by going for a good walk or boxing away at the old punch-bag in the backyard; but at night I was vulnerable. I slept on the inside of the bed, facing the wall, and would lie close to it, for I had the most lustful dreams, dreams in which I visualized women's bodies, and at times seemed to feel them; and often they were the oddest partners: certain neighbours in the street, the strooleen, and more than once Miss Newsham turned up and was most provocative. I would wake up feeling guilty and ashamed.

I was much less tense when I was among my mates, and diversions took my mind off sexual thought. One Saturday evening I went to the first house at the Grand Theatre in Churchgate with a pal called Bert Howarth, whose brother Charlie had told him there was a good comedian. We queued up, then hurried in up the steps to our benches at the back of the gods. But when the curtain went up, and all the bright lights came on the stage, I was stunned by the beauty and dancing of the chorus girls. I was enchanted by the face, figure, and smile of the one fourth from the end on the left-hand side. Her legs were more shapely and she looked younger than the others, although they were all worth looking at. And the way she looked upwards to the gods—it was as though she were gazing at me alone. I had little interest in the comedian or his jokes—although I had to pretend one; all I longed for was to see those dancing girls with their lovely legs.

I knelt as usual to say my prayers that night, but, no matter how hard I tried to concentrate on Our Lady over my Hail Marys, the chorus girls kept breaking in, and especially the one who had been smiling up at me. It seemed that real flesh and blood always got the better of images, no matter how holy. I had heard of the custom of child marriages in India, of how a boy and girl would be matched and married. What a sane and sensible people the Indians must be, I thought—the only nation to understand the needs of a boy my age. Often in bed at night I used to imagine how, if only I'd been born Indian instead of Irish, I might have a lovely dusky girl at my side, instead of lying back-to-back with brother Edward. And not only were they said to be quiet and dignified, which I liked, but most obedient to a husband. To be away from the constant and noisy company of boys, I thought, and to lie beside such a bride every night, seemed to me the most idyllic life that could be imagined.

I became fascinated by the rich variety of feminine beauty, the fresh virginal appearance of some girls, and the earthy appeal of others. Woman herself became most desirable to me. Once I had thought one or two of the young men at the Big Corner to be a bit soft in the head when some girl went by and one or other would groan with appreciation, 'Ooh, look at the luv'ly bum on her!' And often he would fling his cap on the ground to emphasize his feelings, and sometimes stamp on it. But now it seemed that the round swinging rump of a young woman was the first thing about her that caught my own eye. It shocked me to think that I was no different from others. Yet not for anything, I felt, would I deliberately offend God by committing an outright sin of the flesh; what I hankered after was some young woman playing upon my youth and beguiling me into sinful pleasures of one kind or another. Then I'd not only get the agreeable feeling of being led on by another but I should also have some kind of an excuse.

One cold winter evening I was in the home of a pal called Albert when his sister, Emma, a well-shaped lass, arrived home from work: 'Ee, I'm starved with the cold,' she said as she went up to the big coal fire, '—my bum feels frozen.' And with that she lifted up the back of her mill skirt, and turned her plump bottom with its blue bloomers to the fire: 'Oooh, that feels better,' she sighed, waggling about. I tried not to watch what to me was a most erotic sight, more tempting even than bevvies of chorus girls. As for the sin of 'impure thoughts', I secretly came to the conviction that there could be no man that ever walked God's holy earth who, if he thought at all, didn't now and again have impure ones. At times I thought back on my courting days with Alice, and of how happy I had been just to walk beside her, or to hold her hand and sometimes kiss her. How innocent and carefree those times now seemed, compared with the problems of my present self!

There was a Saturday evening in spring, warm and sunny, when I decided to get out to the nearest piece of green field to do some deep-breathing exercises. I set off with a cork in each of my trouser pockets to perform my hand exercises along the way, and so develop a powerful grip. I was just passing the end of the backstreet of the row of houses facing us when Mrs Fairclough came out of the back gate of the corner shop and called to me, 'Willie love—have you a minute?' The Faircloughs, with the aid of Mr Fairclough's war bounty, as it was called—he had served in Mesopotamia and had been demobbed with malaria—had taken over the shop when Mrs Langstaff gave it up, and they were now striving against odds to make a go of it. Mrs Fairclough, her first name was Rose, was a buxom woman of forty, the mother of a family of seven, the boys mates of mine; and as I hurried up to her, and saw the nice womanly bulge of her big apron, and the sleeves of her blouse rolled up above her generous arms with the dimpled elbows, her round face flushed, her small brown eyes shining, the thought struck me that the name 'Rose' suited her perfectly, such a fine well-set-up figure she made.

'Will you take a tray of meat pies up to Ram's Head for me, love?' she said; '—I can't see a damn' one of my lot anywhere.' At once I put on a smile and said I would, for, as much as I disliked the thought of such an errand on a Saturday evening, it would have been unthinkable for me to refuse. I followed her in the back gate, down the little back-yard, and into the back kitchen, where there was a warm smell of baking. She handed me the tray of meat pies, covered with a cloth, 'An' ask 'um will they be wanting any more, will you, love,' she said.

I felt ashamed to be seen carrying a tray of pies to a public house, but with head stooped a little I went up Back Cannon Street, along Peace Street, and crossed Derby Street to the Ram's Head, trusting that my schoolmate, Frank Barrow, whose father was the landlord, would not see me with the tray, covered as it was with a less than immaculate tea towel. I shoved open the big door with the glass panels and was struck by the sudden din—a discord of voices harsh and mostly hoarse. The place was smoke-filled and crowded with excited people, flushed of face and loud and eager of manner. It was a shock to come in from the fairly quiet street and find myself among such a rowdy gathering. Fortunately I managed to catch the eye of the barman, passed the tray to him over the bar, and asked did they want any more. 'Aye,' he said, 'we're busy—tell her we could sell another dozen or more.' I hurried out of the place and back to the Faircloughs'.

I went in the back gate, and was just shutting it and putting the latch in place when I heard a voice calling out: 'Is that you, Willie?' I turned at once but there was nobody in sight. And so I had to reply into the air, 'Yes, it's me,' I said. Then I heard Mrs Fairclough's voice, close but faintly muffled, call out, 'Hang on, love—I'll not be a minute.' Then suddenly, as I heard a shuffle of clogs, I realized she was calling from inside the privy closet. That gave me a strange turn and I went dry-mouthed. There was another sound, then a pause, before she asked, 'What did he say?' For a moment I couldn't speak; it seemed sinful to me to be holding a conversation with a woman seated on a privy closet. 'Oh, he said—he said he could take another dozen an' more,' I got the words out with a stammer. 'Ee, did he!' exclaimed Mrs Fairclough from within, '—that's good. It is that an' all. I'll be out with you in a tick, love.'

The door of the closet was slightly ajar, as they usually

were, since few would shut fully, and also it allowed the occupant a shaft of light from the opening; as I was standing barely a yard away, I felt a stifling sense of intimacy with the woman seated inside. As I heard more sounds coming from within, I felt a flush all over my body, and then a funny tingling feeling. I knew how one was expected to behave in most social situations, but this was a new one to me. I had an idea it might be the proper thing to move away, go down the yard a few steps, but it struck me she might think it uppish of me, as though I was teaching her manners, since she was the one who had spoken first. Also, my feet didn't seem to want to move from where they were. I'll not be able to go to Communion tomorrow, the thought crossed my mind, if this goes on much longer.

Then I heard a creaking of the closet seat as she must have been rising, followed by what sounded like a long satisfied sigh, and a pulling up of underclothes or something; as the door opened I lowered my gaze. When I looked up Rose was stood on the closet step, her greasy black skirt and striped apron level with my eyes: 'Ee, another dozen or more, did he say! By gum, that's a bit of all right, Willie, would you say,' she smiled at me, 'but I'll hatta get a move on.' She gave a shimmy turn or two as she eased herself more comfortably into her skirt and what was under it. 'Now I can tak' them up mysel' an' have the last half-hour in the Snug there,' she said, 'but don't you go yet—I've summat for you.' She got her purse from the large pocket, poked inside it and got twopence out, which she pressed into my palm with her warm woman's fingers. 'There y'are, love,' she said, 'you deserve that.' 'Ta very much, Missis Fairclough,' I said, '—ta,' and turned to open the gate. But my sight seemed blurred, my fingers unsure, and the latch did not stir. 'Stuck is it,' said Mrs Fairclough, and putting an arm over my shoulder, with her big bosom resting somewhere against my neck and head, she flicked it up and the gate opened. 'Mind how you go, love,' she said.

I went off in a strange daze, as though wholly out of touch with my surroundings, yet feeling oddly elated. I was unable to think clearly, and forgot all about my cork-squeezing exercises as I made my way up Higher Swan Lane. When I got away from the streets and among the deserted fields I could not concentrate on the breathing exercises, for I was unable to get out of my mind the image of Rose sitting on the seat inside the closet and myself standing outside. Nor did I, it must be said, for many a long day.

26

The Medical Examination

ONE morning Mr J. V. Smith, the headmaster, came into our classroom of some forty boys, had a word with our teacher Miss Newsham, called us all to attention, and informed us of a medical examination that would take place in two weeks' time. He told us to be sure we didn't miss it, and said that every boy should make sure he was clean and spotless, and if possible wearing a fresh shirt for the occasion, which examination would take place in the school hall or basement. Almost the minute I heard Mr Smith a crafty idea came to mind, which I hatched secretly to discover how I should best go about it.

My brother Edward, four years older than myself, had once had a medical examination, after which it had been recommended that he be sent to Southport Sanatorium for a three-week stay. He had gone off looking pale, weak, and uneasy, and when he returned he had put on eight pounds in weight, his face was tanned, and he exuded an air of strength and confidence. For days he went round the house singing the lively farewell song, 'Goodbye Sanatorium, Goodbye Matron too, | Goodbye all the nurses, and Johnny and his donkey too!' I had been envious of the change in him, and of all the adventures he had had, of the donkey rides on the sands, and all the fun with the nurses. A few of my mates from the street-corner had been sent away, and the change in them seemed almost unbelievable: from thin weaklings they had become rosy-cheeked toughs in three weeks. And now I began a persistent entreaty of prayer—asking God to arrange for something to be wrong with me, so that I could be recommended for three weeks at Southport. I had never seen the sea—apart from the ship journey in the dark in 1914 from Ireland—had never been away on a single day of holiday in my life, and now I longed to get away from home, to be taken care of by nice clean nurses, to enjoy days in the fresh air beside the sea. I became so obsessed with the idea that I actually held my breath for as long as I could, hoping it would throw my heart out of kilter just for the occasion, so that the doctor would recommend a change of air—Southport Sanatorium!

During one of my periods of fervent prayer in the pursuit of some special invocation, when I approached God in a way in which I felt I could draw Him to one side to listen to me, it seemed that sooner or later there was this Voice from within which answered one way or another. The response was always in the nature of an intuitive hint, such as *We'll see* or *Maybe*, with which I could put up; or it might be *Yes I think so*; I had to assess the reply, since they were rarely declared, unless in the negative, such as *No, not a chance! Give it up— Put it out of your mind*. Sometimes I attempted persuasion, but this was risky. I had a painful memory of having once overridden Him. It had been the custom of my Uncle William on New Year's Day to take Edward, May, and myself to the fair on the Town Hall Square, and I had been struck with admiration at the skill of certain youths who could throw the small wooden ball with such accuracy and force that sometimes they would knock off three coconuts out of four balls. I had requested of God that I would knock off only one—and the reply had at last come through, so I imagined, that it would all be arranged. Uncle William was baffled that I should even wish to attempt the feat, but I declared I would knock off at least one. He paid the threepence—it was half-price for boys—and I picked up the four wooden balls, which seemed oddly light. There was a big crowd of on-lookers at every coconut shy, and I didn't bother to balance myself before throwing as I normally would, or even to take proper aim, leaving it all in God's hands, so to speak. I threw badly—normally I was a fair thrower—and missed the coconuts by a foot and more, and inside me I began frantic nudgings of God to get into action. Only as I was throwing the third ball did the message come through that I would have to try myself. It was too late—I had only one ball left, and now I took a good aim and actually hit a coconut, but I scarcely stirred it. I blushed and turned from the coconuts to see all the eyes staring at me with puzzlement. God!—I called within myself—why didn't you tell me you were having me on, instead of letting me make an eejit of myself.

And so now I prayed and prayed, and I cut down on my food—although I was never a big eater—and after a lot of pressing it seemed He gave way and agreed that there would be something wrong with me. On the morning of the examination I gave a great washing to myself in the back kitchen; Mother had washed my school shirt the evening before, and ironed it ready for me to put on. 'Are you feelin' well at all?' she whispered to me in the back kitchen, for she was quick to detect any sign of shiftiness. The scheme I was plotting, together with all the praying and spasms and fasting, was proving a strain. 'I'm fine, Mam,' I said, 'fine—' unable to conceal the hollow note in my voice.

It was after prayers and catechism that our class was led downstairs to the large school basement. The weight and height of each boy was taken by a pleasant young nurse who was assisting the doctor. Miss Newsham wasn't needed and had gone back to the empty classroom, so that there was the usual noisy chat and playing around. I wasn't one for fooling about, nor could I get the sanatorium out of my mind. Next we were told to take our shirts off, and I was surprised to see the white puny chests of the other boys compared with my own, which from daily deep-breathing and arm-swinging exercises had become quite broad. In the clear light of the basement I became aware of a few red fleabites I had on my body, especially so since none of the others appeared to have any. There was nothing they could say about a few fleabites, I reasoned, since fleas were one of the many natural afflictions of life—no doubt we had brought them over from Ireland with us—about which little could be done, except to catch and kill the odd one. However, instead of quietly boasting with my big chest, I now put my shirt over my shoulders and brought the sleeves across over my chest, ready to fling off at the examination time. The young doctor sounded my chest, the nurse made notes—and I prayed they would find something wrong; and right at the end they whispered together for a time, and then let me go, giving me curious looks of what I took to be sympathy. I knew You wouldn't let me down, I thought. Two weeks later Mr Smith came into the classroom carrying a few papers, which were apparently to do with the medical examination. He called two boys out about their eyesight, telling them they would have to have their eyes examined, and one or two others over their ears. Then finally called for me; I hurried out to him, imagining the sea and the sand, the donkey and the nurses. 'Yes, sir?' He had a word with Miss Newsham, and she continued the lesson. He lowered his voice: 'Er, Naughton,' he said, '—it's about your medical examination.' 'Yes, sir?' I said. 'It has been put down here', he went on, 'that you have fleabites on your body.' Fleabites!—that was the answer to all my prayers. I felt a stinging flush of shame fill me, and only with intense effort did I manage to keep my eyes dry.

Mr Smith looked at me, seemed to be sorry for me, and he must have been puzzled too, for I washed my head under the cold tap most mornings, and loved soap and water to a degree remarkable among boys. Certainly no boy in the school *looked* cleaner. 'If you could arrange to have baths more frequently,' he said hurriedly. 'Yes sir,' said I, who had almost to fight my way to the kitchen tap. And yet I was touched in some way to see he was concerned. 'Thank you, sir,' I said, turning to go off.

'Oh Naughton,' he said, '—there was another matter I had been intending approaching you about. There are scholarship examinations for boys to go to St Bede's—the college in Manchester.' I had heard of St Bede's—a boy or two had gone there, to study later for the priesthood. 'We feel you would have a very good chance of obtaining one. All tuition would be free—but there would be certain expenses for the uniform. What do you think?' I had scarcely heard a word he said for the shame I felt. 'Yes, sir,' I said, indicating my interest. 'Then talk it over with your parents,' he said, 'and let me know.'

I wanted to spare my mother the distress it would cause her to hear about the fleabite complaint, and resolved not to tell her, but somehow it came out. She was upset about it: 'God save us,' she said, 'but you might have thought to tell him you stayed with some people in Wigan at the weekend, and got them there.' I felt there was little she could do beyond using flea powder, and I was sorry I had troubled her. Then I told her about the scholarship examination. She seemed worried, and then made what struck me as an odd reply: 'It would be great for you to become a priest,' she said, 'but do you know, I've a feeling the way of poor Uncle William's death—it would go against you for the priesthood, they might think there was something not right in the family.' There was a trace of some Irish truth in it, for they read much significance in family and blood, but it was not the whole truth. She was to me the dearest mother, and I feel sure she had some better reason which she kept to herself, and almost never have I regretted it or felt that she was in any way lacking or to blame. Mr Smith seemed disappointed when I went to him the next day and told him a palpable white lie—that my parents had other plans for me.

27

Scene in Classroom

IT was Friday afternoon of the same week in which I felt the Creator had gone out of his way to play a dirty trick on me. Things were still cool between Himself and myself. I had dutifully said my morning and night prayers, the grace before meals and the grace after, but always in a measured manner without spirit or even struggle—at times almost as if I was slyly cocking a snook at Him—and I never turned inward to enjoy a secret feeling or word with Him, as had been my way. Prayer was nothing compared with the odd moment of recognition, the feeling of unison with Him. In the first stage of chagrin and disillusion I had considered giving up my mission and going in for pleasure. I wasn't sure I even wanted to be there in heaven, hobnobbing with angels and others. I had thought only of enjoyment, of staring at the legs of the woman mopping the dentist's doorstep and getting a right good e'enful, as they said, and of going in for ice-cream and Turkish delight at weekends when I began work, and booking a seat in the front row of the Grand Theatre on Saturday nights to get an upward view of the chorus girls' legs. The only risk was that of being killed sometime, knocked down by a train or something, and being denied the forgiveness of a death-bed repentance, and so spending eternity in hell, a prospect I did not fancy. I had decided I would even go to Confession that evening and to Communion on Sunday, but would keep our understanding on a polite basis, rather in the way I felt many others did. I mean, after all He had as good as promised me He would get me to Southport Sanatorium, within sight and smell of the sea, and heaven knows when I would see it now.

I was seated at my desk on that afternoon, the last desk on

the right in the last row—a desk for two, but by good fortune I had had it to myself for some weeks. I was glad to be on my own, since this made it easier to conceal my pubescent stirrings. Sometimes when I wasn't thinking, my right leg would wedge itself under the desk, the heel of my clog would lift, and I would find my thigh vibrating up and down, shaking the desk. A number of peculiar tics and twitches of the same kind made me grateful I had no boy sharing the desk.

The sexual upset, however, which was impossible to control and difficult to conceal, had eased considerably, and now there had come to life in me an intense awareness of beauty and romance. Poetry, which I had always enjoyed, now yielded up a new richness: 'Whene'er I see soft hazel eyes | And nut-brown curls, | I think of those bright days I spent | Among the Limerick girls; | When up through Cratla woods I went, | Nutting with thee; | And we plucked the glossy clustering fruit | From many a bending tree.' The poem being translated from the Irish gave it deeper meaning for me and also reminded me of my one-time girlfriend Alice, when we once went for a walk in the woods. 'Beneath the hazel boughs we sat, | Thou, love, and I'—I used to repeat that over again, and also the ending, 'That sat with thy white lap full of nuts | Beneath the hazel tree.'

At singing lessons, at which I was hopeless, I found I was deeply moved when the boys around me sang 'Shenandoah' and I mimed the words. Their boyish voices had suddenly taken on a new beauty, as indeed had many of the faces, as they sang with what seemed to me an angelic sincerity. Even boys at the Big Corner began to hint at beauty. Bernard Dunleavy, a year or two older than myself, was tall, slim, and blue-eyed, and some evenings when he came to the Corner straight from the High Street swimming baths, his cheeks rosy and his soft skin glowing, he looked lovelier than any girl. As for girls—they were *beauty* to me, even the least becoming of them. But special were Sister Hyacinth, a most attractive and gentle nun who taught in the girls' school, and also the tall and leggy Peggy Conway, a pupil there, the younger sister of my once favourite teacher. Mill girls, who tended to get greasy and pale skins, seemed to lose their attraction, but they were friendly and I liked them too.

This flurry of new sensations, which I had to keep hidden, made me feel like a man among boys in the classroom, as I watched the antics of those in front of me; it was indeed my feeling on this certain Friday afternoon. I couldn't understand how they seemed unable to concentrate for more than a minute at a time, and were always eager for diversion of some sort from the effort of thought. There was a furtive gesticulating going on, winks and nods, and even at times a guilty whispering. Joe Cassidy, the school's star footballer—Mr Seddon of Standard Seven had recently organized a school team—was demonstrating his feat of taking hold of the top part of his right ear, together with the bottom lobe, and folding the lot into a compressed bundle which he pressed into the earhole, so that it held for a few moments before it suddenly burst out. Tommy Gauley, a short wiry boy, a brilliant dribbler, was encouraging Joe to attempt two ears at once. Another boy was displaying his double-jointed thumb, and another his capacity to lick his nose with his tongue. I had never cared for such a boyish carry-on, and now I felt utterly remote from it, and at times envied the boyish innocence and irresponsibility, which echoed a state I had briefly enjoyed but from which with puberty I was now banished forever—or until my second childhood, whenever that might be.

Playtime was over, and Miss Newsham stood before the class wearing her Friday face and the posh crochet blouse that went with it. Every weekend she went back to her home in Preston, some twenty miles away, and on Fridays she came to school dressed for the occasion, always wearing her fur coat, summer and winter. The clash of our totally unalike natures and upbringing had softened over the four years, and of late my early adolescent stiffening had generated a male defiance, of which she seemed not unaware, so that with more spirit in me, and no longer any real fear of her, it seemed that there was a tacit understanding of sorts.

There was the usual Friday sense of relaxation in the class, and Miss Newsham was not teaching but espousing what was a motto she called on every boy in the class to take up: '"The first I am determined to be,"' she declaimed in a loud clear voice, and then added, '"let who will come second." I remember learning that as a child, and I have always clung to it.' She looked appealingly at us all for some response. I looked at Norman Burke, the boy at the desk ahead of mine. He was my age, thirteen, but looked about eleven, and a puny eleven at that. I looked at his frail figure, the narrow shoulders, the white neck from which the two bones stuck out above his celluloid collar. Norman was gentle and mild, kind and soft-spoken, and I imagined what impression her words could have had upon him, for in nothing at all could Norman ever hope to be the first—not that it ever seemed he would wish to be. At hygiene lesson, when it was customary for the large manikin illustrating the human body to be displayed over the blackboard, I always had to keep an eye on Norman. A minute or two into the lesson Norman had only to look up, see that strange bald figure, consisting of coloured veins, ribs, organs, and a mouthful of large teeth, for him to give a moan and swoon over at his desk—and fall to the floor unless I caught him. I had much sympathy for Norman, since not only had I fainted over at Mass, when the church was hot, the candles bright, and my stomach empty, but I wasn't drawn to the manikin myself. More than once two or three of us had dashed to help, and I had got the others to help lift him on to my right shoulder, and then somewhat proudly I had carried Norman out in the approved 'Fireman's lift' fashion, which I had studied from a cigarette-card on first aid.

Miss Newsham went on about how each one of us should strive to get ahead of all others, and I wished I had the guts to ask her had she never heard of 'the first shall be last; and the last shall be first'. To beat another, perhaps a good mate, would have been the last thing I wanted; not that I would care to be beaten either. It seemed to me that all my contests were within myself—and I was having one with God at the moment. The bell was heard ringing in the corridor, and she

told us that it was now the weekly 'free reading time'. Boys
who had brought their own books to read could start reading, and the rest of us could enjoy our weekly ration of *Ben
Hur*. The ones who had library books, and two boys who
actually had books of their own, started reading, and the
monitors came round with *Ben Hur*. I was addicted to reading the printed word, wherever my gaze met it; I knew by
heart all the screeds on sauce bottles and the Derby salt
packet, and on wet Sunday evenings I would be so desperate
for a read that I would read every word of my mother's
twopenny magazine, *My Weekly*, including recipes and
household hints. Reading seemed to ease a mental hunger
within me. But *Ben Hur*, a story about the coming of Our
Lord, written by an American, Lew Wallace, seemed to block
the flow. 'How to remove ink stains from a white tablecloth' I
could read with interest, but half a page of this famous book
exhausted me. The print was small, the book long, the tone
supposedly religious, the writing stodgy, and the dialogue
skimpy, and although I tried once more to read it I could not
take in a word more.

Miss Newsham left the classroom and there was at once
the usual buzz of talk. The whisper was going round the
class, 'Look up "groin" in the dictionary.' I did: 'The curved
portion of the body between the belly and the thigh,' I read. It
seemed a most suggestive entry, one unfit, I felt, to appear in
such a book. Two good mates, Willie and Arthur, who were
separated by a seat, kept passing a sheet of paper to one
another, on which they added a further few lines of drawing,
and at each addition the one who got it clapped a hand over
his mouth as he chuckled away. I was curious as to what
might be so funny about it, when Thistlethwaite, a boy in the
seat ahead, intercepted it and had a look, grinned and passed
it to me. I did not care to be involved in any underhand affair
but I looked at the paper. I saw a smutty drawing, but a
clever one, for the two naked figures on it were unmistakable,
without the caption underneath. I was tempted for a moment
to tear it up, feeling that it was a most risky drawing to be
around, but I didn't: I shook my head disapprovingly, play-

ing up a bit the adult role which I seemed able to assume. I also gave Willie a cautionary look, and the paper was passed back to Arthur. The chatter ceased instantly as the sound of the latch on the classroom door was heard and Miss Newsham entered. She was sharp at sniffing out such capers, and I saw she gave a quick look in Arthur's direction, but he had slipped the paper out of sight inside *Ben Hur*, and being Friday it seemed Miss Newsham was reluctant to pursue trouble, and she began marking exercise books and tidying up the register and similar tasks.

Arthur made a weak attempt to turn his attention to life in Ancient Rome, but it proved too much for him and, seeing Miss Newsham engrossed in her task at the desk, he took the drawing out and from what I could make out began to add bits to it. Then he exchanged looks with Willie indicating that he was about the pass the paper on. Willie shook his head— the risky venture had already been too much for him, and he needed to settle down. But Arthur insisted, passed it to one boy in between who passed it on to Willie, who let it slip out of his hand, and in desperate haste to pick it up and hide it, caught the eye of Miss Newsham.

'Murphy—' she asked, 'what's that sheet of paper?'

'Er, Miss—, please, M-Miss,' stuttered Willie, 'er n-nothing, Miss.'

'What do you mean—nothing? Bring it out—' said Miss Newsham.

'Er, Miss—please, Miss—' Willie stood, his right hand held up as demanded when addressing a teacher, '—er it's only a piece of paper I've been writing on.'

'Bring it out here at once—' said Miss Newsham, slowly taking on her usual severe manner.

Don't Willie! I cried in alarm within myself, recalling what I had seen, *whatever you do don't let her see it! Tear it up— run off with it—do anything rather than let her see it.*

Willie had been so conditioned to responding with instant obedience to that voice that now, sheet of paper in hand, like someone hypnotized, he made his way slowly and apprehensively between the desks. Arthur, desperate but not as helpless as Willie, grabbed the paper from Willie and called out, 'Please, Miss, it's mine—I passed it to him.' At that first sign of defiance Miss Newsham picked up her cane, and came up swiftly to Arthur, 'Give me that piece of paper!' she exclaimed. The command was too strong for Arthur to resist and he handed it over. She did not look at it at once—and the very thought that she might brought me out in a sweat. She marched Willie and Arthur out in front of the class. 'Now to see what's been engaging your attention so avidly,' she said, and she held the paper in front of her to inspect it. Willie and Arthur looked at each other and went pale. I was aghast, dry-mouthed, as I imagined what Miss Newsham was looking at—a drawing of a naked man with a big moustache, clearly Mr Smith, and a fat female figure, hair done up in Miss Newsham's style, the pair engaged in sexual intercourse. Underneath was written, 'Old Smiteyballs having a do with Fat Ada!' It was deadly silent in the classroom for a few seconds as Miss Newsham looked at the paper.

Her face went almost purple, the one word 'Filthy—' came out, but then she went speechless, and the next thing, with her words smothered in rage and shock, the paper in one hand and the cane in the other, she drove the almost paralysed pair of boys before her, out of the classroom, and along the corridor to that fearful sanctum, the headmaster's room. For a minute there was hardly a sound from the class of boys—they just looked at one another, thanking God, it seemed to me, that they were not in the shoes or clogs of Willie and Arthur. Then came the quieter buzz of talk; the boys in front wanted to know what could have been on the paper to have produced such a reaction. The information was passed around in shocked whispers. Soon the howls of Willie and Arthur could be heard coming from the headmaster's room. It was at that moment that I spotted the sudden sagging of Norman's shoulder to one side, and I made a grab, but was too late to catch him, although I was able to break his fall as he collapsed to the floor.

'Gimme a hand!' I called. 'Sum'dy gimme a hand!' At once three or four boys gathered round, but they got in the way.

'Jimmy,' I said to a close mate of mine, 'you an' Joe lift him—an' I'll carry him.' They lifted up the unconscious Norman, and so deathlike did he look that instead of turning him over on my shoulders I took him in my arms as though taking a child. 'Leave him to me,' I called, for they were jostling around. 'Aye, see if Naughty Billy can carry him,' called Carter.

Although a dead weight, I was surprised at how confident I was in carrying him, with the boys hurrying ahead to open doors. As we were going out we had to stop as Miss Newsham came along, with Arthur and Willie limping ahead of her. They looked a pitiful pair, with Arthur attempting to put on a bold front but failing. 'Norman Burke fainted over, Miss,' my mate Jimmy explained. 'We're taking him on to the steps.'

She looked at me in an odd way, and nodded. I couldn't bear to show off, but enjoyed a situation in which the showing off was done for me; 'silent brag' was the name for it. The boys made way for me, opening the door of Standard Seven, Mr Seddon's class, through which we had to go, then out through the other door and on to the top of the steps that led down into the playground. I stood there in the open air, holding Norman whilst Jimmy went back to get a chair. I looked down at him, at the brittle hair on a head that seemed too large for the body, the pinched face, the white forehead speckled with sweat, the eyes closed as though in death, beneath them the dark half-moons, the small shapely nose and the bloodless lips. I felt a sudden spasm of shame to think that I'd prayed so hard that *I* should have a spell in Southport Sanatorium. Norman, who never said a word against anyone, never boasted or showed off like I did, always gentle, would share his last sweet with anyone. Saint!—that was the real saint, the uncomplaining Norman.

'Here we are, Bill,' called Jimmy, '—put him down theer.'

Between us we lowered Norman on to the chair. A light breeze was blowing, and soon he opened his eyes. 'I'll get him a drink of watter,' said Jimmy, and off he went. I wiped Norman's forehead with my hanky. 'All right, Norman?' I said. He nodded. Jimmy returned with the water. 'Here, Norman,' he said, 'have a sup,' and he held the mug of water to Norman's lips. The water revived him and he made to stand up. 'Hold on a tick,' said Jimmy, 'whilst I have a quick drag.' He took a docker from his pocket, pressed the loose wisps of tobacco in, squeezed it into shape, looked round to see nobody was watching, got a match from a pocket, bent down and struck it against the wall, lit the butt and took a couple of swift draws. 'Smithy had no right to flog 'um like that,' he remarked to me. 'He's got about six kids in all, hasn't he—so he musta done *that there* at least a dozen times with his missis. All they done is *draw* it—but he's *done* it—he can't deny that. He coulda showed a bit of understandin'—after all, it were only a joke.' Then we all made our way back to the classroom. The first thing I noticed was Willie, his face ashen except for the red-rimmed eyes, letting out an involuntary sob followed by a fit of trembling.

Miss Newsham turned to me, 'William,' she said, and I felt some surprise, as it was the first time I had heard her use my Christian name, 'I would like you to take my case to the station. You go to number ninety-three Fletcher Street—you haven't been there before, have you?' She knew well that I had never been, since it was a task usually reserved for one of her favourites. 'No, Miss,' I said, trying to keep any sign of eagerness out of my voice. 'Just knock,' she said, 'and you will be handed the case. Then take a tram in Derby Street to town. You can wait for me at the barrier for Platform Four at Trinity Street Station. Here's twopence for your journey to town and back home.' The boy chosen to take Miss Newsham's case to the station was envied, since he not only got out of school early, but was given sixpence, a right handy sum—two threepenny seats at the pictures.

It was a relief to escape the tumult and yelling of the normal afternoon school turning out. I got her case, then hurried to the tram, feeling rather important carrying the small suitcase. I decided it was too precious to put in the recess for luggage, and I kept it on my knee. Although I felt privileged to be singled out for the task, I also felt uncomfortble, for I had a feeling that this was the way people who were over you used to sweeten you and get you on to their side.

I was waiting at the station when I saw Miss Newsham walking in. She looked smart in her fur coat, and quite a different person from her classroom self. Watching her from a distance I noted the swing of her ample bust, and for a second I wondered had she two warm womanly breasts underneath. She didn't smile at me, not being one given to that sort of thing, but it seemed she treated me with a new respect. She took her purse out of her handbag, hesitated a moment, then took out a shilling and handed it to me.

'Oh no, thank you, Miss—' I began, as I had always been taught, but she waved me to be quiet. 'I'll take it now, William,' she said. I felt it was the olive branch after our years of discord, and I accepted it graciously. As I watched her fairly plump short figure go off, I certainly had no idea that sixty years hence I should still have dreams about the woman.

28

A Right Good Laugh

I DECIDED that instead of going straight home I would cross
the long railway footbridge, then visit St Patrick's Church at
the corner of Johnson Street and Great Moor Street and,
having made things up with Miss Newsham, I'd try to do the
same with God. There was no doubt that now I had got over
the worst I felt better for my humiliation over the fleabites. It
seemed that a regular dose of life going against me kept me in
fettle. I moved cautiously as I was crossing the broad area of
Trinity Street, with workmen repairing the road, and the
usual long line of tramcars waiting to set off on the various
routes. I hesitated before stepping between the rear of one
tram and the front of another, since they set off in unexpected
jerks, and just as I was about to go through the narrow
opening the line of trams did jerk forward: 'Get a bloody
move on!' a tram driver roared down at me from his platform. I darted between the two iron monsters. 'Stubborn
Turks an' Tartars,' I said to myself, 'never trained to offices
of tender courtesy.' That was a way I had of getting level with
his sort, men with loud voices and ignorant ways, to mutter
to myself a few words of Shakespeare or the like.

I was glad of the relative quiet of the narrow footbridge. I
looked down on the trains coming and going, now and again
feeling in my pocket to make sure I hadn't lost Miss Newsham's shilling. Yes, I'd slip into church for a minute or two:
somehow one was more inclined to feel warmly disposed to
God when there was some money in one's pocket; it was as
though one met Him on a more equal footing. In this life it
seemed that you never got what you expected, but then came
some bit of luck you didn't expect. But I must learn to stop
pestering Him—He obviously doesn't like it. 'God's good,'

ny father often said, 'and the devil isn't bad if you'll treat
1im right.' There was surely some kind of understanding
between those two, or else why should God expect me to be
chaste yet allow Satan to fill me with sinful desire? 'Holy
Michael Archangel, defend us in the day of battle;' that was a
powerful prayer heard after Mass, said at the foot of the
altar; 'be our safeguard against the wickedness and snares of
the devil. May God rebuke him, we humbly pray ...'
Rebuke, I had often asked myself, why only *rebuke*? Surely
that meant no more than to scold or tell him off. What kind
of a Church was it that could summon up no more gumption
than humbly to pray to God Almighty that He simply *chide*
Old Nick! It made no sense. Why not put the kibosh on him
altogether and give us all a bit of peace! My reflections were
interrupted by the sight of a young woman who went striding
close by me in heavy clogs. She was of a sturdy build, and had
the swinging walk of one who worked at a brewery or some
such place, and was used to lifting, for her shoulders were
thrust back as she moved along. She wore a short working
skirt, soiled and greasy, which tight shininess flaunted her
two splendid buttocks; at every step, as the hip lifted sharply,
first one and then the other thrust itself out like a solid
dumpling. Watching the regular rise and fall, I wondered was
it deliberate or natural, and did it tire her much. I followed
closely, and could not take my eyes off her and her fat bottom, and was most annoyed when a man in overalls came
between us and blocked my view. It now struck me that
perhaps I had been too confident in my vocation of sainthood, so suddenly could you be lured away or knocked off
your perch. It was certainly not going to be as easy as I had
imagined, nothing so simple as the fate of the early Christian
martyrs, being flung to the lions and all over in a couple of
minutes. Had I bitten off more than I could chew?

I hurried into the small porch of St Patrick's Church, dipped my fingers into the font of holy water—cold but comforting it felt as I blessed myself. The church was different from
that of SS Peter and Paul's, but the atmosphere of peace was
the same, with a soft silence, a candle or two flickering

brightly for the souls of the departed, and an old woman kneeling close to the altar. I paused to take in the full sense of the holy place, then I stepped forward to the centre aisle genuflected, and gazed at the familiar companion light glowing like a tiny red star over the altar: Our Lord is waiting there for me inside the tabernacle. Then I knelt and blessed myself again, and felt something within me open up to God my Heavenly Father. The keen feeling came, made me faintly hoarse in the throat, and then seemed to kindle up inside me It was like going out on a spring morning and feeling the new fresh air after winter. It seemed to pulse through every vein in my body.

Why, I thought, with such joy to be got, should the church be so forgotten. In the silence I could hear the traffic outside the footsteps of people going by, and all the street bustle Soon, when the mill gates opened and let the workers out there would be hordes of them, and not a one with a moment to spare for the Saviour of all mankind. Few indeed knew they had been saved, not that they seemed to care much, one way or another. Hard work all week gave them little time to contemplate—their minds were not on heaven or hell, but on what they were going to have for their tea. They were lucky in that respect; being Protestants they could have what they fancied on a Friday, boiled ham, roast pork, or nice hot meat pies with the gravy spilling down their chops at the first bite, whilst the best I could hope for was a boiled egg, since I didn't like herrings, the only fish that was cooked in our home.

Then I rose to my feet after the swift prayer, for I had learned that it was better not to cling to the feeling, but to slip quietly away, thankful and hoping some breath of it might stay with me. As I knelt down again on the one knee in the aisle, facing the altar, I realized that I had forgotten a prayer for Uncle William. I found that I was reluctant to go against the impulse that had induced me to get up, and then it prompted me: *since you have coppers in your pocket, why not light a candle for him?* Just the thing, I thought, and I rose and went quietly to the brass stand on which candles were lighted for the Holy Souls. There were three tiers of

candle-holders, spattered with dribbles of wax, only two candles burning, and these guttering near their end. I had the
penny clutched in my hand, and now I placed it into the slot
at the lid of the box. The chink of the coin drew the attention
of the old woman who had been praying with her head
stooped; she gave me an approving smile, and I responded
with a bow of my head to her. I took up a candle in my rather
shaky grip and, after lighting it from one of the dying candles,
managed on the third attempt to find a holder into which it
fitted. Suddenly my candle burst into brightness, which
created for me an image of Uncle William's soul: please God
he is out of purgatory by this, I thought. Then I brought to
mind the words of the prayer, 'Out of the depths have I cried
into Thee, O Lord, Lord hear my voice . . .'.

Isn't it a great blessing altogether, I thought, to be born and
brought up a Catholic, and have Jesus, Mary, and Joseph to
turn to in times of trouble, and St Anthony and St Francis at
hand when needed. It seemed we all had need of a bit of
comfort now and again. The only snag was that you were
always asking to be forgiven your sins instead of getting on
with the job. Just the same, I resolved, as I dipped fingertips
into the font of holy water, I must never let myself give up the
struggle. Let them have their juicy steak-and-kidney pies on a
Friday, with the crisp crust; I would keep the day of
abstinence. It would be a sorry way to carry on, I thought, as
I pushed open the church door and felt the fresh air on my
face, to go through life without the Holy Spirit. I made one
more reassuring feel with my thumbnail along the milled edge
of the shilling down safely in my pocket—just to make sure it
hadn't turned into a ha'penny, as they said—and then, warning myself against giving way to 'immodest thoughts and
desires, and the wilful pleasure enjoyed from such', I went
out into the street.

I was walking slowly up Derby Street when from all the
mills about the buzzers began to blow, signalling that it was
half-past-five and the factory gates could be opened and the
workers let out. In a minute or two the street was noisy with
the sharp patter of clogs, and the air alive with the happy

voices of mill girls hurrying home clutching their wages. They didn't seem to look where they were going, and I had to watch out. Then an odd thing happened. A trio of girls, laughing and chatting excitedly, almost bustled me over, as I made to dart off the pavement. Why should I keep giving way to wenches, I thought, being as I'm brimful of the Holy Ghost! 'Sorry, luv,' said one, and another called out, 'How's your mother for soap?' 'Up to the neck in lather,' I answered back. They all laughed, and I tried to laugh, but I couldn't—it seemed that my laugh had gone rusty. 'What're you grinnin at?' said one. 'I'm just thinkin' of the fun I'll have when I'm dead,' I said. They laughed but my face felt too set or stiff to laugh properly. It struck me that I hadn't had a right good laugh for months, ever since those strange sexual feelings had begun throbbing in me. I'll make myself laugh, I thought, and I forced an odd croaky laugh out. The girls were going off and one yelled back, 'Have you got it out at last, luv!' By gum she's right, I thought.

What was up with me—getting so finicky over every little thing—sick with shame about a few fleabites? To hell with the lot of 'um—why not take things just as they come like those mill girls. They work hard in the mill, yet they're nearly always laughing—so I'm going to have a laugh too—even if it kills me. Once the idea was in my mind it seemed that a little smile twitched my lips open, and the funny thing was that just the idea of laughing seemed to make me want to laugh out loud. The mood took hold of me right off, and I felt my mouth spread out into a big grin, and from down in my stomach the laughter gushed up like a spring, eager to break out. Ee, but that feels lovely, I thought, it does that an' all. It seems to flush out your lungs. Just fancy, you can enjoy a laugh by just telling yourself to laugh—who'd have thought it! That's a bit of all right that is—something worth knowing. It's odd the word hasn't got round—you don't need jokes or comedians, you can do it all on your own. The more I gave way to the laughter the more it took hold of me. I'd better tone it down a bit, I thought, or else I'll get carried away— folk are staring. Not that I care.

Then a woman with a shawl over her shoulders and a bonny round face smiled at me, I laughed, and she laughed back. What a nice place this world is, it struck me, when you're laughing. I must remind myself to do this when things are getting me down. I stifled it a bit as I was passing the Big Corner, but when I turned up our street and went in the front door I let it come out—a right burst of laughter, until I felt tears in my eyes. My mother came hurrying out of the back kitchen: 'Musha that was a great laugh, my son,' she said, 'may God bless you.' Her face lighted up, and the warm smile that was now rare spread over it. I was glad to see that. 'Are you yourself again then?' she asked. Mothers must know a lot more than they make out, I thought. 'I'm champion, Mam,' I said, 'champion.' And I went over and kissed her.